CHRIST AND THE WORLD OF RELIGIONS
LESSLIE NEWBIGIN'S THEOLOGY

CHRIST AND THE WORLD OF RELIGIONS
LESSLIE NEWBIGIN'S THEOLOGY

Joe M. Thomas

WIPF & STOCK · Eugene, Oregon

Wipf and Stock Publishers
199 W 8th Ave, Suite 3
Eugene, OR 97401

Christ and the World of Religions
Lesslie Newbigin's Theology
By Thomas, Joe M.
Copyright©2011 by Thomas, Joe M.
ISBN 13: 978-1-5326-8947-5

Publication date 2/17/2020
Previously published by Ekklesia Society Publications, 2011

ACKNOWLEDGMENTS

A book on the theology of Bishop Lesslie Newbigin could hardly have been written without the help and support of several individuals. I want to acknowledge and pay tribute to the works of my predecessors and contemporaries from whom I have benefited much. Anyone who reads this work closely will know how seriously it takes the labors of one or two pioneers who nurtured the Newbigin field through careful articulation and exposition of his theological vision. Among them, particular mention must be made of Professor George Hunsberger, whose dissertation and academic files were important resources for my research.

I owed a special debt to Bishop Lesslie Newbigin himself, whose theological life and our common link to the church in India has been a source of encouragement for me. I think of the refreshing time spent with him in conversation and correspondence.

I owe much to professors Harold G. Wells, John Webster, and Carl Starkloff for the many ways in which they have enriched my academic life. I want to record my gratitude to Professor Wells, whose comments, queries, and suggestions helped in the improvement of this manuscript. I am most grateful for his continued friendship.

I also acknowledge, with deep gratitude to God, the irreplaceable contribution of my late parents to all my work: my mother and my father who first told me of Jesus and nurtured me in the Christian faith. Their wisdom, goodness, and the life of prayer have always inspired me.

Finally, I am thankful to my family, especially my wife Anita, whose love and care continue to strengthen the vision of a Christ-centered family. I acknowledge the support of my children, Susan, Nathan, and Roshan, who continue to give me cause to rejoice in the goodness of God.

CONTENTS

Acknowledgements	i
Contents	ii
CHAPTER 1: LESSLIE NEWBIGIN: AN INTRODUCTION	1
1. Newbigin and His Life Work	3
2. Newbigin's Theological Formation	15
a. Influences of John Oman	15
b. Two Formative Events	20
3. Newbigin's Theological Writings:	
Their Central Concerns and Characteristics	23
a. The Gospel As a Secular Announcement	26
b. The Christian Mission to the World	26
c. Christian Unity	27
d. Secularization and Culture	28
e. Christ and the Powers	29
4. The Method and Goal of the Book	31
CHAPTER 2: CHRISTOLOGY	34
1. Methodological Questions	34
2. The Fact of Christ	41
3. Jesus as Incarnate God	43
4. Jesus and the Trinity	49
5. Jesus, Spirit and the Church	56
6. Jesus and the Coming Kingdom	67
7. The Election of Israel and The Meaning of History	71
8. Jesus as Saviour of the World	82
The Meaning of Salvation	85
9. Jesus as Unique and Final Revelation of God	90
Concluding Critical Comment	97
CHAPTER 3: KNOWLEDGE AND TRUTH	100
1. Epistemological Questions	102

a. Skepticism and the Possibility of Knowing the Truth	102
b. Knowing and Believing	119
2. Revelation and Scripture	131
The Authority of Revelation	134
3. Using Michael Polanyi's Philosophy	140
a. The Need for a Fresh Starting Point for Thought	142
b. The Republic of Science	147
c. Fiduciary Act in Intellectual Inquiry	155
4. Interaction with Peter L. Berger	160
a. Plausibility Structure	161
b. Newbigin's Critique of Peter L. Berger	166
Concluding Critical Comment	169
CHAPTER 4: CHRIST AND CULTURE: A READING OF THE CONTEMPORARY CONTEXT	171
Definition of 'Culture'	172
Concept of Christ	174
1. Relationship Between Religion and Culture	176
a. Their Inseparability	176
b. 'Gospel' and the Criticism of Culture	179
c. The Role of the Church in Cultural Criticism	185
d. The Question of Contextualization	188
2. A Critique of Modern Western Culture	194
a. Roots in the Enlightenment	194
b. The Loss of Teleology in the Modern World	201
c. Dichotomy of Public and Private Life	211
d. The Reality of Secularization	218
e. The Absence of Hope	229
Concluding Critical Comment	236
CHAPTER 5: THE UNITY OF ALL RELIGION: A RESPONSE TO THE PLURALIST CHALLENGE	237
1. Christ and the Religions	237
a. Newbigin's Concept of 'Religion'	240

Schleiermacher	247
Otto	250
b. The Question of `Continuity/Discontinuity'	253
c. Salvation of Non-Christians	264
2. Newbigin's Conversation Partners	269
a. Karl Barth	270
b. Hendrik Kraemer	276
c. Karl Rahner	285
3. NEWBIGIN AND THE PLURALIST THEOLOGIANS	290
a. Wilfred Cantwell Smith	291
b. Diana L. Eck	297
c. Paul Knitter	301
d. John Hick	305
e. Gordon D. Kaufman	311
Concluding Critical Comment	315
CHAPTER 6: THE NATURE OF INTER-RELIGIOUS DIALOGUE	318
1. Exclusivism, Inclusivism, and Pluralism	318
a. Exclusivism	318
b. Inclusivism	323
c. Pluralism	326
2. The Manner and the Goal of Inter-Religious Dialogue	328
a. Types of Dialogue	328
John Hick	333
b. Manner of Dialogue	339
c. Purpose of Dialogue	346
d. Attitude to Non-Christians	348
e. The Quest for the Unity of All Religions	351
f. Christ and the Unity of Humanity	356
Concluding Critical Comment	361
BIBLIOGRAPHY	364

CHAPTER 1

LESSLIE NEWBIGIN
AN INTRODUCTION

Bishop Lesslie Newbigin's theological work is a reference point for theologians of all traditions, and his later writings are widely used in seminaries and colleges around the world. They reveal an intense awareness of the challenges posed especially by religious pluralism. Numerous references to his books by both Catholic and Protestant writers are an immediate clue to his influence on Christian thinkers across the world. His ecclesiology and missiology have been the subjects of several doctoral dissertations. Newbigin's name is certainly a household word among the churches across the world

Religious pluralism and the salvific nature of non-Christian religions have become in recent years an important area of concern in Christian theology. Generally speaking, this concern is most pronounced in the area of Christology. The view that Jesus may be Saviour for Christians, but not necessarily for all people in all cultures, has become a point of controversy. The occasion for this controversy is the impact of religious pluralism, the new widespread awareness of religious diversity, and the continuing vitality of many religious traditions.

Theologians use several models and concepts in their approach to inter-religious dialogue; some of the flag words that describe these models are `Trinitarian', `Christocentric', `Theocentric', and `Soteriocentric'. These models and what they propose have generated much discussion and debate, primarily because some of them challenge the classical Christology on which the Christian church has based its worship, life, and mission.

Some argue that God's revelation through Jesus Christ, as attested in the Bible, is only a stage in the history of revelation which appears in all religions. There can be no absolute religion; all are relative. There can be no exclusive revelation. The language of exclusivism has been judged as arrogant and dogmatic. Some argue that there is no essential difference between Christianity and non-Christian religions. This, however, does not mean that Christianity is not unique. It is unique, but only in the sense that every other religion is unique. Religious pluralism denies the possibility of knowing any ultimate truth in religion and rejects the idea that there is anything superior or normative about the Christian revelation. This assumption is evident in many debates about inter-religious dialogue. Christian faith is said to be merely one of many equally legitimate responses to the same divine reality. For churches or Christian individuals that hold to a traditional exclusivist understanding of the gospel, pluralism has become a perplexing problem, which has to be addressed in a systematic way. This book, which explores the work of Lesslie Newbigin, stems from an understanding of this need.

Newbigin is one of the most insightful analysts of religious pluralism and its consequences for Christian doctrine and Christian mission. Until his death in 1998, he has been an important participant in the discussion of religious pluralism and inter-religious dialogue. His contribution to this area of theology should be seen as a valuable tool which needs to be expounded and developed further for the use of the church. He consistently maintains "the finality of Christ" as a necessary presupposition which must determine the nature and task of the church's dialogue with people of other religions. Evangelicals are increasingly lending an ear to Newbigin's approach to the Bible, theology, and non-Christian religions. Numerous academic references to Newbigin's writings, found in contemporary theological literature, are a clear indication of his importance in this area. An erudite thinker, his methodology makes use of developments in philosophy, natural sciences, sociology of knowledge, and biblical hermeneutics. This interdisciplinary methodology can be seen as a new way of doing theology which, I believe, is becoming increasingly important. An inquiry into the work of Newbigin, i.e., a thorough study, evaluation and critique of his contribution, seems called for. This book will focus specifically on the centrality of Christ in Newbigin's theology, and its relevance for the church and its relationship with people of other faiths.

To appreciate Newbigin fully, it is important to know about his life, world, work, and his cultural context. In this way, one can take a closer look at the make-up of the man and his concern for making theology intelligible in a pluralistic world. In the next few pages I shall offer a brief outline of Newbigin's life and work which began in England and then spilled over into India and other parts of the world.

1. LESSLIE NEWBIGIN AND HIS LIFE WORK

James Edward Lesslie Newbigin was born in Northumberland, England in 1909. If it is true that one's earliest environment shapes a person in decisive ways, the fact that Newbigin grew up in a devout, Presbyterian family and that he received training in a broad range of disciplines both at home and school are significant.

In his autobiography, Newbigin speaks highly of his parents and their commitment to Christian faith[1]. Prayer was very important for his father, who struggled with the question of how to integrate Christian faith with the day-to-day issues of business and

---

[1] *Unfinished Agenda: An Autobiography* (Grand Rapids, Michigan: Wm. B. Eerdmans Publishing Company, 1985), p. 3.

political life. Newbigin's father was an "able and trustworthy businessman" who owned his own shipping company. His mother was an "exquisite pianist" whose roots were in Scotland. Undoubtedly, Newbigin's upbringing in a Christian home, where there were mutual trust and love among its members, had a direct bearing upon the young Newbigin's outlook on life. He describes his mother as the "most loving and devoted mother" that a child could wish for and he lived by its strength and constancy.[2]

For early childhood learning, young Newbigin was sent to the kindergarten of the girls' school and then to a preparatory school where much of the time was devoted to the study of Latin. Later on Newbigin attended Leighton Park, the Quaker public school in Reading, England, where students had a great deal of freedom and opportunity to develop their ideas and interests. The major reason for the choice of this school was that his father "loathed militarism" and therefore wanted to send him to a school which had no Officers Training Corps. As a student, Newbigin was developing different skills and different dimensions of his personality. The school offered him plenty of opportunities for political debate in which he says that he "espoused the Liberal Cause."[3] He remembers a particular teacher called S. W. Brown, who was helpful to students in creating a capacity "to think, to break out of stereotypes, to explore new ideas and to question old ones."[4] Speaking of his academic interests at Leighton Park, Newbigin says that he had the "ambition to be a renaissance man with interests in all directions" and without specializing in any field, he took a wide range of subjects in order to "keep a foot in all possible camps."[5]

---

[2]Ibid.
[3]Ibid., p. 5.
[4]Ibid.
[5]Ibid.

Leighton Park was a Quaker school. In his evaluation of the school life, Newbigin does not speak favourably of the Quaker meetings. Those meetings, in his opinion, were not the best for a schoolboy to encounter the Christian faith. The scripture lessons in the meetings were "in general utterly boring." Nevertheless, they gave him an "experience of quiet, humble, and attentive waiting upon God" which he appreciated. But by the end of the school days he had "abandoned the Christian assumptions of his home and childhood." Reading in historical geography gave him a "broadly deterministic view of history."[6] During this period, two books were of great influence on his life. In his last year at school, Francis S. Marvin's book, *The Living Past*[7] made the "strongest impact" on his thinking. It gave him "a belief in the human story as an upward striving toward growing mastery over all that stands in the way of man's full humanity."[8] *The Will to Believe*[9] by William James was the second book that impressed him, especially at a time when he was wondering about the possibility of belief in God. This has led him to see that "Christian faith was not irrational."[10]

The next stage of Newbigin's education, which began in 1928 at Cambridge University, was very significant in shaping his life work. It was at Queens' College at Cambridge that he came in contact with distinguished political leaders, such as Anthony Eden and George Lansbury. Newbigin was asked by the headquarters of the Liberal party to run for Parliament after he had finished at Cambridge. But it was at this time that his "liberal principles began to shake" and he began to wonder "if socialism was not the real

---

[6]Ibid., p. 6.
[7](Oxford: Clarendon Press, 1917).
[8]Ibid.
[9](London: Longmans, Green, 1912).
[10]*Unfinished Agenda*, p. 6.

way forward."[11]

It was at Queens' that he was attracted to the Student Christian Movement (SCM), which eventually influenced him very highly. There he was drawn into a "personal faith" by a friend called Arthur Watkins, whose "life was a profound devotion to Christ," and "prayer was his deepest being."[12] There Newbigin became a committed Christian and enthusiastically became involved in the work of the Student Christian Movement. Cambridge was a great opportunity for Newbigin to meet many Christian leaders of the time whose visits left "unforgettable impressions" on him. John R. Mott, Jack Winslow from India (who first awakened his interest in India and showed him the "most attractive elements of Indian spirituality"), John Mackay of Lima (who touched him with the vision of Christian discipleship), and William Temple (who said that "it is possible to be comparatively religious but there is no such thing as comparative religion").

Other major leaders that Newbigin had opportunity to receive and entertain were Hendrik Kraemer, Hans Lilje, C. F. Andrews, and John Grosser. Of the experience of his Cambridge days, Newbigin says that it gave him the "thrilling experience of sharing in a worldwide Christian enterprise which was commanding the devotion of men and women, whose sheer intellectual and spiritual power was unmistakable."[13] At this time, Newbigin was becoming a reader of the *International Review of Missions* and his Christian faith was taking an ecumenical understanding from the beginning. He was deeply committed to the cause of Christian unity, a cause which he espoused with greatest passion in the years to come.

---

[11]Ibid., pp. 8-9.
[12]Ibid., p. 10.
[13]Ibid., p. 13.

Newbigin received his formal theological education at Westminster College, Cambridge, where the well-known Scottish theologian John Oman was the principal. Westminster, the theological college for the Presbyterian Church of England, was founded in 1844 and was relocated from London to Cambridge in 1899. On account of the high quality of its ministerial education, Westminster College was a highly prestigious institution. It was able to bring the Church and its faculty and students "into a relation of vital give-and-take with the general flow of English religious thought."[14] Newbigin's time at the College was very significant as it profoundly changed his understanding of the Christian faith. His education changed him from a liberal to an evangelical.[15]

This theological shift did not mean that Newbigin became unconcerned about social and political issues. Rather, his writings as well as his manifold works in India give evidence of his serious concern and commitment to vital social and political issues. He was in frequent contact with Joseph Oldham and his work in preparation for the Oxford Conference on 'Church, Community and State'. During this time, some of Newbigin's own political ideas were changing. For example, he was a pacifist and a socialist. He began to wonder whether pacifism, in the end, was a kind of "escapism." He learned from R. H. Tawney that there was an "inescapable contradiction between Christianity and capitalism." In his last year at Westminster, Newbigin held a study on 'The Kingdom of God and History', a topic which became "the most

---

[14] W. M. Horton, *Contemporary English Theology* (New York: Harper and Bros., 1936), p. 18. Also see Stephen Bevans, *John Oman and His Doctrine of God* (Cambridge, U.K.: Cambridge University Press, 1992), p. 14.
[15] *Unfinished Agenda*, p. 30.

passionate theological interest" toward the end of his study.[16]

Newbigin's Westminster days were not devoted to formal study alone. He also interacted with renowned Christian leaders from different parts of the world. In his opinion, the person who had the greatest influence on the students of that generation was William Temple. Newbigin remembers vividly the day he was the guest of Temple and how they spent a whole long evening "discussing theological issues and unfolding his vision for the future of the Ecumenical Movement."[17] It is true to say that Newbigin's theological and cultural thought was forged in an age of the "steady rise of German militarism, the long-drawn-out failure of the Disarmament Conference, the re-militarization of the Rhineland, and the Italian attack upon Abyssinia and the Hoare-Laval Pact of December, 1935."[18] These events had challenged some of his assumptions.

Newbigin was first licensed to preach the gospel by the Presbytery of Newcastle and was ordained in 1936 by the Presbytery of Edinburgh for service as a foreign missionary to work in Kanchipuram in Madras. Kanchipuram was one of the seven cities counted most sacred in all of India by the Hindus. It was here that Newbigin was exposed to the teaching of Hindu religion, particularly of the school of Vedanta. At the Ramakrishna Mission he attended a weekly study group in which they studied alternatively *Svetasvara Upanishad*[19] and the gospel of John.

The exposure to the teaching of Hinduism in India was very

---

[16]Ibid., 31
[17]Ibid.
[18]Ibid., p. 36.
[19]*Upanishads* are Indian philosophical and religious texts dating approximately from the 9th to 4th centuries B.C.

rewarding, because it gave Newbigin an awareness of the "profound rationality of the worldview of the Vedanta." He says in his autobiography that he had astonished the *Swamy* by saying that "if it could be shown that Jesus had never lived and died and risen again I would have no alternative but to become a Hindu."[20] Undoubtedly Newbigin's life in Kanchipuram and his engagement with the scholars of Hinduism, especially those of the school of *Visishtadvaita*[21], had equipped him in formulating his view of Hinduism. In his view, the doctrine of this school has many parallels with evangelical Christianity and has been termed "India's Religion of Grace" by Rudolf Otto. Of this religion, Newbigin says,

> Even this profoundly moving and gracious form of religious devotion had its roots and its only support in the human need for salvation, not in a divine act of redemption within the real history of which this human life is a part. I am bound to say that as I reflected on these long discussions on religious subjects with gracious and helpful Hindu friends, I became more and more sure that the 'point of contact' for the Gospel is rather in the ordinary secular experiences of human life than in the sphere of religion. I had not then read Karl Barth, and did not know that 'religion is unbelief', but I was certainly beginning to see that religion can be a way

---

[20] *Unfinished Agenda*, p. 57.

[21] This is a theistic form of belief which may be described as 'Qualified non-dualism,' a system of Hindu philosophy whose chief exponent was Ramanuja (AD 1017-1137), according to which ultimate reality, although non-dual, admits the distinctions of God, living beings, and nature. The ultimate reality is a personal God (*Ishvara*, Supreme Lord).

of protecting oneself from reality.[22]

Newbigin's involvement with the Student Christian Movement brought him into contact with an Indian theologian, M. M. Thomas, which Newbigin describes as the "beginning of a personal and theological friendship which has lasted as a very precious gift through the years." From that time onward, both Thomas and Newbigin have been involved in the World Council of Churches.

Newbigin eventually moved to the South India United Church (SIUC) which had been set up in 1908 by a union of Presbyterians and Congregationalists. He worked with this church until it became part of the 1947 union forming the Church of South India (CSI), which included the Anglicans. Newbigin was elected to be one of the bishops of the church and served in the church in this capacity from 1947 to 1959 in the diocese of Madura and Ramnad. He had serious difficulties with the scheme of church union because of the need for accepting the role of the historic episcopate as an element in a new united church. Finally he overcame this difficulty through two important considerations: One, the fact that the Church was constituted by the Gospel, communicated in word and sacrament, evoking the response of faith. Ministerial order was therefore secondary and could not be put in the same level of importance as Word and sacrament. Two, the historic episcopate could be accepted as something given by the grace of God to be the means of unity. But this also meant that one had to reject at the same time any way of interpreting the historic episcopate which made it a *conditio sine qua non* of the fullness of grace.[23] Newbigin's change of view in this matter was aided by the reading of Michael Ramsey's book *The Gospel and the Catholic*

---

[22]*Unfinished Agenda*, pp. 57-58.
[23]Ibid., p. 75.

Church.[24]

In his diocese Newbigin had opportunities to implement his vision of what he calls a "truly responsible Church." As a response to many local people who had no church in their midst and who wanted to embrace the gospel, Newbigin devised a scheme of early baptism, periods of intensive teaching, and the development of the natural and Spirit-identified leadership.[25]

Newbigin's place of work changed in 1959 when he accepted leadership in the International Missionary Council (IMC) during the two years which led to its integration into the World Council of Churches (WCC) in 1961. His work in this capacity as the first director of the WCC's Division of World Mission and Evangelism gave him experience of a wider spectrum of churches, cultures and circumstances throughout the world. After this, he returned to Madras from Europe in 1965 to his responsibilities as the Bishop of Madras.

Newbigin retired from this position in 1974 to England, where he was invited to teach at the Selly Oak Colleges in Birmingham. His main work was teaching 'The Theology of Mission' and 'Ecumenical Studies' to those who have come from a "rich mix of races, nations and denominations." A second responsibility was teaching Hinduism to the students of Westhill College who were taking religious education in the B. Ed. course of Birmingham University. This necessitated a substantial amount of reading, both in Indian history and Hindu classics. He saw that the churches in Britain were "timid" in commending the gospel to the unconverted. Newbigin sees Britain as a pagan society which has excluded the true God and worships false gods. He believes

---

[24](London: Longmans, Green & Co., 1936).
[25]*Unfinished Agenda*, pp. 146-148.

that the development of a truly missionary encounter with this tough form of paganism, which had been born out of the rejection of Christ, should be the greatest intellectual and practical task challenging the church.[26]

Newbigin, after being a bishop for twenty-seven years in the Church of South India, had the "painful necessity" of choosing a church in England. He was invited to become an assistant bishop in the Church of England, but felt it was wrong for him to accept this. Being committed to unity, he applied for admission as a minister in the United Reformed Church (URC) and was accepted. At the 1977 General Assembly of this denomination, Newbigin was elected to be Moderator for the year 1978-79. His work with the church in Britain and his contribution to the British Council of Churches are highly commended by Christians in Britain. A major concern of his Christian vision is to address the need for an encounter of the gospel with Western culture.

During the period of 1985 - 1995 Newbigin continued, on a much larger scale, his schedules of writing and speaking both in Europe and North America. To find a perspective on his own Western culture, to explore an Archimedean point from which he could critically look at his own intellectual and spiritual formation, was a major concern during this period. Newbigin's questions and insights about the underlying assumptions of the post-Enlightenment Western culture resulted in the formation of a movement called *The Gospel and Our Culture* which, both in Europe and North America, has been growing rapidly. At the heart of this movement is the need for addressing the crisis of Western culture from a missiological perspective. Newbigin, who has been in conversation with non-Christian communities in England, was also drawn into several inter-religious issues. He had in mind the

---

[26]Ibid., p. 249.

aim of developing a truly Christian response to the phenomenon of religious pluralism in Western societies. As a part of this challenge in the area of education, he became involved in the Birmingham debate on the school Syllabus, which was directed "towards developing a critical understanding of the religious and moral dimensions of human experience and away from attempts to foster the claim of particular religious standpoints."[27] This was largely the work of John Hick, who was one of the Church representatives on the Standing Advisory Council on Religious Education for the Birmingham Authority. Newbigin notes that Hick was a personal friend whose theological views had been profoundly changing after coming to Birmingham.[28]

During the 1980s Newbigin made two visits to South India. On the second visit, which took place in 1988, he was a participant at the celebration of the fiftieth anniversary of the Tambaram Conference of 1938. This, as he recalls, was not an easy meeting for him, "since the gathering included several very powerful representatives of a (so-called) pluralist theology, particularly Wilfred Cantwell Smith and Diana Eck."[29] In this meeting, Newbigin found himself fighting the same battle that Hendrik Kraemer had fought at Tambaram fifty years earlier.[30] After his return to England, he has been actively involved in a programme of writing and speaking.

To sum up, Newbigin's life as a theologian, bishop, evangelist and teacher has greatly enriched the life of the Christian churches all over the world. He has held many important positions

---

[27] Lesslie Newbigin, *Unfinished Agenda*, 2nd ed. (Edinburgh: Saint Andrew Press, 1993), p. 245.
[28] Ibid.
[29] Ibid., p. 243.
[30] Ibid.

in World Council of Churches, International Missionary Council, and many other ecclesiastical and social organizations which are too numerous to mention here. All his achievements are characterized by his commitment to the centrality of Christ. This is very clear from the recollection of one of his colleagues. Eugene L. Stockwell, former Director of Commission on World Mission and Evangelism of World Council of Churches, refers to a conversation that Newbigin had with him as follows:

> The conversation was brief and he had but one message: keep Jesus Christ central in all that you do, and persist always in reminding the WCC of the centrality of Jesus Christ. Distilled in that counsel was the commitment of a lifetime of a man who had wrestled with countless ideas, who had been the architect of many ecclesiastical structures, who had moved easily from the poverty of Indian villages to the heady realms of theological scholarship, and through it all knew and grew in the conviction that all of it, as life itself, has only one centre and reason for being, Jesus Christ the Lord of all.[31]

This observation of Stockwell should be seen as insight into the underlying motive and guiding principle of Newbigin's life and work. It is difficult to think of any person over the past fifty years who has made a more lasting contribution to world Christianity than Lesslie Newbigin. If Newbigin's influence on people around the world has been decisive, it is equally true to say that he was also decisively influenced by his own teachers and mentors. I believe that it is

---

[31] "In Tribute to Bishop Lesslie Newbigin," in the *International Review of Mission*, Vol. 79 (January, 1990), pp. 95-96.

important to take a brief look at one `mentor' who has been of considerable influence on Newbigin and his theology, and two important formative events.

2. NEWBIGIN'S THEOLOGICAL FORMATION

Newbigin's formative years were influenced by certain special persons and events. Besides his parents, many churchmen and theologians had been influential in shaping the religious thought of Newbigin. Some names, such as Joseph H. Oldham, William Temple, John Oman, Herbert H. Farmer, Nicol Macnicol and Hendrik Kraemer, are more important than others. Among these, Kraemer became a senior colleague in the ministry, whose association with Newbigin will be addressed elsewhere in this thesis. It is not necessary to survey the kind of influence each of these men have had on Newbigin. However, I shall take the name of John Oman as a formative influence upon Newbigin's thinking on religion.

a. **Influences of John Oman**

The strong reason for preferring this name is that he was his teacher of theology and, in earlier days, his parents' family friend and pastor at Alnwick. `Personal God,' as Newbigin recalls, was an important theological truth which Oman had always emphasized.[32] Newbigin's emphasis on `personal knowledge' is related to this idea. However, it should be added here that, since Oman's theology was influenced by Schleiermacher, Newbigin has never espoused his method. Rather, he emerges as a critic of Schleiermacher. How Newbigin sees Oman's ideas in relation to his own and how he uses them in his writings can be briefly considered here.

---

[32] From a Personal Conversation with Newbigin on 24 October, 1994.

John Wood Oman was principal of Westminster College and Newbigin's first teacher in theology. Oman, who was born in Scotland, was a major theologian of persuasiveness and depth. Newbigin, at one place in his autobiography, gives some interesting glimpses of Oman's teaching at Westminster College. He says,

> His lectures were obscure to the point of opacity, but his writings and, above all, his occasional utterances in chapel, were full of profound insight. Every student had to face, twice a year, the ordeal of preaching in chapel and of then having his sermon criticized by the professors. These were, for me, among the most memorable events in the course. When Oman criticized a sermon, he could be devastating; but when he went on to say how he would have expounded the text, he would produce gems of exposition that I could never forget.[33]

At different places in his writings Newbigin refers to the works of Oman. For example, Newbigin's Firth Lectures at the University of Nottingham in November 1964, published with some changes as *Honest Religion for Secular Man*, are a tribute to John Oman by a "former student."[34] The question of 'How do you know?' was very important to Oman. His *The Natural and the*

---

[33] *Unfinished Agenda*, p. 31.
[34] Lesslie Newbigin, *Honest Religion for Secular Man* (London: SCM Press, 1966), p. 10. According to Newbigin, John Oman's own book, *Honest Religion* (Cambridge: Cambridge University Press, 1941) is characteristic of his whole theology. Oman recognized that theologies can become dishonest.

Supernatural was a "superb intellectual achievement by a profoundly honest thinker." According to Newbigin, it appeared just at the time when the rise of the Barthian theology was "sweeping that question under the carpet." We are facing again that question to which Oman devoted his "tremendous intellectual powers."[35]

Oman's is not a traditional christology. Christological questions were subordinate to the understanding of God as personal. As Stephen Bevans comments, in Oman's writings, christology "never receives a sustained, systematic, and definitive formulation."[36] This does not mean that christology was unimportant for him. His Christology is certainly essential to his doctrine of God, however, and a treatment of the doctrine of God is incomplete without a similar treatment of Jesus. Knowledge of Jesus Christ shapes Oman's theology in general, and particularly his doctrine of God. Instead of calling it christocentric, one could call it "Christomorphic."[37] Jesus is the chief cornerstone of the Church, because he "means more for our direct knowledge of God than all others."[38] He is supremely the object of religious faith.[39]

I shall list here at least four areas where I think that Oman has influenced Newbigin. The first one is the significance of a 'standpoint' in any intellectual inquiry, especially in the task of classifying religions. According to Oman, "there is no use in

---

[35] Ibid. Newbigin refers to Oman's classification of religions in his book *The Finality of Christ* (London: SCM Press, 1969), p. 16. Cf. John Oman, *The Natural and the Supernatural* (Cambridge: Cambridge University Press, 1931), pp. 29-42.

[36] *John Oman and His Doctrine of God*, Op. cit., p. 102.

[37] Ibid.

[38] John Oman, *The Church and the Divine Order* (London: Hodder & Stoughton, 1911), p. 321.

[39] Ibid., p. 288.

pretending that we can look out upon the world from any other standpoint than our own."[40] Again, it is the "merest illusion to think that we can transfer ourselves to some absolute standpoint or do more than look out from the highest standpoint we can reach with our equipment of knowledge, experience and ability." And further, "the position we occupy is the position which seems most to have approved itself to us."[41] Therefore, a classification of religion from one's own standpoint alone is what is possible.

Second, both Oman and Newbigin recognize the difficulty in giving a precise definition to the word `religion'. For Oman,

> So wide is the scope of religion that it has been maintained that its essential quality is to be concerned with the mind as a whole and the world as a whole. In that case, it would be a hopeless task to try to distinguish what embraces everything from anything else and, from the start, any attempt to define religion would seem doomed to failure.[42]

With respect to `primitive' beliefs and practices, the task of determining what is religious is difficult and it is almost impossible to say what is not religious. Newbigin echoes the same concern when he says the word `religion' covers an "extremely wide and

---

[40] John Oman, *The Natural and the Supernatural*, Op. cit., p. 358. That Newbigin affirms the same position can be seen in his engagement of John Hick concerning the method of Inter-religious dialogue. See Newbigin's *The Open Secret* (Grand Rapids: Wm B. Eerdmans, 1978), p. 190 where he states that "no standpoint is available to any man except the point where he stands."

[41] *The Natural and the Supernatural*, p. 359.

[42] Ibid., p. 3.

varied range of entities."[43] For both of them, dealing with religion involves dealing with one's ultimate commitments. Religion is a concern with ultimate reality. Newbigin, like Oman, does not believe that 'religion' is something that can be ignored, because it is "much too great and permanent an element in human experience to be swept out of sight."[44]

Third, there is a similarity of views on the question of the reliability of a given tradition. To what extent can the tradition of a community be considered reliable? This is a question with which both Oman and Newbigin wrestle and find some answers. Oman writes,

> Every living creature is itself a record of the past, and instinct as well as knowledge is in a sense history. But man is distinguished from other creatures by remembered tradition. No one builds anything, not even criticism of what he finds, except upon a foundation already provided by those who went before him. This may be social ideals, customs and institutions, but it has been, in increasing measure, what has been handed down by human memory and then written in books. And, from the beginning, this has had to do with the Supernatural.[45]

Oman appeals to the importance of tradition or the "path which others have trod before." One is greatly helped by giving attention

---

[43] Lesslie Newbigin, *The Gospel in a Pluralist Society* (Grand Rapids: Wm. B. Eerdmans Publishing Co., and Geneva: WCC Publications, 1989), p. 171.
[44] *Honest Religion for Secular Man*, Op. cit., p. 9.
[45] *The Natural and the Supernatural*, Op. cit., p. 346.

to this guidance, but one is not infallibly guided by tradition. One needs to break out on one's own and blaze one's own path when the old path seems to be leading into a dead end. This, according to Oman, is personal rational appropriation.[46] In the same vein Newbigin speaks of the authority of a tradition with respect to the community of scientists which stands on the reliability and authority of their tradition.[47] The knowledge of Divine things, says Oman, comes in a cumulative way which means one building on another's foundation.[48] Human beings are historical beings, and therefore "heirs to the past." The past is important and by interpreting and making it live in the present, its importance is maintained.[49] Or as Bevans comments, tradition is being faithful to the meaning of past achievements in the context of the present.[50]

In short, one could say, that although Newbigin and Oman differ significantly, Newbigin's theological writings include some of Oman's important insights. Besides those already mentioned, both are deeply trinitarian in theology, and both address the relationship between theology and science. Finally, for both of them, the clearest and fullest manifestation of God is Jesus' submission to death on the cross. The cross is the highest manifestation of God's love. This leads us to consider two formative events in Newbigin's life which are related to the cross and the atonement.

b. Two Formative Events

A transforming vision of the cross took place in Newbigin's life

---

[46] *John Oman and His Doctrine of God*, Op. cit., p. 48.

[47] *The Gospel in a Pluralist Society*, pp. 39-51.

[48] John Oman, *Vision and Authority Or The Throne of St. Peter*, new rev. ed. (London: Hodder & Stoughton, 1902), p. 98.

[49] Ibid., p. 173.

[50] Op. cit., p. 51.

during the Cambridge years (1928-31). This event occurred in the Rhondda Valley in South Wales, where miners were "rotting for years in hopeless unemployment and destitution."[51] Newbigin joined the programme of The Society of Friends with the aim of bringing some relief and comfort to the miners' community. It was an opportunity to attempt to do something in a hopeless situation. After his summer term at Cambridge, he traveled with Jim Cottle to Trealaw where they were to help in the programme. Newbigin's primary role was to help with a men's recreation club. Anything in the way of religion was excluded from the programme, lest this would be an occasion for proselytizing by taking advantage of men's helpless situation. Newbigin's analysis of the situation has led him to believe that the real issues were political, both national and international. The miners needed some kind of faith, certainly Christian faith, which would fortify them for today and tomorrow against apathy and despair. No mere form of recreation would provide this.

He speaks of a night when the men managed to get a lot of strong drink into the tent. Before long they were drunk and were fighting with each other. Newbigin went to his tent with the feeling of total defeat. He had nothing to contribute. He describes his transforming vision as follows:

> As I lay awake a vision came to my mind, perhaps arising from something I had read a few weeks before by William Temple. It was a vision of the cross, but it was the cross spanning the space between heaven and earth, between ideals and present realities, and with arms that embraced the

---

[51]*Unfinished Agenda*, p. 11. Also see Newbigin, "I Believe in Christ," in M.A. Thomas, ed., *I Believe* (Madras: SCM Press, 1946), p. 106.

> whole world. I saw it as something which reached down to the most hopeless and sordid of human misery and yet promised life and victory. I was sure that night, in a way I had never been before, that this was the clue that I must follow if I were to make any kind of sense of the world.[52]

This vision of the cross was a transforming experience. "From that moment," says Newbigin, "I would always know how to take bearings when I was lost."[53] He would know where to start again when he had come to the end of all his own resources of understanding or courage.

Another decisive and transforming event in Newbigin's life was again at Cambridge, returning from the service in the SCM. This was studying the book of Romans, which he describes as a turning point in his theological journey.[54] Of this experience, he writes in his autobiography:

> I decided that the Letter to the Romans was probably the most complete and condensed statement of the Gospel and I therefore spent several months wrestling with the Greek text of Romans, surrounded by half a dozen of the major commentaries. That was a turning point in my theological journey. I began the study as a typical liberal. I ended it with a strong conviction about `the finished work of Christ', about the <u>centrality and objectivity of the atonement</u> accomplished in

---

[52] *Unfinished Agenda*, pp. 11-12.
[53] Ibid., p. 12.
[54] Ibid., p. 30.

Calvary.[55]

James Denney's work on Romans was the decisive agent in Newbigin's theological shift to the evangelical camp.[56] For Newbigin, Barth was "incomprehensible" and C. H. Dodd made the Epistle palatable by removing the parts where Newbigin found "strong meat." He could not agree with Dodd's "demythologizing of the wrath of God," because if 'wrath' was only an anthropomorphic way of describing the consequences of sin, then 'love' would have to be explained in the same way.[57] Newbigin received another opportunity to build upon his idea of the atonement when he had to do a major Old Testament exegesis[58] at the College. The journey of this man has ever since been guided by the centrality of the cross of Jesus.

3. NEWBIGIN'S THEOLOGICAL WRITINGS: THEIR CENTRAL CONCERNS AND CHARACTERISTICS

Newbigin's writings cover a period of over fifty-five years. His speeches and writings from 1936, in the year he published his first book, have inspired the thoughts of many people throughout the world.

Newbigin's published works are mostly slender volumes,

---

[55] Ibid. Emphasis added.

[56] Possibly what Newbigin refers to is James Denney's commentary in *The Expositor's Greek Testament 2*, 1st ed., London, 1900. Denney (1856-1917) has written extensively on the subject of the atonement. *The Atonement and the Modern Mind* (London: Hodder & Stoughton, 1903) is one of his several publications on the theme.

[57] Ibid., p. 31.

[58] Ex 30:15-16. The passage deals with the atonement money (a half shekel) to be offered to the Lord.

writing during a hectic schedule of work and travelling. Nevertheless, they raise important questions in theology and mission, and have had a wide impact upon both individuals and churches. For example, his first book, *Christian Freedom in the Modern World*,[59] which was a critical response to John Mcmurray's *Freedom in the Modern World* (London, 1935), had a profound effect on M. M. Thomas, who was a reputable theologian of India.[60] Newbigin's *The Household of God* is a discussion of the character of the church from the perspectives of the Roman Catholic, Protestant, and Pentecostal traditions. This book, which was translated into German, French, Chinese, Japanese, and a Russian text, had a considerable impact upon denominations and individuals regarding the nature of the Church. In Newbigin's own words, "I was even told by one of the *periti* of the Second Vatican Council that it had influenced the writing of *Lumen Gentium*.[61]

When considering the body of Newbigin's writings a few observations come to the fore. First, they are the work of a teacher who presents his material systematically and with great precision. They are a presentation of Christian doctrines and thus have a didactic character. Second, he writes as a pastor and missionary. They reveal a person who is fully committed to the preaching of the gospel and active care of the churches. Both theology and missiology find each other in their mutually enriching relationship in Newbigin's work. It could be said, to use language common today, that he is a `praxis' theologian, where ideas arise primarily out of scripture, but always in relation to practical ministry and discipleship, as in the case of many outstanding Christian theologians. His beliefs and concepts are tested by the practical

---

[59](London: SCM Press, 1937).
[60]"In Tribute to Bishop Lesslie Newbigin" in the *International Review of Mission*, Vol. 79 (January 1990), p. 97.
[61]*Unfinished Agenda*, p. 137.

requirements of a preacher, pastor and bishop. Although Newbigin's works exhibit remarkable knowledge and intellectual clarity, they are written for the wider audience, concerning a number of topics, and have been well-received and widely read. Third, Newbigin writes from a global perspective. There is a breadth in his writing which transcends his Presbyterian and Reformed theology tradition. His works are not limited to one school or tradition. They show the possibility of ecumenical theology in the Protestant context. A fourth characteristic of his writing is its location in the Reformed tradition. Central to this is the study and exposition of the Bible as the primary source of doctrine. Because the revelation attested in the Bible is unique and decisive, it serves as the primary ground of all theologizing.

In the early 1980s his interest in Christian witness both in Britain and other Western societies generally reached new intensity. He could see the absence of a clear Christian perspective with respect to issues affecting the future of modern culture. This was coupled with the decline of churches and the lack of active participation in the existing churches. In 1982 Bishop Newbigin was commissioned by the British Council of Churches to draft a programme statement defining the issues that needed to be addressed. The statement was later published as *The Other Side of 1984: Questions for the Churches*. Response to this was immediate and widespread. Within a short time the book had been published in at least seven languages and stirred responses around the world. Through his most recent writing, Newbigin is engaged in challenging some of the underlying assumptions of Western culture on the basis of the gospel.

In his writings Newbigin covers a wide range of subject matter, dealing with Christology, Christian unity, Sacraments, Political life of the church and much more. The centrality of Christ, as a major theme, can be found in all of Newbigin's writings. His books, theological discourses, and essays and addresses on various topics show an undercurrent of this theme. A review of his works would show that there are certain concerns that are basic to his theology. And I shall now briefly highlight some of them.

a. The Gospel As a Secular Announcement

This is a major emphasis in Newbigin's thought. In its original form, the gospel is the announcement of a historical event for the whole of humanity. Newbigin sees this event, i.e., the life, death and resurrection of Jesus Christ as described in the Bible, in "universal, cosmic terms."[62] The divine purpose for the world has been fulfilled in this event. It is the announcement of the Reign of God. Because of its universal intent, it is also decisive for the whole of human life. It concerns the whole human situation, and not merely one part of it. Newbigin's stress on the 'gospel as public truth' is based upon this universal and cosmic character of the gospel. It is public truth because the gospel is an account of things which have happened. However, to affirm the gospel as public truth does not mean that belief in its truth is to be ensured by the use of political power. It does mean that, as public truth, it is meant not only for a person's private life but also for the public dimension of human life.

b. The Christian Mission to the Whole World

Newbigin rejects a narrow-minded, Eurocentric view of mission. He addresses mission from a global perspective and reflects the universal outlook of the whole church. His contribution to a domestic missiology for Western culture is very instructive. In his writings, the nature, purpose and strategy of missions are

---

[62]Lesslie Newbigin, *The Finality of Christ*, Op. cit., p. 48.

clearly defined.⁶³ Mission is the mission of the triune God. It is proclaiming the Kingdom of the Father, sharing the life of the Son, and bearing the witness of the Holy Spirit. In short, it is trinitarian in character with great stress on the work of Christ in a world of religions.

Newbigin does not support a separation of Church and Mission. In his theology, each is integrally linked to the other. For him, the Church is the mission. The dichotomy between the two, as is seen in the practice of contemporary churches, cannot be justified by the teaching of the Bible or by the basic facts of the Christian faith. He argues that the dichotomy between the Church and Mission leads to a situation where 'Missions' came to mean something different from 'Church'. A great task of the contemporary church is the healing of this rift.

Related to this theological perspective on mission is Newbigin's understanding of inter-religious dialogue and he engages several contemporary pluralists such as John Hick, Stanley Samartha and others, who are actively present in this field. Inter-religious dialogue contributes to mutual understanding among people of different religious beliefs. The question of ultimate truth and commitment in religion is essential to understanding his discussion on inter-religious dialogue. For him, the purpose, manner, and basis of inter-religious dialogue rest on the centrality of Christ.

c. Christian Unity

Christian unity is a key concern in Newbigin's Christian

---

⁶³Lesslie Newbigin's *One Body, One Gospel, One World* (London and New York: International Missionary Council, 1958) is a precise theological analysis of the Christian Mission.

vision and writing. In his early years of ministry in India, his search for unity has led him to think and write about it extensively. *The Reunion of the Church* (SCM, 1948), *The Household of God* (SCM, 1953), and *A Faith for this One World?* (SCM, 1961) are explorations of this concern. Newbigin was a powerful force in the preparatory work for the union of churches in South India. He sees mission and unity as the two sides of the same reality.

Newbigin's understanding of unity is that of organic, visible, bodily church unity. It is a unity in Christ. The notion of unity stems from the doctrine of reconciliation. During the years of 1982-92, he kept reaffirming the commitment to the quest for the visible unity of all Christian people.[64] He saw that the development of local unity was the point at which growth was possible and therefore had to be encouraged. He was deeply involved in the Anglican-Reformed International Theological Commission which met in 1983 for considering the questions of unity. In his report on this meeting, Newbigin placed the question of Christian unity within the doctrine of God's Kingdom.[65]

d. Secularization and Culture

Secularization has been a major theme in Newbigin's writing. When, after many years of service in India he returned to Europe to work with the International Missionary Council, he found the new changes in Europe very shocking. The book *Honest Religion for Secular Man* (SCM, 1966) was written during this period. In 1974, when he finally returned to England he saw Britain as a pagan society. He was coming home to a society which was deeply resistant to the gospel message. During this period there came out two books, *The Other Side of 1984* and *Foolishness to*

---

[64]*Unfinished Agenda*, 2nd ed., p. 242.
[65]Ibid., p. 243.

the Greeks (WCC, 1986). They offer a considerable critique of secularization. While he gives warning against secularization, he does not ignore its positive aspects in a country like India. But Newbigin is a strong critic of western secularized societies which have excluded God from their reasoning and assumptions, and writes about the need for an encounter between western society and the gospel.

e. **Christ and the Powers**

Newbigin's works indicate a serious concern for political theology, dealing with issues such as 'Christ and the powers', the concept of 'Welfare State', and the need for 'unmasking the ideologies' of our time. On various occasions he examines in an interesting way the claims of liberation theology and its use of Marxist analysis. He sees the need for bringing the political structures into an encounter with the claims of the gospel, for Christians must speak the truth to Caesar. The 'powers' stand for the given structures - political, economic, etc. - which have been created in Christ and for Christ for maintaining justice and order. When they claim absolute authority, they assume demonic character and become agents of the 'ruler of this world.'[66] They are disarmed in Christ, but not destroyed (Col. 2: 15; 1 Cor 2. 8). The Church has to respect their role in maintaining justice and has to recognize at the same time that all of them have been judged in the event of the Cross of Christ. This is a foundational thought for Christian political action in the world. He admired the dogmatic theology of the Barmen Declaration and its immense political consequences.[67] The church's political task implies naming and

---

[66] Lesslie Newbigin, "Politics and the Covenant," in *Theology*, Vol. 84, No. 701 (September 1981), p. 358.

[67] Lesslie Newbigin, "The Welfare State: A Christian Perspective," in *Theology*, Vol. 88, No. 721 (January 1985), p. 179.

rejecting the false ideologies of our time. The question is not whether or not Christians should be involved with public affairs, but whether their responsibilities in the public sphere are to be discharged under the rule of Christ, or under the rule of the evil one. In all his discourses and writings on political and economic matters he maintains a strongly Christ-centered view.

In short, it can be said that Newbigin's writings are a clear evidence of a man who was actively engaged himself with every facet of church life and thought. His theological method makes use of developments in the natural sciences (Michael Polanyi), sociology of knowledge (Peter Berger), biblical hermeneutics (Walter Wink), and philosophy (Alisdair MacIntyre). In a Review of Newbigin's *The Gospel in a Pluralist Society* (WCC, 1989), George A. Lindbeck speaks of it as at the "forefront of a new theological trend: one that acquired profile only in the 1980s and which, some people think, will become increasingly prominent in the next decade and century."[68]

Because of Newbigin's keen cultural analysis and his commitment to orthodox Christianity, churches have been paying closer attention to his works, which reveal his struggle to interpret the Christian revelation in relation to new and changing contemporary situations in the world. His firsthand experience of various cultures and religions, coupled with a brilliant mind, has made Newbigin "one of the most perceptive analysts of the consequences of pluralism for Christian churches."[69] He does theology with a vision of the "cross of Jesus as the one place in all

---

[68] *International Bulletin of Missionary Research*, Vol. 14, No. 1 (January 1990), p. 182.

[69] Alister E. McGrath, "The Challenge of Pluralism for the Contemporary Christian Church" in the *Journal of the Evangelical Theological Society*, Vol. 35, No. 3 (September 1992), p. 361.

the history of human culture where there is a final dealing with the ultimate mysteries of sin and forgiveness, of bondage and freedom, of conflict and peace, of death and life."[70]

4. THE METHOD AND GOAL OF THE BOOK

I want to show in this book that Newbigin maintains the centrality of Christ as the fundamental paradigm for all his life and work. He views the gospel not as another religion, but an occurrence in secular history which contains the clue to all history. All his writings turn on this axis. It is the centrality of Christ in his theology that determines the nature and manner of theological dialogue with people of other religions. In this work, I shall contend that Newbigin's contribution to this area of theology is unique in the way in which he employs a Christ-centred/Trinitarian framework to test the presuppositions and truth claims of non-Christian religions and various models of inter-religious dialogue. On the one hand, Newbigin recognizes the grace of God at work in the lives of those who belong to other religions and the need for inter-religious dialogue and cooperation in society for the welfare of all. On the other hand, he rejects any attempt to deny or subordinate the lordship of Christ for the purpose of dialogue with other religions and ideologies. While reaching highly positive conclusions about the value of his work, I shall also offer critical comments aimed at even greater clarity for a Christian theology of religions that is centred in Christ. Lesslie Newbigin's writings will be the primary source of this book.

I have indicated at various places above that the 'centrality of Christ' is a recurring theme in Newbigin's works. In one of the

---

[70] *Unfinished Agenda*, p. 254.

essays,[71] he clearly affirms this centrality in three areas of life, namely, theology, religion, and society.[72] He proposes that we have to take the story of Jesus as the starting point for a "radically new, revolutionary understanding of the world."[73] With this clue, one should set out, not only to understand the world, but also to change it. This is what most theologians cannot do, complains Newbigin. Jesus Christ is not their starting point, but one of the pieces that has to be fitted into the total pattern of a philosophy of life. But Christ cannot be so fitted, as he explains:

> He is only rightly known when he is honoured and obeyed as cause and corner stone of the universe, the one starting point from which we can begin to make sense of the whole of our baffling and perplexing world, and from which we can begin to *change* the world in the direction of God's purpose. Real theology *begins* where that decision of faith has been made.[74]

Newbigin, in speaking of the centrality of Christ for religion, strongly criticizes those who claim to have the knowledge of God without Jesus Christ. Religions can be studied by ordinary methods of observation, but God cannot be studied the same way. Therefore, by suppressing the finality of Jesus among religions, one does not bring unity among the religions.[75]

---

[71]Lesslie Newbigin, "The Centrality of Christ," *The Fraternal*, No. 177 (October 1976), pp. 20-28.

[72]Using Colossians 1:15-20 and 2:13-15, he speaks of the "centrality, the sovereignty, and finality" of Jesus Christ. Ibid., p. 20.

[73]Ibid., p. 25.

[74]Ibid.

[75]Ibid., p. 26.

Not only for theology and religions, but for the whole of society Christ must be central. All things have been created in Christ, through Christ and for
Christ. Social structures have been treated as if they were outside the sphere of the

gospel. Christ is before all things, and therefore, sovereignty belongs to Christ alone.

Because of the work of Christ on the cross, neither the political order, nor the economic order, nor law, nor religion, nor custom can claim absolute authority again. "Final authority, sovereignty, belongs to Jesus alone."[76] Newbigin argues that Jesus is the "Lord of the Universe and his Cross is final for all things in heaven and earth."[77] It is with this observation of Newbigin's view of Christ that I proceed to examine his christology.

---

[76] Ibid., p. 27.
[77] Ibid., p. 28.

CHAPTER 2

CHRISTOLOGY

Christology occupies the centre of the Christian faith. It is true to say that there is an organic unity and relatedness among all Christian doctrines, and yet there is a particular sense in which the knowledge of Jesus Christ as the incarnate Lord is the central point of Christian truth. The incarnation and the work of atonement are at the heart of Christian truth. The special revelation of God in Jesus gives particular and distinctive meaning to all other doctrines. As God's special revelation, Jesus stands in a mediatorial relation between God the Father and humanity. Here there is a bi-directional movement involving Christ. In the movement toward humanity, he reveals God, manifests his saving power and relates God to human beings; and in the movement toward God, he leads and relates them to God. As the one mediator between God and humanity, he brings the true knowledge of the invisible God. As the Bible teaches, Christ is both the wisdom of God and the power of God (1 Cor. 1:24, 30), and grace and truth came through him (Jn 1:14, 17). One can say that both revelation and redemption are found in Jesus as the Christ. Therefore it is logical to say that within the trinitarian framework there is a special place for Christology.

1. METHODOLOGICAL QUESTIONS

Newbigin ascribes a special role to Christology within the trinitarian framework, because the doctrine of the Trinity "depends upon Christology."[1] It is "only because of Christ that we have learned to speak of God as triune."[2] We see the Son in relation to the Father, and the Son in relation to the Spirit. Trinitarian doctrine has at its centre the incarnation of Jesus. So he affirms: "For me, Christ is absolutely central."[3]

Although Newbigin has not produced a special treatise on Christology, he nevertheless works out of a christology which, if gathered up from his many writings and addresses, assigns the person of Christ the incomparable place as the final and unique revelation of God to the world. Every major theme in his writing is connected to the person of Christ, which can rightly be seen as his 'christological basis'.[4] Newbigin is concerned that most often christological discussions are based upon an idea of God which has been derived from sources other than the Bible. But he wants to begin his thinking about God with Jesus, and by listening to Jesus, he wants to learn who God is. Let us explore, then, the main elements of Newbigin's theology of Jesus Christ.

Newbigin affirms the incarnation, divinity, atoning work, resurrection, and second coming of Jesus Christ. These essential biblical doctrines are foundational for his whole theological understanding, including his approach to other religions. Moreover, Newbigin's christology can be said to have developed, at certain

---

[1] From a personal conversation with Newbigin at Duke University, on 24 October, 1994.
[2] Ibid.
[3] Ibid.
[4] See, for example, the work of John Reilly, S.J., *Evangelism and Ecumenism in the Writings of Lesslie Newbigin and Their Basis in His Christology, Excerpta ex dissertatione ad Doctoratum in Facultate Theologiae*, (Roma: Pontificia Universitas Gregoriana, 1979), p. 15.

points, precisely in response to and in dialogue with non-Christian religions and ideologies. The biblical picture of Jesus is being brought into a sharp focus against certain non-Christian interpretations of Jesus. He rejects the Hindu view that Jesus is one of many names among the pantheon of deities.

Newbigin believes that in the New Testament "there is a variety" of Christologies, but there is not an unlimited variety.[5] It is a fact that there were differing ancient traditions about Jesus, but not all of these became canonical for the historic Christian church. The canonicity was determined by the belief that the name of Jesus referred to a real human person who lived at a specific time and specific known place in history. The church struggled to verify the various traditions about Jesus against the testimony of original witnesses or of those who were related to the original witnesses by a continuous tradition of public teaching. Concerning the completion of the canon, Newbigin has this to say:

> Those which were accepted, varied as they are, were united by the fact that they were judged to be reliable reports about the same person. The inclusion of a variety of differing accounts, and the absence of any attempt to iron out these differences so as to create
>
> a single picture, is evidence of the fact that the controlling fact was the actual person who had lived - not the doctrines about him.[6]

The fact that there are several Christologies in the New Testament

---

[5]Lesslie Newbigin, *The Open Secret* (Grand Rapids: Eerdmans Publishing Co., 1978), p. 175.
[6]Ibid., pp. 175-176.

is "not an unfortunate defect to be regretted or concealed." On the contrary, recognition of this is important for a "faithful doing of Christian theology."[7] It makes clear the fact that "Christology is always to be done *in via*, at the interface between the gospel and the cultures which it meets on its missionary journey."[8] In his words,

> It is of the essence of the matter that Jesus was not concerned to leave as the fruit of his work a precise verbatim record of everything he said and did, but that he was concerned to create a community which would be bound to him in love and obedience, learn discipleship even in the midst of sin and error, and be his witnesses among all peoples. The varied Christologies to be discovered in the New Testament reflects the attempts of that community to say who Jesus is in the terms of the different cultures within which they bore witness to him.[9]

Newbigin does not want "one definitive Christology framed in the *ipsissima verba* of Jesus himself," because this would bind the gospel perpetually to the culture of first-century Palestine.[10] This would create a situation similar to that of the Qur'an, where the New Testament would have to be regarded as untranslatable. In the end, one would be dealing with a different kind of religion altogether. Therefore the variety of Christologies is "part of the fundamental witness to the nature of the gospel," namely the destination of the gospel in all the human cultures. The New Testament contains, "not every Christology," but "only those which

---

[7] Ibid., p. 176.
[8] Ibid.
[9] Ibid.
[10] Ibid.

were judged to be faithful to the original testimony."[11] Thus the New Testament has a unity which reflects the origin of the gospel in the one unique person of Jesus.

Newbigin suggests that when the New Testament is read in the context of the Old Testament, it provides us, in the variety and unity of its interpretation of Jesus - with the canon, the regulator and guide of our Christology. He says,

> It shows us that Christology must always be something *in via*, incomplete, but it shows us that the road has a real starting point in the historic fact of Jesus Christ who lived, taught, died, and rose again under Pontius Pilate; that it has a real destination in the universal confession of this Jesus as Lord; and that the two conditions for the journey are faithful confession within the varied cultures, and faithful mutual openness within the ecumenical fellowship.[12]

At this juncture there can arise questions about the possibility of a reliable knowledge about the historic fact of Jesus. Such knowledge might enable one to speak of a known starting point for the journey of Christology. Issues such as these always spring from the sphere of the modern critical study of the New Testament.

According to Newbigin, the application of the modern methods of critical historic research to the contents of the New Testament involves two issues. First, it involves the greatly improved tools for examining the origins of each tradition and the factors which have shaped its formation and influenced its

---

[11] Ibid.
[12] Ibid., p. 177.

transmission. Second, it involves the presuppositions which control the use of the tools. Against the background of these two issues, Newbigin firmly asserts that the attempt to write history involves "assumptions about what is significant," and therefore "assumptions about the ultimate meaning of the story."[13] Therefore Newbigin rightly holds to the fact that the question of the ultimate meaning of history is the question of one's ultimate faith-commitment. The skepticism of the modern Western critic about the possibility of a reliable knowledge of the Jesus of history arises, not from a vacant mind, but from an implicit faith-commitment based on the post-Enlightenment culture.

Newbigin unhesitatingly gives credibility to the original writers of the New Testament corpus, affirming that the writing was formed within a community which believed that the ultimate meaning of the whole human story had been declared in the total fact about Jesus as the first witnesses had known him. Within the limitations of the historical methods available to the community within their culture, they sought to create and hand on a record which was faithful to the original testimony of those who had known Jesus in the flesh and who were witnesses of his resurrection. The selection and handling of the material was controlled by the fact that in Jesus the meaning of God's whole story is revealed.[14]

Presuppositions are important in doing Christology. Newbigin derives these, not from the modern scientific world view, but from the gospel itself.[15] He believes that theology has become captive to the University and the academic world, where

---

[13]Ibid.
[14]Ibid., p. 178.
[15]"The Centrality of Christ," in *The Fraternal*, No. 177 (Oct. 1976), p. 20.

the criteria of what is credible are not drawn from the "figure of Jesus Christ."[16] Newbigin does not want to devote his energies to critical, literary and historical studies, where scholars use presuppositions and axioms derived from outside the Bible. They feel that the story about Jesus has to be sifted and interpreted in the light of these axioms and presuppositions. Newbigin charges that some theologians write as if they had a secure basis for understanding human existence and that from this basis they can assess the evidence about Jesus and decide how much of it can be accepted and how much can be rejected.[17] A serious consequence of this approach is that it produces a dichotomy between *geschichte* and *historie*, as is typical of Bultmann, i.e., a distinction between the kind of interpreted record of Jesus available in the New Testament and the kind of record considered acceptable to `scientific' historical research.

A serious objection to this distinction is raised by Newbigin, because, in his words, it "drives a wedge between the scholar and the believer, between Jesus of historical research and the Christ of faith."[18] This dichotomy hurts a preacher who is trying to speak the truth to a believing congregation. Newbigin rejects this dichotomy because it rests on the assumption that scientific methods can produce a kind of history which would consist simply of objective facts, free of all value judgments. But the ultimate reality with which we have to deal is God. For the modern scholar, these assumptions and presuppositions have become a substitute for God. Thus the interpreter has to fit Jesus into this picture of reality. But, he argues, Jesus has to be the starting point, and not a piece to be fitted into the total pattern of a philosophy of life.[19]

---

[16]Ibid.
[17]Ibid., p. 21.
[18]Ibid.
[19]Ibid., p. 25.

Newbigin's view of Christ is based upon the foregoing affirmations, which is drawn from the New Testament. Here he often refers to what he calls the `total fact about Jesus.' Since this expression is found frequently in his writings, it is appropriate for us to introduce and examine the meaning of this phrase in the following section.

2. THE FACT OF CHRIST

The `fact of Christ', or sometimes the `total fact of Christ,' is a concept which Newbigin uses as a standard or criterion for his discussions in Christology.[20] The source of this phrase is Newbigin's own teacher Dr. Carnegie Simpson[21], who meant by this `the life, death and resurrection of Jesus interpreted by the apostles.'[22] Simpson, in presenting this fact of Christ, goes back to the questions of Jesus at Caesarea Philippi: "Who do people say the

---

[20] Lesslie Newbigin, *Christ Our Eternal Contemporary* (Madras: The Christian Literature Society, 1968), p. 23. Newbigin shows that the word `fact' is derived originally from the Latin *factum*, which means something which has been done, and having been done, is there and cannot be changed. See his "Confessing Christ in a Multi-Religion Society," in *Scottish Bulletin of Evangelical Theology*, Vol. 12, No. 2 (Autumn 1994), p. 126.

[21] *The Fact of Christ* (London: Hodder & Stoughton, 1901). Simpson views the fact of Christ as a "fact of history, of conscience, and of spiritual experience." Christ is even more than "a fact of ancient history," he is an "ever-living fact of present or personal experience." Simpson says that `the Christ of history' and `the Christ of experience' are to be held and stated together. See pp. 43, 44, 45.

[22] Lesslie Newbigin, *The Finality of Christ*, p. 75.

Son of Man is?" and "Who do you say I am?" (Mt 16: 13b, 15b). These questions are a "critical issue for religion and its proper point of departure,"[23] because they are not about God or about morals or about principles but about Jesus himself. "Jesus," says Simpson, "absorbs the highest principles into his own personality."[24] He came not to elaborate a system of theology or ethics but to introduce himself to human minds. Simpson argues that the foundation of Christianity is not theological or ethical ideas but the person of Christ.[25] The "most patent and accessible of data" for Jesus' followers was himself, the person standing before them.[26] Simpson maintains that The data of His religion were and are in a positive fact. What are the data? Unverifiable sentiments or ideas in the inscrutable region of faith? Not so. `Whom say ye that I am?' `What think ye of Christ?' `I am the truth.' `Come unto Me.' Here are the data of Christianity. They are in an historical person, a fact as available as any other fact.[27]

The fact of Christ contains the "data of Christianity" and it is a "fact of conscience as well as history." It calls for a moral decision. One must "meet that fact with moral as well as mental candour," and must meet it with not only a "mind open to historical facts but also a will honest with moral issues."[28]

Both Newbigin and Simpson speak of the `fact of Christ' as accessible historical data. For Newbigin, as he uses it on various occasions, the `fact of Christ,' is what gives credibility to Christianity which deals with the particular happening of the

---

[23] *The Fact of Christ*, Op. cit., p. 3.
[24] Ibid., p. 6.
[25] Ibid., p. 45.
[26] Ibid., p. 12.
[27] Ibid., p. 13.
[28] Ibid., p. 48.

living, dying, and rising of Jesus at one time and place.[29] This concept, which is a broad term, is used as a starting point even to question his own accepted beliefs. It helps him in answering the 'why' and 'what' of life's serious questions. If the great sages of India have begun their religious inquiry with the 'experience of realization' or the 'universal religious consciousness,' Newbigin begins with what he calls the 'fact of Christ.'[30] He justifies this by saying that Christ laid hold upon him in his time of perplexity and failure and the search for a firm standing ground, "the one reality that can span the whole dimension, the height and the depth, the length and the breadth of human experience" is the cross of Christ.[31]

Newbigin ascribes a 'particularity' to the fact of Christ and he is aware of the possible objections to this starting point. Nevertheless, he has sufficient grounds for justifying the use of this concept as his starting point for thought.[32] First, the particularity rests in the fact that God has revealed himself in a person. It has to be a particular person, a particular deed, and that means a particular place and particular time. Second, there is a particular centre for human history. There is no compelling reason to deny the possibility that human history in all its vastness and perplexity might have a single centre from which alone it could all be fully understood.

3. JESUS AS INCARNATE GOD

The incarnation of Christ - what God has done in Jesus Christ - is a fact of history which is accessible to us. This is

---

[29]Lesslie Newbigin, *The Open Secret*, p. 57.
[30]*Christ Our Eternal Contemporary*, Op. cit., p. 23.
[31]Ibid., p. 23.
[32]Ibid., p. 24.

"ultimate reality" and as such it is central in assessing everything else.[33] All historical facts, according to Newbigin, are judgments of historical evidence. But he confesses that the story of Jesus does not have any "bare facts," if this means uninterpreted facts.[34] Newbigin works with the data, which are the testimonies of those who believed in him as the Lord and Saviour.

The basic biblical text on the theme of incarnation is the prologue of the Gospel of John. In his exposition of the fourth Gospel[35], Newbigin describes the prologue as an "overture" that announces the themes which will be developed as the story unfolds. The themes such as 'life,' the 'light and darkness', 'truth,' 'glory,' etc., have an important christological association. His exposition of the fourth Gospel is important for his understanding of the meaning of the incarnation of God in Jesus Christ.

The Johannine language describes God as eternally existing. God was before time was. Everything came into existence by God's Word. Newbigin says that the fundamental philosophical question "Why is there not nothing?" can be answered only in this way: "In the beginning was the Word." This Word, both creative and revealing, was with God before time was. Here the creative Word of God is God, for none but God can create. Likewise the revealing Word of God is none other than God, for none but God can reveal

---

[33] Lesslie Newbigin, "Confessing Christ in a Multi-Religion Society," in *Scottish Bulletin of Evangelical Theology*, Op. cit., pp. 126, 128.
[34] Lesslie Newbigin, "The Centrality of Jesus for History," in Michael Goulder, ed., *Incarnation and Myth* (London: SCM, 1979), P. 198.
[35] Lesslie Newbigin, *The Light Has Come: An Exposition of the Fourth Gospel* (Grand Rapids: Wm. B. Eerdmans Publishing Co., 1982).

God.³⁶ The 'Word' which has been referred to here is not a philosophical abstraction. The Word is "He," Jesus. He is the one "who is God's word, who is God, and who was with God" from before time was. The Gospel is the story of a "man among men, occupying one place and time in the created order of time and place," and yet it is the story of the "one who stands beyond all time and space." ³⁷ The incarnation constituted the pre-existent Son a member of the human race.

To call Jesus "the Word" might convey different images to human minds such as the creative Word of Genesis, the Word of God in the mouths of the prophets and evangelists, the *logos* of the Stoic philosopher and of the various schools of thought which sought to use that concept as a point of fusion between Greek and Hebrew thinking. This 'Word' Jesus is "not merely declarative," but "creative and life-giving." The incarnation of God has overcome the dichotomies of the ancient world into which the Gospel came. The ultimate division of things into "natural" and "spiritual" has been overcome by the incarnation in Jesus, for all that is has its unity of origin and purpose in Jesus. This is one of the most decisive implications of the incarnation, which gives rise to Newbigin's integral Christian worldview.

As God Incarnate, Jesus reveals the very character of God. He is the bearer of God's life and light. As the Father has life in himself, so has he granted the Son also to have life in himself (Jn 5: 26). The life of Jesus is not for himself but for the life of the world. He gives "eternal life," "life in his name," to those whom the Father gives him. The life of God is also the light of truth. The light which shone in Jesus, and which shines on as the name of Jesus is preached, is none other than the light of God himself.

---

³⁶Ibid., p. 2.
³⁷Ibid., p. 3.

Newbigin notes that the Johannine language, although it carries a "timeless" dimension, is intertwined with plain narration of history. It is "in this history that the eternal reality of God is present, active, and manifest."[38] The incarnation of the eternal Word of God is the centre which gives history its meaning and apart from that one centre, life has no meaning.[39] In other words, the incarnation is a historical event and Jesus is "the true, the authentic, the real light" which was coming into the world. This light is the light which enlightens everyone. In what sense does this light enlighten? This question is pertinent, because

> There is a long tradition which understands this enlightenment as the inner illumination of reason and conscience, thus bringing it into line with Stoic ideas about the *logos* being a seed within each one capable of developing into full understanding. More strangely still, it has often been assumed that this inner illumination is to be identified with the various religions of mankind. Nothing in the text suggests this.[40]

So, the text must be interpreted in line with the consistent usage of the evangelist throughout the Gospel. It does not refer to inner illumination of conscience and reason. Therefore, one cannot take a moralistic approach to the work of Christ, so that he is seen as the Saviour of the good, and not as the Saviour of sinners. Jesus is "the true light" and he is the light of truth which shines upon every human being, including non-Christians, bringing all under

---

[38] Ibid., p. 5.
[39] Lesslie Newbigin, "Christ and the World of Religions," in *Churchman*, Vol. 97 (1983), p. 28.
[40] *The Light Has Come*, p. 6. Cf. "Christ and the World of Religions," in *Churchman*, Op. cit., p. 28.

judgment. There are not different varieties of light, but there is only one light, namely, that which enables us to see things as they really are. Newbigin's understanding of the universality of grace arises from this incarnation of light that shines upon all.

The incarnation of God in Jesus is a movement "in opposite direction," which means it is from God to humanity and not from humanity to God. This was necessary because to pass from darkness to light and to lay hold on the life of God is "beyond the power of flesh and blood and of the human will."[41] God himself became a human being and "pitched his tent" among the humans. It is *shekinah* which revealed the presence and glory of God. What the incarnation reveals is the same glory which was revealed in the "tent of meeting" where God met with his people (Ex 40:34-38) and that filled the temple of Solomon (1 Kings 8:10 f.). The incarnation is the fulfillment of the divine promise to Israel: "... I am coming and I will dwell in the midst of you" (Zech 2:10). Now the promise has been fulfilled for those who have been given eternal life. The glory of God, which tabernacled among human beings, is the "glory as of the only Son from the Father." Jesus glorifies God and receives glory by his humble obedience, even to the point of death. All the pagan conceptions of glory are eliminated in the manifestation of the true glory of Christ. The true glory is revealed in the figure of a slave humbly washing the disciples' feet, and finally offering his life itself in obedience to his Father's will. What we see in this great event is "not the self-glorification of a supreme monad which egocentric man fashions in his own image," but "the ceaseless and limitless giving of love and honor to the other within the being of the one God."[42] Newbigin asserts both the divinity and humanity of Christ within the trinitarian framework.

---

[41] Ibid., p. 8.
[42] Ibid., p. 9.

The specificity and the particularity of the incarnation within history is important for understanding Newbigin's stance on the nature of inter-religious dialogue. Throughout Newbigin's writings one finds this insistence on the specificity and particularity with respect to the incarnation. It is the "actual presence" of the Word through whom all things were made.[43]

The incarnation was also a crisis of religion, because God Incarnate was rejected by the most religious people of the time. Those who claimed to see rejected the light of God in Christ. Newbigin calls this the "terrible paradox of human existence" that "Religion" in its "purest and loftiest form is found to belong to the area of darkness."[44] Nevertheless, God's movement toward humanity in Jesus has brought eternal life to those who believe in his name. Thus,

> There is a fresh creative act when, in a world that is in darkness because men have turned away from the one true light, the *fiat lux* is spoken again and men turn to the light and become children of the light. The coming of Jesus into the world of "flesh and blood" was the fresh creative act of God himself, and it has as its result the existence of a company of men and women whose life is a kind of extension of his, a new life which is no achievement of human desire or human power, but a sheer gift of God.[45]

What we see here is not a philosophical exercise, but a biblical, practical understanding of the incarnation which is central in

---

[43] Ibid., p. 10.
[44] Ibid., p. 7.
[45] Ibid., p. 8.

Newbigin's understanding of Christ. Most often, the debate about the incarnation is carried out on the basis of an idea of God derived from sources other than the Bible. For some pluralists, natural theology is the source. But the God of natural theology could not possibly become incarnate.

4. JESUS AND THE TRINITY

The trinitarian doctrine of God is an essential constituent of Newbigin's theology. His articulation of this doctrine becomes lively and useful in the context of mission and dialogue with people of other faiths. It is the doctrine of the Trinity that offers what Newbigin calls the "true grammar of dialogue" between members of different religions.[46] A "fully and explicitly trinitarian doctrine of God" is a necessary framework to understand what God is doing in the secular events of history.[47] The Christian understanding of God as Father, Son and Holy Spirit offers resources to meet the challenging perplexities of our time. The engagement of the missionary movement with the culture has brought the question of the uniqueness and finality of Jesus Christ into a sharp focus. From the perspective of missiology, a true doctrine of missions must have a large place for the work of the Holy Spirit and of God the Father.[48] However, he believes that a "church-centric" view of missions has to be corrected, because this has perhaps been "too exclusively founded upon the person and work of Christ".[49] But the missionary period which was known for

---

[46]*The Open Secret.*, p. 207.

[47]Lesslie Newbigin, *The Relevance of Trinitarian Doctrine for Today's Mission* (London: Edinburgh House Press, 1963), p. 31. The American edition *Trinitarian Faith and Today's Mission* (Richmond, Virginia: John Knox Press, 1964) has no change of contents.

[48]Ibid.

[49]Ibid.

this church-centric view, nevertheless, had "immense importance and fruitfulness." For Newbigin, a true perspective of the Christian mission is based upon a trinitarian framework. His book *The Open Secret*[50] is a more thorough outworking of this framework.

Historically, it was when the early Church began to communicate the message of salvation through Jesus Christ that it felt the need for fully articulating the doctrine of Trinity. Newbigin considers it a significant fact that the great doctrinal struggles about the nature of the Trinity, especially about the relations of the Son and the Father, developed right in the midst of the struggle between the Church and the pagan world.[51] The Trinitarian doctrinal struggles were indeed an essential part of the battle to master the pagan worldview at the height of its power and self-confidence. It was a world which interpreted human life mainly in terms of the interaction between 'virtue' and 'fortune,' or to put it in modern terms, the interaction of the human person's intelligence, skill and courage with the forces of the environment. In that Graeco-Roman cultural milieu, it was the doctrine of the Trinity which the Church used as the key to the theological debate. "In other words," says Newbigin,

> [I]t was in terms of this doctrine that Christians were able to state both the unity and distinctness of God's work in the forces of man's environment and God's work of regeneration within the soul of man. The vehemence of the doctrinal struggles which centred

---

[50]The third chapter of the book is about the mission as the mission of the triune God. More specifically, mission has to do with proclaiming the Kingdom of the Father, sharing the love of the Son and bearing the witness of the Spirit.

[51]*Relevance of Trinitarian Doctrine for Today's Mission*, Op. cit., p. 32.

on the formulation of the trinitarian doctrine and especially on the question of the relation of the Son to the Father is evidence of the centrality of this issue for the whole Christian witness to the pagan world of that time.[52]

If the early Church had regarded the doctrine of the Trinity as an important subject for its life, by contrast, this doctrine has not occupied a comparable place in Christian thought during the era of `Christendom.' This was never in dispute during the theological struggle which led to the Reformation. The reason for this, says Newbigin, is not any widespread tendency to deny the doctrine, but simply that it has been regarded as a "venerable formulation" handed down from the past or as a "troublesome piece of theological baggage" which is best kept out of sight when trying to commend the faith to unbelievers.[53]

But this doctrine is not something that can be kept out of sight. Rather, it is the starting point of preaching outside the Christendom situation. Even in the simplest form of missionary preaching, one cannot escape dealing with this doctrine. When preaching Christ in a non-Christian culture, which has in its vocabulary the word `god,' the framework of Trinity is essential. Trinity is a reference point to explain who Jesus is in a non-Christian context.[54] Jesus is to be preached as the Son, the only begotten from the Father. The doctrine of the Trinity is the *arche* for the preaching, because it reveals who Jesus is. Therefore, the preaching must "presuppose an understanding of the triune nature of God."[55]

---

[52]Ibid.
[53]Ibid.
[54]Ibid., p. 33.
[55]Ibid., p. 34.

However, Newbigin realizes the fact that even in the New Testament, an "explicit trinitarian theology" is not found. Although there is no "formally developed doctrine of the Trinity," there is a "trinitarian pattern" present in the language of Saint Paul. A true restatement of the missionary task in a pluralistic, polytheistic, pagan society rests, as the New Testament rests, upon the revelation of God as Father, Son and Spirit.[56] This trinitarian conception, as we shall see in the next chapter, is to be a new guideline for facing the crisis of modern culture.

Most importantly, Newbigin examines the importance of the relationships within the Trinity as follows:

> The Gospel records, and the New Testament as a whole, show us Jesus as the Son of the Father, as the 'Beloved Son,' as the 'Only begotten from the Father.' It is impossible to think of him or to speak of him truly apart from the Father. He reveals God by showing us the love and obedience of the Son to the Father. No account of the gospel which does not put this in the centre can be accepted.[57]

Here he examines the distinction between the Father and the Son and their mutual relationship. God's fatherly rule of all things is a fact that comes at the heart of Jesus' teaching. As the Son, Jesus loves and obeys the Father and submits himself to his ordering of events. He does not seek to take control himself of world history. Although the Father alone is in control of all events, the coming of the Son is the event by which the Father has chosen to bring all things to the point of decision, to the issue of judgment and

---

[56]Ibid.
[57]Ibid., p. 35.

salvation.[58]

Jesus is also related to the third person of the Trinity, the Spirit. The Father calls human history to its final issues by the Son, and this, by the presence of the Holy Spirit. Newbigin makes reference to the descending of the Spirit on Jesus at his baptism and the words of the Father who affirms his sonship as a decisive event of the Trinity.[59] Jesus was anointed by the Spirit and it is as one anointed by the Spirit that he stands up in the Synagogue at Nazareth (Lk 4: 16 ff.) to announce the year of the Lord's favour. Newbigin observes:

> And it is not blasphemy against the Son, but blasphemy against the Spirit speaking and working in him that becomes the occasion for final condemnation. Likewise for the disciples also, it is the Spirit who is the witness. It is by his presence that they receive the gift of sonship and are enabled thereby to continue in the world the ministry of the Son.[60]

There are implications of this understanding of Jesus and the Trinity for the calling of Christians. They are to continue through history the ministry of Christ, "looking up to the Father as those who share his Sonship, accepting the Father's disposition of events as the form in which their mission is to be accomplished, rejoicing in the presence of the Spirit who gives them the foretaste of God's completed purpose and therefore confronts the world with the most powerful witness to that purpose and with the necessity to accept

---

[58]Ibid., p. 36.
[59]Ibid., p. 37.
[60]Ibid.

or reject it."⁶¹

The trinitarian framework gives clarity and direction to Christian mission in the world. The Christian is always faced with the need for explaining who Jesus is in a religiously plural world. The question of the identity of Jesus becomes a pressing one particularly in a Hindu religious context. The doctrine of the Trinity, as has been stressed above, is a reference point which identifies the Christian mission as the mission of the triune God.⁶² For a Hindu, Jesus is a *jeevanmukta*, one who has attained in this life the full realization of the divine. For a Muslim, he is a messenger of Allah. Modern Western people may see him as one of the religious leaders of the world. Some Tamil preachers might call him *Swamy* ("Lord"), or *Satguru* ("the true teacher"), *avatar* ("incarnation of God") or even *Kadavul* ("the transcendent God"). But, by these words, people try to place Jesus "within a world of ideas which is formed by their tradition and which is embodied in the language of the people."⁶³ But these names are qualitatively different from the biblical words such as *Kurios* and Yahweh. The relationships in the Trinity offer a language to answer the question about the identity of Jesus.

The confession of who Jesus is, such as that of Peter,⁶⁴ is not the work of "flesh and blood" but a gift of the Father.⁶⁵ It is the

---

⁶¹Ibid., p.44.
⁶²*The Open Secret*, p. 20.
⁶³Ibid., p. 21.
⁶⁴Simon Peter answered, "You are the Christ, the Son of the living God."
(Mt. 16:16)
⁶⁵Jesus replied, "Blessed are you, Simon son of Jonah, for this was not revealed to you by man, but by my Father in heaven." (Mt. 16:17)

primary work of the Spirit himself.[66] It is the work of the Spirit of God to reveal who Jesus is in particular cultural situations.

Three things can be noted in the Gospel of Mark (1: 1-15) to speak of Jesus and the Trinity. First, Jesus announces the reign of God (Mark 1:25). God was already known in Israel as the one who reigns. Israel had to "say among the nations" that "the Lord reigns" (Ps 96: 10). Newbigin points out that

> Through centuries of crushing defeat and humiliation a remnant in Israel had kept alive the faith that the sovereign Lord would in the end reveal his hidden kingship, tear aside the illusions behind which evil carries on its work, dethrone the idols, and come to reign in justice over the nations.[67]

Jesus is not the initiator or founder of the Kingdom, but the one who is sent as "herald and bearer of the kingdom."[68] Second, Jesus is acknowledged as the Son of God. Jesus used the word *Abba*, as an intimate mode of speech from a son to his father. Though Jesus is the bearer of the kingdom, he is yet at the same time the obedient Son. The sovereignty which Jesus brings is not exercised in his own name but in the name of the Father. This sovereignty is exercised by one who looks up in loving obedience as a son to a father. The third point to be remembered is that Jesus was anointed by the Holy Spirit. What is seen in the anointing of Jesus by the Spirit is the fulfillment of all the Old Testament promises about the Holy Spirit resting on him in a unique way to be the agent of God's

---

[66]Therefore I tell you that no one who is speaking by the Spirit of God says, "Jesus be cursed," and no one can say, "Jesus is Lord," except by the Holy Spirit (1 Cor. 12:3).

[67]*The Open Secret.*, p. 23.

[68]Ibid.

justice.⁶⁹ This is also clear from the interpretation of the prophetic words by Jesus.⁷⁰ Jesus is the Son, sent by the Father and anointed by the Spirit to be the bearer of God's kingdom to the nations.⁷¹

God cannot be understood as a "timeless, passionless monad beyond all human knowing, but as a trinity of Father, Son, and Spirit."⁷² The understanding has not been the result of speculative thought, but of "the revelation in the actual historical life and work of the Son."⁷³ According to this revelation, the work of the Son who offered the ultimate and obedient sacrifice to the Father on the cross is not the Father, but he is truly God as the Father is God. The word *homoousios*, a word which, according to Newbigin, "expressed in the language of contemporary philosophy the conviction that the being of the Son and the being of the Spirit are the very being of the Godhead and are not intermediate between a remote and ultimately unapproachable Supreme Being and the known world of nature and history."⁷⁴

5. JESUS, SPIRIT AND THE CHURCH

Newbigin presents a vibrant picture of the Church within the

---

⁶⁹"Here is my servant whom I uphold, my chosen one in whom I delight; I will put my Spirit on him and he will bring justice to the nations" (Isa. 42: 1).
⁷⁰"The Spirit of the sovereign Lord is on me, because the Lord has anointed me to preach the good news to the poor" (Isa. 61: 1).
⁷¹*The Open Secret*, p. 26.
⁷²Ibid., p. 28.
⁷³Ibid.
⁷⁴Ibid., p. 29.

trinitarian framework of the Father's reign over the world, the redemptive work of the Son, the creative work of the Holy Spirit, and the eschatological consummation with the second coming of Christ. He presents the Church in this way both in its universal and local manifestations. In his thought, ecclesiology depends on christology.[75] Since so much has been published on this interrelated theme, it is not feasible here to make a comprehensive presentation of all that Newbigin has said about Jesus in relation to the Spirit and the Church. What is attempted in the following pages is the crux of his thought from a Christological point of view.

We cannot properly understand Newbigin's christology or the centrality of Christ in his thought without reference to his ecclesiology and pneumatology. He believes that everything in the life of the Church is determined by the "dying and rising of the Lord Jesus Christ."[76] The name of Jesus Christ is inseparable from the notion of the Church, because "only a church that lives by and under the cross of Jesus Christ is truly the Church."[77] In the Bible studies based on 2 Cor 4 and Mt 10: 5-8, 16-20, 24-28, 32-33, given at the Consultation on Church Union, Newbigin sees the dying and rising of Christ as an essential pattern for the life of the Church.[78] The point that he stresses is the way in which the Church becomes at the same time the bearer of the dying of Jesus and the bearer of the life of Jesus. The Church received its life and mission

---

[75] Lesslie Newbigin,"Christ, Kingdom and Church: A Reflection on the papers of George Yule and Andrew Kirk," Unpublished paper (c.1983), p. 4.
[76] Lesslie Newbigin, "The Bible Study Lectures," *Digest of the Proceedings of the Ninth Meeting of the Consultation on Church Union*, ed. Paul A. Crow, Jr. (Princeton, New Jersey: Consultation on Church Union, 1970), p. 193.
[77] Ibid.
[78] Ibid., p. 203.

from Jesus Christ who said, "Receive the Holy Spirit."[79] The Church is the "visible form of the action of God the Holy Spirit" drawing all to Christ and sending them out into the world.[80] To reproduce the life of Jesus in the life of the world is the mission of the Church. The Spirit of God is the witness to Christ, and the Church's mission is rooted in the very nature of God as Father, Son and Holy Spirit. Newbigin, in his exposition of 2 Cor. 6: 3-10, observes:

> There is an authentic picture of a Church renewed for mission, a Church which is poor yet makes many rich, is dying and yet gives life, has nothing yet possesses everything.[81]

This truth of dying and giving life should be referred back to the teaching of Jesus in the days of his earthly ministry when he promised the power to heal and to give life and also promised that for themselves there would be suffering and death.

We see that Newbigin holds to a doctrine of the Church which is inseparable from the doctrine of Christ. This is because, according to a working definition, the Church is "provisional

---

[79] Lesslie Newbigin, "The Life and Mission of the Church," in *We Were Brought Together*, ed., David M. Taylor (Sydney: Australian Council for the WCC, 1960), p. 59.
[80] Ibid.
[81] Lesslie Newbigin, "Bible Studies," *Renewal for Mission*, edited by David Lyon and Albert Manuel (Madras: The Christian Literature Society, 1967), p. 203.

incorporation of mankind into Jesus Christ."[82]

The phrase "into Jesus Christ" implies a three-fold reality. First, by this, reference has been made to the Jesus who lived and taught and died and rose again under Pontius Pilate. Second, it refers to the risen Christ who is present in the midst of his Church. Third, it refers to the coming Christ who will gather up all things into himself at consummation. The incorporation is provisional, because those who make up its membership are only a small part of humankind. Nevertheless they are there, not for themselves, but for the sake of all humankind. They are the *pars pro toto*, the "first-fruits" which is intended to include all others. Newbigin believes that the Church cannot accept the status of a *cultus privatus*.[83] The visible form of the Church is only provisional. The Church does not yet reflect in its forms the full richness and variety of humanity. Moving from here to the work of the Spirit, one notices that Newbigin is equally concerned with the doctrine of the Holy Spirit in the life of the Church. In the preface to his work *The Holy Spirit and the Church*[84], he complains that even though all Christians are familiar with the name of the Holy Spirit, yet for many Christians, the coming of the Spirit means very little or nothing.[85] Therefore, Newbigin is trying to clear up any misunderstanding about the Spirit and his work in the Church and in the lives of individuals. Before we consider the Spirit in relation to Jesus and the Church, it would be appropriate to have a look at what Newbigin thinks of the biblical language of the Spirit.

---

[82]Lesslie Newbigin, "The Form and the Structure of the Visible Unity of the Church," in *So sende Ich Euch: Festschrift für Dr. Martin Porksen zum 70. Geburtstag*, ed. by Otto Wack et al., (Korntal bei Stuttgart: Evang. Missionsverlag, 1973), p. 127.
[83]Ibid., p. 128.
[84](Madras: The Christian Literature Society, 1972)
[85]Ibid., p. iii.

The Hebrew word *ruach* is translated in the English Bible as `Spirit,' which means `wind' or `breath.' It described the breath of God, the mighty life-giving breath of God, by which the human being became a living being. But South Indian translation of this word, as Newbigin notes, is problematic. The Tamil translation renders the word *avi* and the Telugu, *atma*, which is the word for `soul.' Malayalam language, Newbigin says, transliterates the Hebrew word.[86] He finds *uyir* as translated by the Madras University Lexicon a better word which comes closer to the Hebrew word. However, the Spirit of God is the creative power of God.[87] Newbigin's survey of the word `Spirit' both in the Old and New Testaments is not what concerns us here, but how the `Spirit' is viewed in relation to Jesus and the Church. The reference point for this is the baptism of Jesus.[88]

This was baptism with both water and the Spirit. The Spirit of God who came upon Jesus was the Spirit who would lead him to complete his baptism by the way of the cross, lead him to give himself up as a sacrifice for the sin of the world. The character of the Spirit given to Jesus (Mark 1:10-11) is the Spirit of sacrifice, the Spirit of humble service, the Spirit who will lead Jesus by the way of the Cross to be the Saviour of the world. Jesus was anointed by the Spirit (Lk 4:18 f; Acts 10:38) for the purpose of carrying out the task which the Father has entrusted to him.

The Spirit of God is given to Christ's disciples as the gift of

---

[86]Ibid., p. 2. I believe that Newbigin is in error here with respect to Malayalam translation. Malayalam Bible renders *atma*, most often with a prefix which means `Holy.' It is the Malayalam Syrian Christian prayer books which transliterate the Hebrew *ruach*.
[87]Ps. 33:6; 104: 29-30; Gen. 1:2, 2:7.
[88]Mark 1: 10-11.

the crucified and risen Lord. On the day of Pentecost, Peter reminds the crowd that the great new event is the consequence of what has happened in the dying and rising of Jesus. The Holy Spirit was given to enable the Church to fulfill its mission.[89] The Spirit would enable the disciples to continue Christ's work of bringing conviction of sin and forgiveness to those who are under its power. This is so because the gift of the Holy Spirit is given in the closest possible connection with the gift of forgiveness. Peter's sermon on the day of Pentecost reveals the connection between the Spirit and forgiveness (Acts 2: 38). In Newbigin's understanding, repentance, baptism, forgiveness and the gift of the Spirit are all inseparably linked.[90]

The Spirit of the Lord rests upon the Messiah, and Isaiah 11: 2 indicates that it is the Spirit of wisdom. According to Newbigin,

> It is by the Spirit that we know that Christ is truly the power and the wisdom of God; it is by the Spirit that we recognise the cross as the power of God for salvation; it is by the Spirit that we are able to recognise and understand the gifts which God gives to each of us.[91]

The work of the Spirit is to take the things of Jesus and show them to the believers (Jn 16:14). The gifts of the Spirit are not to be understood apart from the work of Christ. In other words, the Spirit's work is to glorify Jesus by giving true testimony to him. The crucified Jesus is the King and Lord of all. That testimony is the mark of the presence of the Spirit in the Church.[92] Using the

---

[89] *The Holy Spirit and the Church*, p. 12.
[90] Ibid., p. 14.
[91] Ibid., p. 18.
[92] Ibid., p. 17.

metaphor of body, Newbigin suggests that God intends a variety of gifts and endowments in the body of Christ for the sake of unity. Therefore the Church is to be a fellowship of human beings all sharing the life of one body through the power of one Spirit, a life into which they are introduced through the one baptism of Jesus Christ for the sin of the whole world. As Christians, baptized by the one Spirit into the one body, confessing the one Lord Jesus Christ, they are sharers in the Spirit.[93]

The twin nature of the Church, which Newbigin impresses upon us, is at once "eschatological and missionary."[94] The doctrine of the Church, as he wrote in 1953, has come to occupy a central place in theological discussion. The reason for this is to be found in several closely related factors such as the breakdown of Christendom, the missionary experience of the Churches in the lands outside of the old Christendom and the rise of the modern ecumenical movement.[95] There can be no true ecumenical movement except that which is completely missionary in nature, because the ecumenical movement has been a result of the missionary experience of the Church. Related to this is the fact that there can be no true doctrine of the Church which is not held, so to say, in the tension of urgent obedience between the Saviour and the world he came to save.

What is the nature of the Church and how shall one define it? It can never be defined in static terms and it can be defined only

---

[93] Ibid., p. 27.
[94] Lesslie Newbigin, *The Household of God: Lectures on the Nature of the Church* (London: SCM Press, 1957), p. 9. First published in 1953.
[95] Ibid., p. 11.

in terms of "that to which it is going."⁹⁶ This is the eschatological and missionary perspective. As the "pilgrim people of God," it is hastening to the ends of the earth, with a call to be reconciled to God, and hastening to the end of time to meet its Lord who will gather all into one. There is a meaning to the present age, which is between the first coming and the second coming of Christ. The powers of the age to come are already at work in this age to draw all peoples into one in Christ. When the Church ceases to be one, or ceases to be missionary, it contradicts its own nature. The missionary and eschatological perspectives must be understood as a new obedience to, and a new possession by, the Holy Spirit, who works in the Church now. Both the mission and the unity of the Church are two aspects of the one work of the Spirit.⁹⁷

It is important to note here that Newbigin has a strong sense of the Church as a community or society of Christians saved by the work of Jesus Christ. This community, which has been placed among other human communities, has "discernible boundaries."⁹⁸ This human community implies both the visible and invisible Church. When we speak of the Church,

> We are not speaking of an abstract noun, or of an invisible platonic idea. It is true that the Church includes those who, having died in faith, are now beyond our sight, but await with us the final day of

---

⁹⁶Ibid., p. 25. Newbigin rejects a `static' conception of the Church in favour of a "directional" society which is in movement. See also Lesslie Newbigin, "The Life and Mission of the Church," in *We Were Brought Together*, Op. cit., p. 59 and "The Future of Missions and Missionaries," in *Review and Expositor*, Vol. 74, 2 (1977), p. 213.
⁹⁷*The Household of God.*, p. 26.
⁹⁸Ibid.

judgment, resurrection and victory.[99]

Those who are now living should recognize and join the visible community on earth. This, God's visible community, is truly known only to faith because it is constituted in and by the Holy Spirit. This congregation is precisely as visible and temporal as the Christian. Newbigin views the core of the biblical history as the story of the calling of a visible community to be God's own people, his royal priesthood on earth, the bearer of his light to the nations.[100] Although Israel, in spite of all apostasy, is one of the petty tribes of the Semitic world, it is God's people and possession. Likewise, in the New Testament, there is an actual, visible earthly company which is addressed as the people of God, the Body of Christ. This community has been entrusted with the work of salvation through Jesus. This community is the Church and the Church is called together by the deliberate choice of Jesus and recreated in him.[101]

As the bearer of salvation, the Church is not an end in itself, but it is something "living and moving, as the visible form of the action of the Holy Spirit in drawing men of all kinds to Christ."[102] It is a place where we have "joy and peace through Christ."[103] The Church's existence and its growth as a community is on account of the work of Jesus. Therefore,

---

[99] Ibid.

[100] Ibid., p. 27. Here and elsewhere in Newbigin's writings, there is a strong and repeated emphasis on the Church as the human community of God. See, for example, his emphasis on 'Being God's People' as the community of God in his *Honest Religion for Secular Man* (London: SCM Press, 1966), pp. 100 ff.

[101] *The Household of God*, Op. cit., p. 27.

[102] *Honest Religion for Secular Man*, p. 108.

[103] Ibid., p. 108.

The Church does not depend for its existence upon *our* understanding of it or faith in it. It first of all exists as a visible fact called into being by the Lord Himself, and our understanding of that fact is subsequent and secondary. This actual visible community, a company of men and women with ascertainable names and addresses, is the Church of God. It was present on the day of Pentecost, and the Lord added to it day by day those that were being saved."[104]

The phrase *ecclesia theou* tells us nothing more than the English words 'meeting' or 'gathering.' What is needed is to say who called the meeting or who attended it. The character of the Church is not derived from its membership, but from its Head, not from those who join it but from Him who calls it into being. Therefore the Church is God's gathering. Newbigin says that it is possible to use either singular or plural with respect to the term *ecclesia*. One can speak of God's gathering in Smyrna or of God's gatherings in Asia. However, this does not mean that the Church of Asia is made up of a number of local churches, or the local churches are subordinate branches of the Church regarded as a whole. It means that God is gathering his own alike in Ephesus and Smyrna and in all Asia. 'Congregation of God' is an equally appropriate title for a small house-church and the whole worldwide family. This is because its real character is determined by the fact that God is gathering it. Christ's words were "Where two or three are gathered together in my Name, there am I in the midst of them" (Mt. 18:20).

Newbigin, in agreement with Schmidt's exegesis, says that

---

[104] *The Household of God*, p. 27.

basileia tou theou has an analogy with *ecclesia theou* or *Christou*.[105] It is the congregation which God is gathering in every place. It is the congregation of God which is called into the fellowship of his Son.[106] The Church is constituted in God's love. In constituting the Church, there is the work of the Holy Spirit. Looking at the very nature of the congregation, one might wonder how an "unholy concourse of sinful men and women can be in truth the Body of Christ." But this is the same problem as how a sinful person can at the same time be accepted as a child of God. In other words, *Simul justus et peccator* applies as much to the Church as to the Christian.[107]

Newbigin's ecclesiology presents an organic relation between the works of God the Father, the Son and the Holy Spirit. For example, the Church is constituted by God's atoning acts in Jesus Christ. This includes the incarnation, life, death, resurrection, ascension, session at the right hand of God and the gift of the Holy Spirit.[108] His understanding of the nature of the Church has three inter-related truths. Christians are incorporated into Christ by hearing and believing the gospel. They are incorporated by sacramental participation into the life of the historically continuous Church, and finally, they are incorporated by the receiving and abiding in the Holy Spirit.[109] All three of them are to be kept in the right perspective without taking any single one of them alone as the

---

[105]Reference is to Karl Ludwig Schmidt's work in the *Theological Dictionary of the New Testament*, Vol. 1, ed. Gerhard Kittel. English edition translated and edited by G. Bromiley (Grand Rapids: Eerdmans, 1964), pp. 574-593.
[106]Ibid., p. 29.
[107]Ibid.
[108]Ibid., p. 30.
[109]Ibid.

clue to the Church's nature.[110]

6. JESUS AND THE COMING KINGDOM

Jesus and the Kingdom of God are intrinsically linked in the thought of Newbigin. His idea of the Kingdom of God is biblically based. The concept is fundamentally important in both the Old and New Testaments of the Bible. There is a struggle in contemporary Christianity to address the relation between the gospel and the Kingdom of God. Some Christians would look at the message of the Kingdom as something wider, more inclusive, and less sectarian than the message of salvation through Jesus Christ. In one of his books, *Sign of the Kingdom*,[111] he is trying to identify and suggest an alternative for these struggles. In this book, he treats the theme of the Kingdom of God in historical, biblical and missiological perspectives.

In Newbigin's opinion, contemporary Christianity is subject to severe tensions between those on the one hand who see their faith as mainly concerned with the life of the spirit and think that 'politicization of Christianity' is a deviation from the truth, and those on the other hand who regard a purely private and 'spiritual' religion as a betrayal of the biblical revelation. He wants to correct both extremes by saying that the proclamation of the Kingdom of God, or the Reign of God, is something which embraces the whole

---

[110] This three-stranded understanding of the nature of the Church is an innovative approach which depicts the Church in its biblical wholeness. This approach can be a solution to the problem of what may be called a 'single-nature' emphasis of each Christian tradition.

[111] (Grand Rapids: Eerdmans, 1981). This book was originally written in preparation for the World Council of Churches meeting in Melbourne, Australia, with its theme, "Your Kingdom Come."

of life.[112] It cannot be reduced to some aspects of human life. It is all pervasive; its scope far exceeds the area of religion.

Newbigin's understanding of the Kingdom of God is based upon the preaching of Jesus.[113] In a meditation on the Good News of the Kingdom, he emphasizes the fact that the Kingdom of God which has come near in Jesus is the Reign of God.[114] It is present supremely in the cross and resurrection of Jesus.[115]

In the development of monarchy in the Old Testament, the kingship of Yahweh was fundamental to the faith of Israel.[116] In later Judaism, there are two distinct strands of thought pertaining to the kingship of Yahweh.[117] According to one, Yahweh is now and always king over all, but it is possible for people to be ignorant of his kingship, or fail to acknowledge and live under it. The second strand is the theme of the Davidic kingship which would continue in a Son of David who would rule over Israel and even over the nations in the future. The key word in both these strands is *malkuth*, which refers primarily to the `fact of rule' and only secondarily to the sphere of rule. In this respect, the Greek word *basileia* is a correct translation of the original *malkuth*. This refers to the Reign of God which Jesus preached.

---

[112]Ibid., p. viii.

[113]Mark 1: 14-15: After John was put in prison, Jesus went into Galilee, proclaiming the good news of God. "The time has come," he said. "The Kingdom of God is near. Repent and believe the good news!"

[114]Lesslie Newbigin, *The Good Shepherd* (Grand Rapids: Wm B. Eerdmans Publishing Co., 1977), p. 63.

[115]Ibid., p. 65.

[116]*Sign of the Kingdom*, Op. cit., p. 22.

[117]Ibid., p. 23.

The centre of Jesus' preaching is the Kingdom of God, which calls for repentance and faith. The faith to respond to the Kingdom is given to those who are called by Jesus. The secret of the Kingdom is given to those who have been chosen and called; to the rest it is riddles (Mk 4:10-12). The Kingdom of God is Christ-centered. The announcement of the Kingdom by Jesus is not the "propounding of an ideology or a philosophy or a religious doctrine."[118] It is an announcement of an event the subject of which is the *malkuth Yahweh*. This rule of Yahweh is not limited to the private sector of life, but it has cosmic scope. The fact that Yahweh is King is not in itself news, because this is already part of the fundamental faith of Israel celebrated in Psalms and liturgy. Here the news is that this sovereignty has now become present reality with which one has to reckon. It is "no longer something remote, something belonging to the end of time, or to a transmundane sphere of reality."[119]

There are parables and 'mighty works' in the teaching and public ministry of Jesus. They are pointers to the mystery of the Kingdom. "Jesus," says Newbigin, "in the contingency and particularity of his human being, is the presence of the Kingdom; but that very presence can be a riddle or a scandal."[120] The parables and mighty works of Jesus culminate in the "supreme parable and supreme mighty work," namely, the crucifixion. Here Jesus is either the corner stone or the stumbling block. The crucified Lord is the presence of the Kingdom of God in wisdom and power.

It is in the light of these biblical considerations that Newbigin charges the liberal Christianity of the 1920s with

---

[118] Ibid., p. 24.
[119] Ibid., p. 25.
[120] Ibid., p. 28.

separating the Kingdom of God from the name of Jesus.[121] That era, says Newbigin, was so eager to talk about the coming of the Kingdom but very reluctant to speak of the second coming of Jesus. It was eager to pray `Thy Kingdom come' but was reluctant to pray `Come, Lord Jesus.' The problem of this separation was that the name of Jesus was seen as something sectarian and divisive, but the notion of the Kingdom was seen as all inclusive.[122] Separating Jesus from the concept of the Kingdom of God has created an ideology with a vision of the worldwide spread of what was called modern civilization. The "centrepiece" should be "personal discipleship of Jesus" and "the total fact of Jesus - his life, ministry, death and resurrection."[123]

The name of Jesus and the Kingdom are inseparable in the thought of Newbigin. Accordingly, the language of the Kingdom cannot be used to cause a transfer from the Gospel about Jesus to a programme based on an ideology. This, however, does not mean that the Kingdom of God does not have social implications. Newbigin believes that a preaching of personal salvation should lead individuals to challenge the monstrous injustices of society. At the same time, he does not want to identify particular political or social programmes with the Kingdom of God, as this would betray people with false expectations. The name of Jesus has to be seen at the centre of the Kingdom. In his words,

> To separate Jesus from the Kingdom, to preach Jesus without the Kingdom, or to preach the kingdom without Jesus, is to betray our generation and it is to divide and destroy the Church. The gospel is this:

---

[121]Ibid., p. 32.
[122]Ibid.
[123]Lesslie Newbigin, *Mission in Christ's Way* (Geneva: WCC Publications, 1987), pp. 7, 8.

that in the man Jesus the Kingdom has actually come among us in judgment and blessing. It is now the reality with which we have to deal - whether in our most private devotion or in our most public actions in the life of society.[124]

What happens when the message of the Kingdom of God is separated from the name of Jesus? Newbigin warns us against two distortions.[125] First, it results in the preaching of the name of Jesus as one who brings a religious experience of personal salvation without involving one in the costly actions of public life. This is preaching of cheap grace which does not go the way of the cross. The second distortion is that the action of the Church in respect of the evils in society becomes a mere "ideological crusade."[126]

In Jesus we find both the presence and the proclamation of the Kingdom. His works of healing, action for justice, etc. are not an end in themselves. They are signs which point away from themselves to a greater reality. For Newbigin, the Reign of the Kingdom gives him the mandate to address both public and private spheres of human life. Since Christ is the cornerstone of the Kingdom, he has authority over all things.

7. THE ELECTION OF ISRAEL AND THE MEANING OF HISTORY

Newbigin's christology and the centrality of Christ in his theology has to be seen in connection with his doctrine of election. Election, according to Bishop Newbigin, is a most essential

---

[124]Ibid., p. 10.
[125]Ibid., p. 9.
[126]Ibid.

theological foundation for understanding the story of the Bible. That this is an important theme can be seen in its emergence at critical points in Newbigin's writings.[127] In order to see this doctrine clearly, one has to look at the whole way of understanding the human situation which is characteristic of the Bible. This doctrine, which "permeates and controls the whole Bible"[128] captures an important place in the missionary theology of Newbigin. It refers to the choosing action of God, particularly concerning his election of Israel to be his people and of the church to be his witness.

One of the researchers on Newbigin's works has rightly identified this theme as an important thread running through his missiology.[129] Hunsberger points out three periods in Newbigin's

---

[127]Some important works are, "The Duty and Authority of the Church to Preach the Gospel," *The Church's Witness to God's Design*, Amsterdam Assembly Series, Vol. II, (New York: Harper & Brothers, 1948), pp. 19-35., *The Household of God: Lectures on the Nature of Church* (London: SCM Press, 1953), pp. 110-114; *Sin and Salvation* (London: SCM Press, 1956), pp. 43-46; *A Faith for this one World?* (London: SCM Press, 1961), pp. 71-83; *The Finality of Christ* (London: SCM Press, 1969), pp. 112-113; *The Open Secret: Sketches for a Missionary Theology* (Grand Rapids: Wm B. Eerdmans, 1978), pp. 75 ff; *Foolishness to the Greeks* (Grand Rapids: Wm B. Eerdmans, 1986), pp. 50-64; *The Gospel in the Pluralist Society* (Grand Rapids: Wm B. Eerdmans, 1989), pp. 80-88.

[128]Lesslie Newbigin, *The Open Secret*, p. 75.

[129]George R. Hunsberger, *The Missionary Significance of the Biblical Doctrine of Election as a Foundation for a Theology of Cultural Plurality in the Missiology of J. E. Lesslie Newbigin*, Ph. D. Dissertation (Princeton, New Jersey: Princeton Theological Seminary, 1987).

life which may be identified in regard to the way in which election figures as an important theme in his lectures and writings.[130] Although it is important to identify the various stages of its development, this section seeks to find the integral relationship of election and the meaning of history. Therefore, under this title, I shall formulate Newbigin's view of the election of Israel and its significance for history.

In one of his essays, "Christ and the World of Religions," Newbigin says that the Bible "seems to teach consistently that God's gift of salvation (which is certainly intended for all) works by the principle of election, one being chosen to be the means of God's saving grace to others."[131] Election is the key to the relation between the universal and particular.[132] Election is the rationale for biblical authority to preach the gospel.

---

[130]Ibid., pp. 80 - 111. The early period includes the late 1940s and most of the decade of the 1950s, the years of his work in the Church of South India. The middle period includes the late 1950s which shows the new concerns which he had to deal with as he moved back to the West. In this period, which includes the 1960s and running into the 1970s, according to Hunsberger's analysis, there was less direct reference to the doctrine of election. But it was implicit in his thought and it gave a basis for his growing attempt "to forge a sense of the meaning of history, especially the world history which the contemporary world increasingly shared as one history." The third period begins with his "retirement" to a plural England in the mid-1970s where he found the necessity of a gospel-culture encounter. In this period also he has seen the doctrine of election as a foundation for Christian faith in a pluralist society. See Hunsberger, pp. 78- 79.

[131]*The Churchman*, Vol. 97, p. 23.

[132]*The Open Secret*, p. 75.

Newbigin's *The Gospel in a Pluralist Society*[133], presents the 'logic of election' as a main theme in the biblical history. The discussion of this theme is not only aimed at clearing the misunderstanding of this doctrine by some Christians, but is also for raising the need for a different approach by which the human person must be understood as a relational being, and not as autonomous being.[134] In the Bible

> Human life is seen in terms of mutual relationships: first, the most fundamental relation, between man and woman, then between parents and children, then between families and clans and nations. The Bible does not speak about "humanity" but about "all the families of the earth" or "all the nations." It follows that this mutual relatedness, this dependence of one on another, is not merely part of the journey toward the goal of salvation, but is intrinsic to the goal itself. For knowing God, for being in communion with him, we are dependent on the one whom he gives us to be the bearer of this relation, not just as a teacher and guide on the way but as the partner in the end.[135]

Newbigin's point is that every human person depends on others for receiving the message of God. Because of this interdependence and human relatedness which involve one with another, there can be "no private salvation." God's saving revelation does not come to a person without the involvement of human mediation. It can come, for example, from a neighbour, who communicates the gospel with us. But this is not the same as in the case of Hinduism, where one

---

[133] pp. 80-88.
[134] Ibid., p. 82.
[135] Ibid.

has to search for a teacher of religion.

The reference made to Hinduism is very important as Newbigin develops the 'logic of election' in interaction with other views such as that of Hinduism, and modern Western culture. He realizes that there are certain false assumptions which come at the root of this doctrine of election. For example, one might question the need for depending upon others for one's own salvation. Could this not be a matter between the individual and God? According to Hindu traditions, the knowledge of God and the path to salvation in the last analysis is a matter for the individual soul.[136] The seeker of salvation needs a spiritual guide, but in the end the journey must be made alone. Here the initiative is to be taken by the seeker of salvation who may go from one teacher to another until he or she can find a guru. But the guru is not sent out by God to seek and find lost souls. It is the individuals who are to seek him.[137]

Newbigin proceeds to an exegetical consideration of Romans 9 through 11 which deals with the question of election.[138] Here the apostle is convinced that God has chosen Israel uniquely among all the nations. But Israel as a nation has rejected the chosen Messiah. It does not mean that God's purpose has been rejected or God has rejected his chosen people. It is important to realize that God retains his freedom. Election does not give us claims against God. Not all descendants of Abraham are chosen. Newbigin points out that no one can find fault with God for this. Paul argues that God has the freedom to dispose of his creation as he will. Newbigin comments:

He *could* make some vessels for honor and some for

---

[136]Ibid., p. 81.
[137]Ibid.
[138]Ibid., p. 83.

destruction. Paul does not say that he has done so, but only that, if he did, we would have no ground for complaint. This is where false conclusions have been drawn from Paul. The whole passage makes clear that God has *not* done what he might have done. He has not made some for honor and some for destruction. What he has done is to consign *all* men to disobedience in order that he may have mercy on *all* (11:32).[139]

Newbigin's logic of election is found in what Paul suggests about Israel's rejection of the Messiah. God has hardened the heart of Israel so that the gospel which they reject will "bounce off to the Gentiles."[140] This truth was demonstrated in the preaching of Paul in city after city: when he was turned out of the synagogues, he went to the Gentiles. The apostasy of Israel has resulted in the salvation of the Gentiles. This, however, does not mean God's rejection of his chosen people. Rather, he has kept a remnant as pledge that Israel is not cast off. The hardening of the heart of Israel is until the full number of the Gentiles comes in (11: 25). Newbigin says that, in the end, it is through the Gentiles that Israel will be saved. The logic of election is complete by this conversion. In the end, the chosen people, the elect, receive salvation through the non-elect. Newbigin's point here is that salvation involves us with others who are bearers of his message.[141]

Newbigin believes that election is not election to privileged status before God, but for responsibility.[142] In several passages in the Old Testament, says Newbigin, there are descriptions of God's

---

[139]Ibid., p. 83. Italics original.
[140]Ibid.
[141]Ibid., p. 84.
[142]Ibid.

undying love for Israel. But this love is intended for all the nations. When Israel interpreted this love as a license to do as it pleased, chastisement followed. An illustration for this truth in the Old Testament is found in Amos: "You only have I known of all the families of the earth; therefore I will punish you for all your sins" (3:2). To be God's chosen people means not privilege but suffering, reproach, humiliation. With special reference to the New Testament, Newbigin states,

> Israel is called to embody in her own life God's agony over his disobedient world. And in the New Testament this comes to its final manifestation in that God's chosen one is called to suffer the ultimate agony of a death which carries God's curse, on behalf of all peoples.[143]

The doctrine of election has been greatly misunderstood by Christians when they think that they, as Christians, have a special claim on God's love which others do not have. God's election of a people or calling of a community suggests the universality of his saving love for all peoples. God's truth and love cannot be communicated except as they are embodied in a community which reasons and loves.[144] The Christian community, which is called by the grace of God, is the bearer of God's universal salvation.

Of particular interest to us here is that the doctrine of election has a Christocentric basis. This doctrine should not be separated from the doctrine of Christ.[145] Newbigin says that "as on every theological topic," the doctrine of election should have as its

---

[143]Ibid.
[144]Ibid., p. 85.
[145]Ibid., p. 86.

starting point "what God has done in Jesus Christ."[146] Because,

> It is in Jesus Christ that, as Paul says, we are elect from the foundation of the world. Jesus is not a latecomer into the world. He is the one in whom and through whom and for whom we and all things exist. And the things that happened when he took our human nature and came among us as a man make clear what the meaning of God's election is.[147]

Further it is at the cross of Jesus that the whole of humanity is exposed to the wrath of God, but also to the forgiveness of God. There is a particularity and specificity to the work of Christ. The "universal and unbounded grace of God" could only be expressed through this historic deed that took place at one specific point in history and at one point in the world. This particularity and specificity of God's work in history can only be made known to others by witnesses telling others. Jesus did not appear to everyone, but only to those who had been chosen beforehand as witnesses. They were not chosen for themselves, not for their own privileged status before God, but to be the bearers of the secret of God's saving work for the sake of all. In Newbigin's opinion,

> The logic of election is all of one piece with the logic of the gospel. God's purpose of salvation is not that we should be taken out of history and related to him in some way which bypasses the specificities and particularities of history. His purpose is that in and through history there should be brought into being that which is symbolized in the vision with which the Bible ends - the Holy City into which all the

---

[146] Ibid.
[147] Ibid.

glory of the nations will finally be gathered.[148]

The Christian community or the universal Church is a "particular community among all the human communities."[149] It uses as its starting point and permanent criterion of truth the self-revelation of God in Jesus Christ. This community is the one chosen and sent by God for the purpose of universal mission. The particularity of the Christian community may seem scandalous, but it is inescapable. It is aimed at the universality of God's saving work.

The mention of universality should not be understood as a kind of universalism, which means that in the end all will be saved. Newbigin is aware of what he calls the "universalist ring" in Romans when it speaks of "the full number of the Gentiles has come in," and "so all Israel will be saved" (11: 25, 26). However, Newbigin does not support universalism. He knows that on the one hand the apostle Paul says in one place that "as one man's trespass led to condemnation for all, so one man's act of righteousness leads to acquittal and life for all" (Rom 5:18). The same apostle says on the other hand that he should exercise the strictest discipline "lest after preaching to others I myself should be disqualified" (1 Cor 9:27). Newbigin sees a tension between these two and the whole nature of the gospel requires us to maintain this tension.[150] It should not be resolved by a rationalistic universalism which denies the possibility of finally missing the mark, or by increasingly fruitless arguments about who will and who will not be saved. Newbigin wants to avoid a kind of confidence which leads to complacency, and a kind of anxiety which leads to selfish efforts to save oneself. The Christian life should be characterized by a "godly

---

[148]Ibid., p. 87.
[149]Ibid., p. 88.
[150]Ibid.

confidence" and a "godly fear." The contrast between these is not a contradiction.[151] He explains this as follows:

> If I know that God in his limitless grace and kindness has chosen and called me to be a bearer of his grace for others, my trust in him will not exclude the awareness that I could betray his trust in me, and that very awareness will drive me closer to him. This is a deeply personal relationship. It excludes, I think, the kind of rationalistic universalism which I have referred to. It also excludes, I think, any temptation to set limits to God's grace, or to write off any human being as beyond God's redeeming love.[152]

A final point may be stated about Newbigin's view of the doctrine of election in a religiously pluralist context. Newbigin believes that there is only one election by God and that election is "in Jesus Christ." This means that the choosing is in Christ and "not otherwise." "There is no election apart from Christ, as some theologies have seemed to suggest."[153]

The doctrine of election is inseparable from the doctrine of Christ. Since the doctrine of Christ is rooted in the universal history of the world, history has meaning. Newbigin views the logic of election as "one piece with the logic of the gospel."[154] Therefore, a discussion of the doctrine of election can logically lead one to what Newbigin calls the meaning of history, which I shall briefly outline in the following lines.

---

[151] Ibid.
[152] Ibid.
[153] *The Open Secret*, p. 79.
[154] *The Gospel in a Pluralist Society*, p. 87.

History has meaning, because it has a goal. The Old Testament writers look forward to a glorious and terrible consummation of history. Newbigin says,

> History does not reach its goal by the development of the forces immanent within it. Human existence is not to be understood in these terms. On the contrary, all human life is a gift from God and all things exist by his will. History, therefore, is not the story of the development of forces immanent within history; it is a matter of the promise of God. History has a goal only in the sense that God has promised it.[155]

Newbigin's attention is turned to the theme of promise and fulfillment which runs like a thread in the Bible. The mysterious promise to Adam that humankind will crush the power of evil (Gen 3:15), the promise to Noah that the world of nature will be preserved for all time, and the promise to Abraham that in him and in his posterity all the nations will be blessed, and all the other promises in the Bible, make it abundantly clear that there is to be a final culmination of all history, both human and cosmic.[156]

For Newbigin, Jesus is the clue to history. In Jesus, the final representative of the apocalyptic tradition, the end has come. Therefore, he points out that in Christ history finds its meaning. Since there is a centrality of Christ in the understanding of history, the meaning of history is bound up with Christ. Meaningful action in history is possible only when there is some vision of the future goal. But the ultimate future, either that of the individual or of the world, is hidden from us because of death. But through Christ, the

---

[155]Ibid., p. 103.
[156]Ibid., p. 104.

ultimate goal of history is the Holy City which the New Testament reveals as the goal of the whole story of civilization.[157]

8. JESUS AS SAVIOUR OF THE WORLD

Newbigin depends on the biblical record about Jesus to interpret the person and work of Christ. What I shall do in this section is to extricate from various writings of Newbigin his interpretation of biblical texts on the theme of Jesus as the Saviour of the world.

In a book of meditations on the nature of ministry, Newbigin proceeds with the Old and New Testaments to explore the saving work of Christ.[158] He draws from the roles of premonarchic leaders and warriors of Israel who rose to deliver the people from their enemies and establish their role as a pointer to the real Saviour Yahweh. Although Newbigin is fully aware that the great acts of liberation in the Old Testament, such as the exodus event, or the return of the exiles from Babylon, reflect something of the saving power of Yahweh, none of these particular salvation acts exhausts the saving power of God. These saving acts, as Newbigin sees, are only a prefiguring of the final manifestation of the saving work of God by which he will have defeated all his enemies.[159] Not only in the Old Testament but also in the New Testament there are

---

[157] Ibid., p. 115.
[158] Lesslie Newbigin, *The Good Shepherd: Meditations on Christian Ministry in Today's World*, p. 148. Also see Newbigin's "Address on the Main Theme, `Jesus, Saviour of the World', at the Synod Assembly of January 1972." *South India Churchman* (February 1972), pp. 5-8.
[159] *The Good Shepherd*, p. 148.

descriptions of how God acts as Saviour. Here the focus is on the work of Jesus, who brought liberation and healing to the people around him.

Newbigin has some interesting points to make with respect to the theme of salvation. He says that God shows himself as Saviour in concrete secular events of history. The healing and liberations which Jesus brought are acts of salvation and yet, according to Newbigin, these do not exhaust the significance of his saving work. The concept of salvation has also a future tense, that is, there are meanings of salvation which are not yet apparent.[160]

The word 'Salvation' should not be restricted to the deliverance from our present distresses. Its meaning has been subjected to a one-sided and unbiblical interpretation. The expression 'being saved' has been used by some Christians to refer to a "purely inward experience between the individual soul and God" which does not have implications for physical and social dimensions of human life. On the other hand, there are those who, fearing the distortion of this term, stand in the opposite camp of social service to the needy, purely within a secular framework. Newbigin wants to avoid the dangers of both extremes and wants to work out the question 'What is the biblical meaning of salvation?' from a biblically balanced perspective. What does it mean to say that Jesus of Nazareth is the Saviour of the World?

Jesus is Saviour because "he will save his people from their sins."[161] He vanquished the ultimate enemy, the devil, who stands behind the particular ills of human life. Only Jesus is singularly qualified to deal with the enemy. Even the secular acts of salvation,

---

[160] Ibid., p. 149.
[161] Matt. 1: 21. Newbigin has a well defined concept of sin which I shall consider in this section at a later stage.

such as the healing of the sick and the deliverance of those who are in bondage, Jesus interprets as consequences of the fact that he alone has been able to 'bind the strong man', the power that has held men and women in bondage. Newbigin certainly has an exclusivist understanding of Christ as the Saviour, because "he and he alone has power to deliver men from bondage to sin, death and the devil."[162]

Salvation, therefore, is salvation from bondage to sin and the thraldom of the devil. It has to do with the totality of the human person in the totality of the person's needs.[163] In terms of the New Testament, salvation means healing, life, freedom and hope. The manifestation of the saving power of God cannot be restricted to what Newbigin calls a "new spiritual experience" but it must be applied to all areas of human need, showing its total victory over the ills that oppress men and women and deprive them of their humanity.[164] Newbigin believes that Jesus is the Saviour of the whole world and as such he should be acknowledged, adored and served in the Church.[165]

In order to understand what it means to be the Saviour of the world, it is important to take a brief look at Newbigin's soteriology, which deals with the nature of the human person in relation to God, the concept of sin and guilt and the work of the Saviour who brings salvation. Newbigin wrote a small book[166] originally published in Tamil for the use of Church workers in the Tamil dioceses of the Church of South India. It is a simplified form of a systematic presentation of the doctrine of salvation which deals with and tries

---

[162]Ibid., p. 150.
[163]Ibid., p. 151.
[164]Ibid.
[165]Ibid., p. 155.
[166]*Sin and Salvation* (London: SCM Press, 1956)

to correct the inadequacy of the Tamil Bible translation of the words 'sin' and 'salvation.'[167] Although this was written for the use of village teachers, its contents and format resemble that of a textbook in systematic theology. It offers an interesting insight into the meaning of the word 'Salvation', because Newbigin traces its connection with the Sanskrit root *sarva* meaning 'wholeness'.[168] In the light of the common Tamil misunderstanding of the term and in the light of the Bible teaching, it is justifiable to develop the concept of 'salvation' in terms of 'making whole.'

The Meaning of Salvation

Newbigin works with the term 'contradiction'[169] to describe the state of humanity. There is a contradiction against the natural world, and against fellow-human beings. This is evident in the hostility between nations, between classes, and between races. Instead of being one united family, the human race is torn by 'fratricidal strife.'[170] But there is an inner self-contradiction, which wages war against mind and body. This contradiction, as St. Paul says,[171] is between 'what one knows one ought to do' and 'what one

---

[167]The Tamil Bible rendering *pavam* for sin and *ratchippu* for salvation are inadequate, because, in Newbigin's opinion, the former carries much less of the idea
of personal guilt and responsibility and much more the idea of misfortune than is proper for an equivalent of the biblical word 'sin.' Similarly, the Tamil translation for salvation carries merely the idea of sustenance and support. See Ibid., p. 8.

[168]Ibid.

[169]Ibid., p. 11.

[170]Ibid., p. 13.

[171]"For what I do is not the good I want to do; no, the evil I do not want to do- this I keep on doing" (Romans 7: 19).

actually does.' But there is a more fierce contradiction, which is against God. It is a human revolt against a holy God. By this revolt, the human persons have cut themselves off from God, the very root of their being. They choose not to obey God, or depend on Him. Rather they trust in themselves, in their own strength and their own virtue.

What Newbigin describes here in simple terms is the state of alienation and estrangement resulting from the fact of sin. This fact is fundamental to his christology. It is the denial of this contradiction and the resultant alienation which leads Newbigin to criticize Marxism, which does not have a biblical understanding of `sin' and `grace'. In Marxism, evil is external to oneself, and not internal. And evil is the `class enemy' which constitutes the *locus* of the evil against which the Marxist has to fight. Consequently, there can be no thought of forgiveness and reconciliation.[172] So Newbigin is in fundamental disagreement with the Marxist understanding of human nature. Marxism sees human beings as the `oppressor' and the `oppressed' and makes no provision for "transcendent righteousness" which can judge and forgive both the oppressor and the oppressed.[173]

The consequences of sin are bondage and death. The message of salvation is the offer of freedom from this bondage and the victory over the contradictions. Newbigin says that the Greek word which we translate as `save' means `to make whole' and comes from the same root as *sarva,* which means "the healing of that which is wounded, the mending of that which is broken, the setting free of that which is bound."[174]

---

[172]Lesslie Newbigin, "Christian Faith and Marxism," in *Madras Christian College Magazine*, (Madras 1974), p. 24.
[173]Ibid., p. 25.
[174]*Sin and Salvation*, p. 14.

Salvation is the restoration of the original divine purpose of living in harmony and in the knowledge and love of God. Newbigin views salvation as `whole' and many-sided, as it embraces every area of human life. It provides a `oneness' of the human race in its fellowship with God. It means the cessation of wars and hatred, and in the end, there shall be no more sorrow or sighing. It means the victory over death, and eschatological peace. In consummation, it is the very dwelling of God with humankind. Christians know the first-fruits of salvation because the earnest of this is given to them as they wait for the completion of it, when God has completed what he has begun.[175]

It is true that the meaning of salvation cannot be understood apart from the meaning of sin and vice-versa. Therefore the discussion of one leads to the other. In *Sin and Salvation*, Newbigin discusses the concept and nature of sin from the perspective of the book of Genesis.[176] Genesis 1:26-27, which says that "God created man in his own image" is a fundamental text in Newbigin's teaching about sin. The image of God in the human person depends upon a relation between the two. The humanity of the human person depends upon loving trust and obedience towards God. The fall of human beings was on account of their desire to be like God. The result of transgression brought them to a state of alienation from God. Sin is a corruption of the nature due to this alienation and estrangement from God.[177]

Newbigin says that sin is a corruption of the very centre of human nature. Evil deeds and words are only the "outward symptoms" of the corruption of the centre of human life. "Sin," he

---

[175]Ibid., p. 15.
[176]Ibid., p. 16.
[177]Ibid., p. 23.

says, "is something which is seated at the very centre of the human personality. It is a corruption of the heart and soul of man."[178] Sin is both personal and communal. Original sin and corporate guilt are integral aspects in Newbigin's view of sin.[179] The human person is unable to extricate himself or herself from the net of sin and it is in this predicament that the need of a Saviour becomes essential.

The good news of salvation is encapsulated in the verse which states that "God so loved the world, that he gave his only begotten son that whosoever believes in him shall not perish but have everlasting life" (John 3:16). God is the author of salvation, which springs from his love for the world.[180] Although the whole world is in the power of sin, and as a result, in a state of enmity against God, God loves the world. Newbigin clarifies the misconception some might have of the role of the cross of Christ in the salvific work of Christ. There is both love and wrath in God. But the cross of Christ should not be construed as something from outside of God. The love that secured salvation also comes from God.[181] God is the author of salvation and Christ is the one who accomplished the redemption and the Holy Spirit is the one who applies the redemption to believers. It is true to say that Newbigin's theology of salvation ascribes to Christ the centrality that is characteristic of his whole theology. He says,

> The cross is the place where the decisive battle between Christ and sin took place, where the powers of Satan brought all their strength to the attack, and where they were defeated. It is the place where the wages of sin were accepted on behalf of

---

[178]Ibid., p. 24.
[179]Ibid., p. 36.
[180]Ibid., pp. 56-57.
[181]Ibid., p. 57.

the whole human race.[182]

The cross of Christ is "the centre and focus" of Christ's work. The "centre and heart of God's saving acts" is the death of Jesus Christ on the cross.[183] While it must not be isolated from the whole work of Christ, it is important to hold to Christ's centrality in the whole plan of salvation. Newbigin expresses it in the following way:

> Without his incarnation there could be no cross and no salvation. Without His words and works we should not know who it was that died for us there. Without His resurrection the cross would not be known to us as victory but as defeat. Without His ascension to the Father and the gift of the Spirit, we who live at other times and places could have no share in Christ. All these things are parts of the one complete work of Christ for the salvation of the whole world.[184]

The plan of God's salvation includes the vicarious death of Christ as a ransom for the redemption of sinners.[185] His death was in full agreement with the will of God. While it was a judgment on the world, it was also a means of life to the world.

In conclusion, it must be noted that Newbigin works with a soteriology which is thoroughly biblical in its basis. In his view, "sin is not a mere illusion which could be cleared away by mere illumination." Rather, it creates a situation which is "real and

---

[182]Ibid., p. 60.
[183]Ibid., p. 62.
[184]Ibid., p. 61.
[185]Ibid., p. 62 ff.

terrible" both for human beings and God.[186] The Hindu doctrine of *karma*, in which Newbigin sees an element of truth, is "not wholly true." Its teaching that everyone must bear his or her own *karma* is not acceptable.[187] The truth is that, God has bound us up together in such a way that we may and must bear one another's *karma*. God has made humanity so that it was possible for Jesus to bear our *karma*. However, Newbigin accepts one strand of its teaching, namely, that human sin produces "a result which cannot be evaded, or ignored, but must be expiated and overcome."[188] Nevertheless, it is a "fatal mistake" to believe that all roads lead to the same end. Newbigin asserts that there is a road that leads to life and there is a road that leads to death. The way of sin certainly leads to death.

Newbigin attributes to the work of Christ perfection and efficacy which is central and final. Because Christ alone has completed the work of atonement, he alone is able to bring salvation to the whole world. And this salvation is holistic, i. e., it embraces every dimension of human life. Sin is pervasive and so also is the effect of salvation.

9. JESUS AS UNIQUE AND FINAL REVELATION OF GOD

The theme of the uniqueness and the finality of Christ in Newbigin's writing has to be seen in the context of the doctrine of election. No matter how scandalous the particularity of the gospel, Newbigin insists that God, who is the creator, sustainer and judge of all peoples, does not accomplish his purpose of blessing for all people by means of a revelation simultaneously and equally available to all.[189] Newbigin is well aware of the different lines of

---

[186]Ibid., pp. 32, 33.
[187]Ibid., p. 33.
[188]Ibid.
[189]*The Open Secret*, p. 75.

search for a universal faith for the whole humankind, as are advanced by S. Radhakrishnan, William E. Hocking and Arnold Toynbee.[190]

It is important for us to take a brief look at how Newbigin views Hocking's search for a universal faith. This exercise is useful for us here, as it reveals how vigorously Newbigin guards the uniqueness of Christian revelation. The Christian message is that God has performed this act, an "act of utter self-abasement" for the sake of the human person. Therefore an exclusive claim can be made by the Christian, not for himself alone, but for that act of God in universal history. What comes at the centre of the exclusive claim is "the total fact of Christ."[191] It provides "the only point at which the final issues of human life are exposed and settled."[192] The language of 'uniqueness' is often given a different twist by pluralists, and they have a ground for doing so. Every religion, including Christianity, is unique in the sense that there is only one of it and there is therefore nothing else exactly like it. In this context, it is often better to speak of as 'unsurpassibility' or 'unsubstitutability.'

Newbigin picks up William Hocking's study of the relations between Christianity and the technological civilization which it has begotten.[193] Technological civilization, according to Hocking, no longer depends upon its parent for spiritual sustenance. Hocking is searching for a world faith which would match this technological civilization. In his study Hocking says that Christianity can offer that faith upon two necessary conditions. Christianity should come

---

[190] *A Faith for this One World?*, pp. 30-55.
[191] Ibid., p. 46.
[192] Ibid.
[193] William E. Hocking, *The Coming World Civilization* (London: Allen and Unwin, 1956), p. 63.

to terms with its own offspring in its own house, and show itself to be as universal as the technological civilization it has produced. Hocking, however, does not suggest that Christianity should shed its history, because it belongs to the essence of Christianity that its world view is being actualized in history. Nevertheless, for Hocking, history is the history of the human person's appropriation of the idea, not the history of the idea itself. Accordingly, the vision of the eternal, not the eternal itself, must have its history.[194] Hocking, in looking for a world faith, came to the notion that we can look forward to a time when the particular names and places associated with the human vision of the eternal can be, if not forgotten, at least removed from a position of absolute significance. Newbigin criticizes this approach of Hocking, because it does not allow the Christian to insist on the specific name of Jesus.

Further, Newbigin argues that Hocking's conception of the word 'faith' is not biblical, because it is understood as an individual experience of timeless reality.[195] To put it more specifically, the centre of the picture is the individual and the history of his apprehension of the eternal love, and not the living God. Newbigin asserts that in the Bible, "the eternal emphatically *has a history*," and is actively involved in the history of humankind. Newbigin does not see in Hocking's view the "masterful, living, sovereign Lord."[196] He agrees that, according to Hocking, God is love, but God can give no sign of it, for God is not allowed to have a history. The most crucial implication of this view is that there is no permanent or absolute place in Hocking's view for the name of Jesus. However, for Newbigin, the criterion of 'the total fact of Christ' is that which gives credibility to Christianity. The truth of

---

[194] Ibid., p. 85.
[195] *A Faith for this One World?*, p. 48.
[196] Ibid.

the preaching of the gospel is inseparable from the fact of Christ. The 'central content' of the preaching is precisely this fact of Christ. The story of Jesus is "not one of the particular historic illustrations or concretions of a general religious truth" available to humankind.[197] This is why Newbigin rejects the legitimacy of a universal mystical experience in the human race, to which Hocking appeals. Without denying the reality of this experience, Newbigin warns that the cultivation of a pure mysticism apart from the influence of the historic revelation in Jesus Christ, leads eventually to a total pessimism about the world, and to the development of religious practices designed to free the soul altogether from entanglement in the process of history. He adds,

> I must simply say that I do not know of grounds apart from Christ upon which it is possible to build a strong and enduring faith that self-sacrificing love is really the sovereign power that rules the world. I have not yet met anyone who could show them.[198]

For Newbigin, God's "final and decisive claim" is made in Christ. Christ makes exclusive claims about himself. Newbigin says,

> Before the High priest he accepts the identification of himself with the Son of Man whom Daniel had seen coming with the clouds of heaven. He tells his disciples that to acknowledge or deny him before men means being acknowledged or denied before God, and that he alone knows the Father and can give that knowledge to others. He tells them that to die for him means being assured of life. In the face of these and other similar sayings which disclose his

---

[197] Ibid., p. 51.
[198] Ibid., p. 52.

own thought about himself, the old alternative *aut Deus aut non bonus* becomes inescapable.[199]

Newbigin asserts that the apostolic faith is not a faith of which Jesus was one of the teachers and exemplars; it is faith in Jesus at whose name every knee should bow and every tongue confess his Lordship to the glory of God the Father.

Newbigin believes that Jesus Christ is the final and unique revelation of God. In his discussion of the gospel as a secular announcement, he speaks of it as the announcement of an event which is decisive for all and for the whole of their lives.[200] It is an event which is described in "universal, cosmic terms." This event, says Newbigin, is "not a religious message which brings to completion and perfection the religious teachings of all the ages."[201] This announcement concerns the end of the world. The true meaning of the word `finality' in Jesus, according to him, will be found by penetrating into the meaning of the gospel announcement. Speaking in the context of Christianity and world religions, Newbigin asserts that the gospel, which announces the decisive encounter of God with human history as a whole, is unique. It concerns the consummation of all things. Its character as `final' lies in this fact.[202]

In his book *The Finality of Christ*, Newbigin recognizes the difficulties associated with using the word `finality' in respect of

---

[199]Ibid.
[200]*The Finality of Christ*, p. 48.
[201]Ibid.
[202]Ibid., p. 49.

Jesus Christ.[203] For example, in modern scientific culture, which has created a real sense of the vastness of space and time, would it not be arrogant to use the word `finality' for something that happened a few centuries ago in an obscure part of the earth? The human knowledge of history is but a moment in the life of the universe which counts time in millions of years. There can be another difficulty in terms of the contemporary scientific methodology according to which every final conclusion is a starting point for further research. In such a situation, a scientist can hardly use the word `finality.' The question is: Can the Christian use the word `finality' with respect to Christ? There can also be difficulties in terms of the development of the science of history which proposes that every epoch in history has to be interpreted in the background of its time. Thus there are objections to the finality-language of the Bible being carried over into the twentieth century without a thorough process of interpretation. Another difficulty in asserting the finality of Christ in modern Western culture can be the new awareness of the non-Christian religions and what they teach, which hitherto have been relatively unknown to the Western culture. Christianity, in a multi-religious fabric, is not something totally *sui generis*, but is one of the many religions.[204]

Newbigin's assertion of Christ's finality is understandable, but he does not show very clearly on what basis this finality rests. He certainly speaks of the cross and resurrection in the public history of the world, but his vantage point is his own commitment to Christ.[205] He believes that if religion deals with one's ultimate

---

[203] The introductory part of this book is an examination of the possible difficulties and problems one might raise and the vantage point from which the author tackles these questions. See pp. 9 - 22.
[204] Ibid., p. 11.
[205] Ibid., p. 20.

commitment, then a religious person does not have a point of view which transcends that commitment and which enables him or her to judge other religious commitments impartially. Newbigin is not making any attempt to demonstrate the finality of Christ, but exploring what it means to claim finality for him. For him, the question of the finality of Christ is not simply a question of the relation of Christianity or of the gospel to other religions. Rather it is the question of the place of Christ in universal history. Therefore to speak of the finality of Christ is to speak of the Gospel as the clue to history.[206]

The finality-language of Newbigin should not be misunderstood as attributing finality to Christianity, because "Christianity is a changing and developing corpus of belief, practice, association, cultus, which is all the time assimilating new elements from other religions and other world views."[207] To claim finality to Christ means "to endorse the judgment of the apostles that in this life, death and resurrection God himself was uniquely present and that therefore the meaning and origin and end of all things was disclosed."[208] It is the substance of the apostolic faith that in God's dealing with the human race, "this time and place were made ready, this people was prepared, these men were chosen and trained in order that they might be the witnesses and interpreters of this unique and decisive event."[209] That which is disclosed in Jesus is the very character and will from which all that proceeds. The Christian's commitment to Christ, by the work of God's Spirit, is the criterion by which he or she judges all else. This commitment arises out of a person's total personal experience or new birth in which the person is brought to stand before the Cross

---

[206] Ibid., p. 65.
[207] Ibid., p. 73.
[208] Ibid., p. 77.
[209] Ibid., p. 76.

of Christ. To one who has made this commitment, the disclosure of God in Jesus is "determinative of his interpretation of all the events of history."[210] So Newbigin asserts that "Jesus Christ is the sole criterion." And there is "no other source of revelation, once we have known Christ."[211]

To claim finality for Christ is to claim that this is the true clue to history. To speak of commitment to the service of God through Jesus Christ is to approach the question of conversion. This is to ask one to forsake other claims to ultimate loyalty and be converted to him. This, Newbigin believes, is the point at which the claim to finality becomes actual and threatening.[212]

Concluding Critical Comment

In conclusion, one can say that Bishop Newbigin's christology, his theological view of the person and work of Jesus Christ in relation to the Christian believer, the Church, and the world, stays close to the thought and language of the Bible, which is both relational and functional. His view of Christ is practical in the sense that it is directly concerned with the redemptive activity of God in Christ and human responses to God, and with personal relationships with God and humanity through Christ. As John Reilly rightly observes, Newbigin "was not so much concerned with the metaphysical conditions within man and the material world that make possible such activities and relationships between God and man, after the manner of much post-biblical thinking."[213]

---

[210]Ibid., p. 83.
[211]Ibid., p. 84.
[212]Ibid., p. 87.
[213]*Evangelism and Ecumenism in the Writings of Lesslie Newbigin and Their Basis in His Christology*, Op. cit., p. 24.

Newbigin's writings show that the relational and experiential dimensions are as important as the metaphysical questions.

Newbigin affirms the incarnation of God in Christ, his atoning work, death and resurrection, and the second coming. These elements are essential in constituting his position against a `Theocentric' scheme of inter-religious dialogue. The incarnational starting point makes his christology a `Christology from above.'[214] Yet he is fully affirmative of the historical reality and theological significance of Jesus as a human being in history. He affirms that history has a centre from which it takes its meaning and coherence and that centre is Jesus Christ.

Newbigin does not offer any substantial Christological work, or original contribution to Christology. However, there is a strong emphasis in his writing on the relational and experiential dimensions of Christ, a characteristic which is missing in many christological discussions. Our purpose here was to be clear about the basis and centre of all his theological thinking, especially his thought on Christ and the world of religions. We have seen that his christology can be called `orthodox' and he exhibits an awareness of problems arising in modern theology and biblical scholarship.

Although this writer is in substantial agreement with Newbigin about his view of Christ, he may be thought to be vulnerable to criticism. Some scholars would find him naive in his

---

[214] The distinction between "Christology from above" and "Christology from below" may be seen in the work of Wolfhart Pannenberg, *Jesus - God and Man*, trans. Lewis Wilkins and Duane A. Priebe (London: SCM Press, 1968), p. 33. A "Christology from above" has the starting point in the divinity and the incarnation of Jesus, whereas a "Christology from below" rises from the historical man Jesus to the recognition of his divinity.

attitude about what can be known with assurance about the `fact of Christ'. Some would argue that he is dogmatic in his single-minded commitment to Christ as the Truth. To assess this we now turn to Newbigin's view of knowledge and truth.

CHAPTER 3

KNOWLEDGE AND TRUTH

It is impossible to engage in `dialogue' with other religions and other truth claims without claiming to speak the truth. Jesus Christ, who said, "I am the way and the truth and the life (Jn 14:6)," is the Truth and the criterion of our knowing. However, this centering upon Jesus Christ as the truth is not to avoid penultimate sources of knowledge and truth. By turning to the sciences and sociology of knowledge, Newbigin brings together important scientific and sociological insights to demonstrate the art of knowing. His reliance on the sciences is quite reasonable, because the scientific culture in general and the Newtonian science in particular has contributed to the shaping of modern Western culture both in its philosophy and in its way of organizing public life. The modern European mind, which has been shaped by the Newtonian science, still holds to a mechanistic view[1] of the world, even if this view is now theoretically outdated.

Moreover, science has assumed the characteristics of a religion with the ultimate answers regarding truth, belief, and salvation from the ills of the world. It has "become more than

---

[1] It is an understanding of the universe in which all phenomena are explained solely in terms of their quantifiable properties and are systematized in accordance with Newton's laws of motion. According to this, nature consists of tiny entities which are externally connected to one another through strictly causal relations. A major problem that Newbigin has with this conception of the universe is that it develops a notion of science itself, in which the criterion of purpose is absent, and the person of the scientist is excluded.

merely an organized body of knowledge or a basis for technical progress."² Newbigin says:

> It has become itself a kind of religion. Multitudes of people look to the sciences as the ultimate source of truth. They see in science a body of finally reliable thought as contrasted with the myths and superstitions of religion. And if they have any hope of salvation from the ills that flesh is heir to, it is rather based on the achievements of science than on the promises of religion.³

Newbigin's theology, as we shall see in this chapter, shows no dissonance with science. Theologians and believing scientists have sought for a *modus vivendi* between science and religion. This is nothing but seeing the same reality in two different ways.⁴ The necessary precondition for the birth of science, however, was the belief that the universe is rational and contingent. "If the world is not rational," says Newbigin, "science is not possible; if the world is not contingent, science is not necessary."⁵ There is the role of faith in scientific investigation. The scientist is sustained by faith in the search for truth. The faith commitment is essential to understanding the truth. It is these epistemological concerns that I will be dealing with in this chapter. Since Newbigin allies himself with Michael Polanyi, and to a certain extent, Peter L. Berger, I shall briefly set forth in separate sections the relevance of their thinking for Newbigin's view of knowledge and truth.

---

²*A Faith for this One World?* p. 15.
³Ibid.
⁴*Foolishness to the Greeks*, p. 66.
⁵Ibid., p. 70.

1. EPISTEMOLOGICAL QUESTIONS

a. Skepticism and the Possibility of Knowing the Truth

When Newbigin uses the word `truth' in its theological context, his concern is with the gospel as public truth. It is not only good news but also true news. It is from this perspective that he discusses the question of `truth' in one of his recent books.[6] There are two main reasons for stressing the gospel as public truth. First, the Christian Church has not been regarded by modern societies as a source of true knowledge, but rather as an agency which stands for good values. Secondly, there is what Newbigin calls, "skepticism" in modern culture about the possibility of knowing truth.[7] Modern pluralist societies are marked by subjectivism and therefore the claim that the gospel is public truth has been viewed with skepticism. And yet, Newbigin asserts that the claim to know truth can never be ignored, because all living creatures must come to terms with a reality beyond themselves. Therefore to reject the hope of speaking truthfully about reality is "to abandon the adventure of life,"[8] and certainly to abandon any significant form of inter-religious dialogue.

What are the arguments for skepticism in modern societies? Newbigin tries to identify some factors which lie at the root of skepticism. A major cause of the problem might be the confusion of `the gospel' with the phenomenon of `Christianity'. Newbigin

---

[6]*Truth to Tell: The Gospel As Public Truth* (Grand Rapids: William B. Eerdmans Publishing Co., and Geneva: WCC Publications, 1991). This book is the result of the Osterhaven lecture series given at Western Theological Seminary, Holland, Michigan.
[7]Ibid., p. 2.
[8]Ibid., p. 4.

distinguishes clearly between the two. The reason for making such a distinction is the fact that Christianity is a "constantly changing phenomenon," while the gospel is "news about things which have happened."[9] The gospel is "unchanging," although the way we understand what has happened changes.

Further, at the root of the skepticism lies the cultural misconception that the gospel is simply a confused record of a variety of religious experiences. According to this misconception, what is accessible to the reader of the gospel is not what actually happened, but the faith of the disciples cast into the form of narrative. Of course, Newbigin does not deny the fact that the New Testament 'represents' the faith of the disciples, that is, their faith about "what really happened."[10] Some also argue that the culture of first century Palestine is so remote from modern times that the reader of the gospels cannot expect to understand what they were trying to say. But this is not a valid argument, because in Newbigin's view, it is a denial of the fundamental unity of the human race.

Another reason for the prevailing skepticism, which is related to the above argument, is the belief that during the time of writing the gospel, it was a custom to tell stories to authorize or validate current projects or practices, but those stories were not "history" as is understood today. This charge is "absurd," because ancient writers show themselves perfectly capable of distinguishing between fact and fiction. Furthermore, if it is understood that alleged facts are fictions, fiction loses its usefulness. Fiction is useful only in a truth-telling society. Therefore this argument should be rejected, because it would abolish one's claim to know

---

[9]Ibid., p. 5.
[10]Ibid. p. 8.

anything reliable about ancient history.[11]

Now the question arises as to how one may begin to deal with the problem of skepticism. The notion of the `Christian community' and its interpretive task is essential to addressing this question. In Newbigin's view, the Christian community is a community of a tradition, which is rooted in the authority of the Scripture. This tradition, like the scientific tradition, embodies and carries forward particular ways of looking at things, particular models for interpreting experience.[12] Newbigin is drawing a close parallel between the ways in which the authority of tradition works within the scientific community and the Christian community. But there is a difference in the parallel. While the scientific tradition has to do with human learning, writing, and speaking, the Christian tradition is concerned with the action of God in history. These actions are themselves the reality which faith seeks to understand. The interpretive task of the Christian community has to be seen in the light of Newbigin's working definition of history, which he borrows from historian Edward. H. Carr.[13] According to this definition, history is a "continuous process of interaction between the historian and his facts, an unending dialogue between the present and the past."[14] Carr points out that the historian is "necessarily selective" with his facts. Take, for instance, modern history of the mediaeval people, who were deeply concerned with religion. Carr argues that what we know as the facts of mediaeval history have almost all been selected for us by generations of chroniclers who were professionally occupied in the theory and practice of religion. They selected the facts which were supremely important to them, and recorded everything relating to it, and not

---

[11] Ibid.
[12] *The Gospel in the Pluralist Society*, p. 49.
[13] *What is History?* (London: Macmillan & Co. Ltd., 1961).
[14] Ibid., p. 24.

much else.[15] Therefore,

> The belief in a hard core of historical facts existing objectively and independently of the interpretation of the historian is a preposterous fallacy, but one which it is very hard to eradicate.[16]

Following Carr, Newbigin argues that if Jesus had written a book, there could not be a real conversation. Instead, he created a human community whose responsibility it is to interpret all that concerned himself. As this community of Christ went out into the world with their varying languages and cultures, they would be led, according to his promise, into the fullness of the truth. Newbigin does not envision the problem of inauthenticity in Christian community with respect to the Christian message. Are there cases where members of the community water-down the original message of the gospel? Should a community consistently be homogenous and consistent in its belief and practice? Newbigin does not address these questions. Sometimes, communities can be inauthentic by their apostasy and their dodging the issue of radical conversion.[17] Nevertheless, he rightly holds that it is the task of the community to tell the Christian story afresh for each age, to interpret it and to live by it. The telling of the story is not a repetition of some statements, but an expression of truth by a community which has been transformed by *metanoia*. Radical conversion is essential here.

The role of *metanoia* or 'radical conversion' is of crucial

---

[15]Ibid., p. 8.
[16]Ibid., p. 6.
[17]Bernard Lonergan, in his *Method in Theology* (Toronto: University of Toronto Press, 1971), p.162, makes a distinction between authentic and inauthentic traditions.

significance in the search for truth. Newbigin has sufficient reasons for stressing this point. *Metanoia* and the skepticism which is prevalent in modern culture are irreconcilable and diametrically opposed to each other. A new 'fact' can only be grasped in terms of one's mental resources, and, when brought to one's attention, calls for at least the possibility of a conversion of the mind. The significance of the fact can be grasped only by relating it to the vast background of one's tacit knowledge which has been acquired since infancy. This concept of the change of mind in radical ways (*metanoia*) which Jesus calls for at the beginning of his ministry, can be applied to the matter of making sense of the gospel. This concept of the change of mind is "as radical as is the action of God in becoming man and dying on a cross."[18] Nevertheless, it is possible to take note of a fact without experiencing this conversion in any radical way. Historical 'facts' about Christ can be recorded without the person being changed by the facts.[19] Without conversion the story is too implausible to be regarded as part of real history.[20]

Newbigin's assertion of the gospel as public truth could be criticized for equating it with public recognition of the gospel. But he does not want this to be misunderstood as a "self-serving exercise," or as an arrogant affirmation aimed at the self-promotion of the Church's interests. He says,

---

[18] *Truth to Tell*, p. 10.

[19] An example cited by Newbigin is Cornelius Tacitus, the Roman historian, who recorded the crucifixion of Christ under Pontius Pilate in the reign of Tiberius. This early Roman reference to Christ and to the persecuted Christians under Nero may be found in Tacitus, *The Annals of Imperial Rome*, Bk XV.44, trans. Michael Grant (Harmondsworth, England: Penguin Books, 1956).

[20] *Truth to Tell*, p. 11.

> But when the Church affirms the gospel as public truth it is challenging the whole of society to wake out of the nightmare of subjectivism and relativism, to escape from the captivity of the self turned in upon itself, and to accept the calling which is addressed to every human being to seek, acknowledge, and proclaim the truth.[21]

Yet the question 'How do we know?' can never be ignored in the understanding and presentation of the Christian faith. What is the source of authority by which a person says about anything, 'I know'? There is always an authority behind the act of knowing. Therefore, Newbigin tries to answer the question of knowing in the context of what he calls, 'the problem of authority'. The following affirmations lie at the root of Newbigin's view of knowledge. Here Newbigin is drawing insight from the epistemological

thought of Michael Polanyi,[22] whose work we shall explore more fully later.

First, knowing is a skill which has to be learned.[23] Some know more quickly than others. The process of knowing begins from very early childhood, when a baby tries to make out the shape of things, tries to distinguish between objects which can be separated from the background, and so on. Whether in linguistics or science, knowing is an art and it does not come automatically. There is no situation in which the reality of things imposes itself on a person so that whether he likes it or not the person is bound to

---

[21] Ibid., p. 13.
[22] *Personal Knowledge* (Chicago: The University of Chicago Press, 1958), *The Tacit Dimension* (Garden City, New York: Doubleday & Co., 1966).
[23] Lesslie Newbigin, *Christ Our Eternal Contemporary*, p. 7.

know. The act of knowing requires that the knower has to take an active and conscious step to go out and get what the knower wants to know. He argues that

> Having mastered a subject, for example a mathematical process, the results of which can be put into formulae which can in principle be fed into a computer and stored for future use, does not obviate the problem of learning for the next person who comes along. There is no formula by which the results of learning can be systematised in such a way that learning becomes unnecessary. All knowledge is acquired by the skill of learning.[24]

Second, the skill of learning is exercised only in a community.[25] Every community has a tradition, which guides and disciplines the process of learning. In the Christian community, the authority of the tradition stems from God's acts in Jesus Christ.[26] This starts at home when a child learns and accepts everything from parents uncritically. If a child is isolated from human community from its birth, it would not grow into a human being. In a scientific community, even to the most advanced stages of scientific research, learning is a communal affair. Scholarly activities take place in a "shared world of experiences and of beliefs and of commitments."[27] In this community of shared experiences and beliefs, every finding is valued and scrutinized.

Third, all knowing involves commitment and therefore an

---

[24] Ibid., p. 8.
[25] Ibid.
[26] *The Gospel in a Pluralist Society*, p. 12.
[27] *Christ our Eternal Contemporary*, Op. cit., p. 8.

element of risk.[28] Even to frame a sentence, one has to have the framework of thought which has created that language. Newbigin gives the example of learning a language other than one's own mother tongue. In this case, the learner has to accept and start with the given words, even though the ideas of these words might be criticized later. In this process, there is a critical reflection that grows within the learner about whether a certain concept can be maintained and the learner criticizes that concept. But that concept has been criticized by means of other concepts which are not criticized for the moment. Newbigin affirms that in every process of thinking, every process of learning, there is risk of using concepts, of accepting ideas, which may prove to be wrong.[29] All significant knowing involves the commitment of the knower to an understanding of reality which may be wrong.

Fourth, in the process of knowing, there is both creative activity (imaginative leap forward, formulation of experience in new ways, etc.) and destructive activity (activity of doubt, of skepticism, of questioning, of checking and experimenting and

---

[28] Ibid., p. 9.

[29] To support this fact, Newbigin cites Michael Polanyi's account of the Morley-Michelson experiments of 1887 on the speed of light which Albert Einstein mentions in support of his theory of 'relativity'. See Polanyi's *Personal Knowledge*, pp. 9-12 for a summary of how Einstein discovered 'relativity' after ten years' reflection. The point which Newbigin wants to make by referring to this scientific account is the fact that the theory of relativity has been an immense imaginative leap forward in human thinking, but was not something imposed upon the mind of Einstein by the pressure of so-called facts. Rather it was an imaginative leap, a commitment to a concept which not only might be wrong, but was regarded as wrong by many scientists when it was first explained. See *Christ Our Eternal Contemporary*, p. 10.

recasting, etc.).[30] Knowledge does not grow simply by skepticism and doubt. It grows by the activity of these together with the creative element, the element of commitment, which in religious language may be called 'faith'. Faith and doubt are necessary elements in the act of knowing. Distinction has to be made between 'rational doubt,' which presupposes faith and 'agnostic doubt.'[31] The capacity to doubt, to question what seems obvious, is an important element in the effort to know reality as it is. But its role is only derivative and secondary.[32] Doubting all one's beliefs at the same time reduces a person to an imbecile. A person is able to doubt one belief only by accepting other beliefs uncritically for the moment in which one is engaged in doubt. Total skepticism, doubting that it is possible to make any truth claims at all, is an "intellectual pose" and not a genuine belief.

Newbigin tries to ask and answer the question, 'How do we know?' and 'What is the authority for the whole body of belief' from the perspective of natural sciences? He says that science does not claim infallibility for any of its conclusions, because everything is subject to re-testing and re-examination. Science does not deal with infallible truths. He notes,

> The authority of science does not rest upon any supposed infallibility. The authority of science rests on the confidence that the public has in the integrity of the scientific community, in its honesty in dealing with all the facts and in the success that scientists have had in solving the practical problems

---

[30] *Christ Our Eternal Contemporary*, p. 10.
[31] Lesslie Newbigin, *Proper Confidence* (Grand Rapids: Eerdmans, 1995), pp. 24, 25.
[32] Ibid., p. 25.

that human beings have to deal with.³³

The whole movement of modern science rests upon certain beliefs and faith commitments which cannot be logically demonstrated. Examples would be the belief in the significance and rationality of the created world, belief in the human power and the right to control nature, and belief in the fundamental integrity of other callings and other scientific disciplines resting on past findings.

There are always unquestioned beliefs which are the commitments of the knower in the process of knowing. These beliefs, argues Newbigin, are taken over by the knower from the culture without questioning, even without being conscious of them.³⁴ Embedded in every culture are different ideals of knowledge which one assimilates without being conscious of them. These ideals seem to give authority to one in the process of knowing.

Human societies have different ideals of knowledge. In some cases, this could be the knowledge of the physical world which can in principle be reduced to mathematical formulae. Accordingly, other ideals can be accepted as reliable only if they adapt and shape up to this particular ideal. Newbigin also cites other ideals of knowledge such as that of Indian classical thought, according to which the knowledge of ultimate reality is to be found by withdrawal from all the experiences of the senses. This might be withdrawal into a world of pure subjectivity, but the assurance of its certitude is found in the mystical experience of the unity of the conscious self. Finally, there is also the biblical ideal of knowledge in which 'to know' means to know another person. It may be explained as the mutual knowledge and mutual self-revelation of

---

[33] *Christ Our Eternal Contemporary*, p. 12.
[34] Ibid., p. 13.

persons. This is the ultimate point of mutual knowledge.[35]

Of the different kinds of ideal, the biblical ideal of knowledge is the ultimate one, according to Newbigin. Like other kinds of knowledge, it involves commitment and risk. Here is found "the deepest, truest and most intimate of personal relationships" between one person and another. The answer to the question 'How do you know?' can be found in the "experience of personal relationship, in the adventure of trust and commitment to another person".[36] Again, he is using concepts drawn from Polanyi, though Newbigin applies them explicitly for his own theological purpose.

Newbigin believes that in the knowledge of another person there opens up a new dimension of knowledge. He draws a distinction between knowing an inanimate object and knowing a person.[37] In the former case, the knower is the only active subject, and the object of knowledge is a passive object which offers no resistance. This knowledge is attained by a process of observing, testing and experimenting. The knowledge of a person is not achieved in that way. This is not to negate the knowledge which one receives by observing and testing a person. However, there is a difference between <u>knowing</u> a person and knowing <u>about</u> a person. A person is known when that person speaks. It is possible that a

---

[35]Ibid., p. 14.
[36]Ibid.
[37]See Martin Buber, *I and Thou* (New York: Charles Scribner's Sons, 1958), where he explores two fundamental relationships: 'I - Thou' and 'I - It.' Newbigin believes that it is an important insight into the world of relationships. We are not fully human until we meet, and are met by, other human beings as persons, as 'Thou.' The latter category is for inanimate objects and the former for human beings and God.

person may refuse to speak or reveal himself or herself to another person. The knowledge of a person involves something more than the knower's commitment and investigation. This knowledge is possible only if the object of knowledge speaks or reveals himself or herself to the knower. This is what Newbigin calls the `ideal of revelation.'[38] This ideal of revelation is essential as it is related to knowledge. Newbigin says,

> The point at which the idea of revelation becomes not only proper but necessary is the point at which we are dealing with the knowledge of a person. A person can only be known if he reveals himself.[39]

In the framework of the biblical ideal of knowledge, the concept of revelation has an important place. The question `How do you know?' can be answered by calling attention to words and acts of God in history. As Newbigin answers,

> I know because of what he did; I know because of what he said; because he opened up his mind to me and because his word and his deeds were consistent with each other and because they revealed the same kind of person, because over a long period what he has said and what he has done have both opened up the same kind of person to me. Because of that I know him and know that I can trust him.[40]

The answer to the question ` How do you know?' should have a central place for the knowledge of persons and therefore for the concept of revelation. The discussion of the nature of

---

[38] *Christ Our Eternal Contemporary*, p. 15.
[39] Ibid.
[40] Ibid., p. 16.

knowledge has its key in the mutual knowledge of persons. To determine the importance of the knowledge of persons in the whole human knowledge of the world, one has to see that persons are only part of the world and we do not know persons except as part of an impersonal world. One does not even have contact with persons except by sharing in an impersonal world of 'visible, measurable and ponderable things'.[41]

Newbigin says that this is one of the great divides of human thought about God and about the world. He points out a certain stage of human development in some parts of the ancient world (as revealed by early Greek legends, Rig Veda of ancient India, etc.), where the people were content to accept the fact of multiplicity, of incoherence as one of the facts of life. They had their multiplicity of deities, each of them having independent powers in relation to the natural world and were apparently content to live in a world in which there was this kind of incoherence. In these cases, from 'multiplicity and incoherence,' there was a journey in search of coherence. For example, in the case of ancient India, this was the road from the Rig Veda to the Vedanta: the search for coherence by withdrawing from the incoherent, visible world, by seeking and finding within the human mind the secret of unity. At the end of that road, says Newbigin, the visible world becomes practically a veil that hides the unseen reality within it. The key to unlock the hidden reality or the mystery of the world is the power of the human mind to transcend and unify the whole of experience in a single consciousness. In the recesses of self, this leads to an ultimate unity with the centre of all things - *athma* and *brahma*.

According to Newbigin, this Hindu way of travelling from incoherence to coherence is very vulnerable for three reasons.[42]

---

[41]Ibid.
[42]Ibid., p. 17.

First, it is self-centred. The clue to coherence is found within oneself, in the capacity of the human mind to transcend and unify in a single consciousness the whole multiplicity of experience. Second, according to this view, time ceases to have any significance. It is not a continuous movement in one direction. The coherence has already been achieved, but is hidden. The natural world is characterized by a cycle of birth and growth and decay and death. The human life also falls within this cycle. Because of this cyclical conception of the world and life, the histories of nations and empires and civilizations follow that same cyclical pattern and return again to the point from which they started. In this cycle of movements, we are involved in the movement of the circumference of a great wheel which in the end returns to the starting point. The way to real knowledge is to find the way from the circumference of the wheel to the center where everything is at rest. Therefore, it does not matter which of the many spokes that connect to the centre one follows. They are equally valid, as they lead to the centre and at the centre there is rest. Third, according to this approach, personality, the distinction between two persons, everything that is involved in a tension and clash of a personal relationship, is part of the world of unreality which ultimately is not important. Newbigin says that this solution to the problem of incoherence is for many people what the word 'religion' means.[43]

What Newbigin wants to stress here is the biblical view of knowledge, which is clearly based on the notion of revelation. Here there is a clear path from incoherence to coherence. The Hebrew people of the Bible began with much the same kind of polytheistic world, yet there has emerged a majestic conception of a living personal God who is the Creator and Ruler and Consummator of all nations. The difference here is that it is not in the power of the human mind that the clue to coherence has been found. Rather, it is

---

[43]Ibid., p. 18.

in the experience of a personal relationship of love and truth and faithfulness. This road takes off in the opposite direction from the road we looked at earlier. This road, firstly, recognizes the existence of a Reality present behind the confusion of the visible world. There exists a personal God and the secret is in his mind who will bring order out of all the chaos and who will sum up all things in Christ. Secondly, time is of the essence of the matter. Time is real, because God is working in history and there is a purpose in all that he is doing. The time which he takes to work out his purpose is real time. Therefore the symbol is not a wheel but a road that leads to a City, which God has prepared for his pilgrim people. The clue is in the mind of God, whose purpose is worked out in history, and that secret can be known only in a personal relationship with him.[44] Newbigin's argument reaches its climax by introducing the concept of a personal, living God, who revealed himself in the person of Christ. This scheme of thinking binds the concepts of personal God, personal knowledge, and the person of Christ in an integral way.

The Bible, says Newbigin, reveals God's plan for human persons and God has made it possible for human persons to know his purpose. This is the heart of knowledge as the Bible depicts it. The Bible presents three great revelatory actions: the deliverance of the Hebrew people out of slavery in Egypt, the experience of captivity in Babylon and deliverance, and the experience of the coming of Jesus, his death and resurrection. Newbigin says,

> These events recorded in the Bible are not recorded for us as illustrative stories from which we can deduce something about the nature of God. They are not recorded as symbols of the timeless truth about God. They are recorded as the actual events by

---

[44]Ibid., p. 19.

which God did the decisive things by which He has been revealed to us and we are saved.[45]

These are not only historical events but are also summonses to people. They inform us that God is committing himself to humankind in order that they may commit themselves to him. This is a call from God to share in his deeds. We do not know, says Newbigin, except in so far as we do share. We do not know simply by a pure act of celebration; we know in the act of commitment to participate in what God is doing.

According to Newbigin, this is the conception of knowledge which the Bible puts forward. At its centre is the clue to the whole meaning of knowledge in its relationships of mutual trust and mutual commitment. It is noteworthy that Newbigin attributes the centrality of Christ to the whole question of knowing when he says,

> The climax and the centre of the whole story is, of course, the coming of Jesus Christ. When the Christian is asked, `How do you know?' here is the place where he takes his stand. In all the welter and confusion of the world, when there is so much that is incomprehensible, when there is so much of which one simply has to say `I do not know', when it is so hard to know where you can start and where you can find a firm foothold to begin the climb, so to speak, this is the place where the Christian stands.[46]

Newbigin says that Jesus has laid hold of the Christian, saying, `You did not choose me, but I chose you.' So the answer to the

---

[45]Ibid., p. 20.
[46]Ibid., p. 21.

question 'How do you know?' may be answered as follows:

> I know because of what He is; because of what He has shown Himself to be; because of what He has done; because of these things I trust Him. I do not pretend to know all about Him. I know only a little, a very very little. But what I know is enough to make me sure of Him, make me sure that everything else that there is to know about Him will be true, to make me sure that He will lead me in the end to know Him as He now knows me.[47]

Newbigin says that this is the only kind of assurance that the Christian possesses, and that is enough. Referring to Saint Paul (2 Tim. 1: 12) who says, "I know whom I have believed and I am persuaded that He is able to keep that which I have committed to him against that day," Newbigin affirms that this is the true pattern of knowledge. It is a "commitment, in response to Him who has committed Himself to us, and it is therefore an adventure upon which I will joyfully stake all that I have."[48]

There is a convergence of knowledge, truth and freedom in the person of Jesus Christ. In modern pluralist societies, freedom is understood to be the liberty to do what a person wants. It is the absence of limits. However, over against this, Newbigin believes that a society in which any kind of nonsense is acceptable is not a free society.[49] Freedom is necessary for grasping the truth about the real world. The fundamental relation between truth and freedom is that enunciated by Jesus when he said, "The truth shall make you free" (Jn 8:32). Freedom is not the natural endowment of every

---

[47]Ibid.
[48]Ibid., p. 22.
[49]*Truth to Tell*, p. 60.

person, but something to be won by the acknowledgment of the truth,[50] and in the end the truth is something given in the grace of God to be received in faith. The biblical notion of freedom is not the individualistic model of freedom; it is experienced by the forgiveness of sins and set free from guilt to follow Christ. The proper freedom of the church is inseparable from its obligations to proclaim the sovereignty of Christ over every sphere of life.[51]

b. Knowing and Believing

Newbigin recognizes in the modern pluralist societies a distinction, or dichotomy, between knowing and believing.[52] According to this dichotomy, knowledge has been attributed to the public realm, and belief to the private and personal life. Consequently, knowledge is associated with natural science and belief is associated with religion. This eventually results in the dualism between science and religion. Science is what one knows and religion is what one believes. In Newbigin's scheme of thinking, this dualism, or dichotomy works against a many-sided and yet integral understanding of human knowledge. He constantly criticizes this dichotomy of knowing and believing and works towards a harmonization of the two, trying to trace the point at which the line of demarcation between knowledge and belief was drawn. There was a time, claims Newbigin, when no such dichotomy existed. For most of history, knowledge was considered to be one. Accordingly, theology was as much a part of human knowledge as natural sciences. For example, Isaac Newton was as much involved in theology as astronomy and physics.

The invention of the telescope and perhaps the microscope

---

[50] Ibid., p. 61.
[51] Ibid., p. 72.
[52] *The Gospel in a Pluralist Society*, p. 27.

has given rise to the new worldview.[53] These inventions revolutionized the thinking of subsequent generations of scientists and intellectuals. Things were not exactly what they had appeared to be. 'How are we to be certain that we are not deceived by appearance?' This question, argues Newbigin, has triggered the whole programme of the past three hundred years of European history, a program of systematic skepticism, according to which it has become normal to critically examine every truth afresh. And old dogmas are to be submitted to the tests of critical doubt, and only what survives should be retained.

The pioneer of this movement, according to Newbigin, was René Descartes, who sought passionately for a firm foundation for knowledge, something that no rational person could doubt, and for a way of building systematically on that foundation by means of clear and distinct ideas, words and concepts whose meanings were determinate. The ideal was to be found in mathematics, where everything is absolutely clear and distinct and everything is related to everything else in a coherent way which reason can grasp. Descartes' famous statement *cogito ergo sum* ("I think, therefore I am.") was his starting point for thought.[54]

Newbigin's severe criticism of Descartes' program is threefold. First, in it Newbigin sees already a great act of 'faith'. He asks,

> How do we know that things are such that we can ever expect to enjoy this kind of total insurance against error? Why should we rule out the possibility that things are such that human life is intended to require the taking of risks? It seems, in

---

[53]Ibid., p. 28.
[54]Ibid.

fact, that both human and animal life requires taking risks. What grounds are there for thinking that this idea of total certainty is anything other than an illusion, a piece of wishful thinking which has no relation to reality?[55]

Second, even if Descartes' statement is considered proof against doubt, it is so only because it makes no contact with any reality outside the thinking self. Mathematics is taken as ideal of a kind of thinking which is not open to doubt. But, says Newbigin, mathematics is itself a construct of the human mind.[56] Third, Descartes' "clear and distinct ideas" needs to be examined. It is Newbigin's opinion that ideas can be handled only by the use of words. We may have clear and distinct visual images and no verbal description will be a substitute for these. But ideas have to be expressed in words if they are to be interpersonal. Newbigin says,

> If the meaning of words was to be absolutely clear and distinct, there would have to be as many words

---

[55] Ibid.

[56] Ibid., p. 29. Albert Einstein's observation about the special esteem of mathematics among other sciences is being used here by Newbigin. This is because mathematics affords a measure of certainty to natural sciences. Puzzling questions arise at this juncture: "How can it be that mathematics, being after all a product of human thought which is independent of experience, is so admirably appropriate to the objects of reality?," and "Is human reason, then, without experience, merely by taking thought, able to fathom the properties of real things?" The answer is: "... as far as the propositions of mathematics refer to reality, they are not certain; and as far as they are certain, they do not refer to reality." See Einstein's *Ideas and Opinions* (New York: Crown Publishers, 1954), p. 233.

as there are things in the universe. Every word we use is useful only insofar as it is part of a whole language, and every language is a distinct way of grasping and ordering the experience of the people who use it. This is true even at the simplest levels.[57]

Newbigin follows here the argument of Michael Polanyi, who says, "Only words of indeterminate meaning can have a bearing on reality."[58] If the meaning of words was determinate, all verbal statements would be tautologies. Newbigin points out that the full sense of a word depends on the culture in which the language has been shaped. An example is how the word "dog" has distinctly different meanings in the two cultures: In one culture it could be seen as a member of the household and an object of affection; while in others it is primarily a scavenger and an object of contempt. The full meaning of the word can never be exhaustively specified.

Newbigin's discussion of knowledge and belief interacts with the statements of others who argue along the line of scientific methodology. One such commentator on scientific methodology is Bertrand Russell, who says:

In arriving at a scientific law there are three main stages: the first consists of observing the significant facts; the second in arriving at a hypothesis, which,

---

[57]*The Gospel in a Pluralist Society*, p. 29.
[58]*Personal Knowledge*, p. 251. In speaking of `The Tacit Component' in knowing (p. 88), Polanyi quotes A. N. Whitehead, *Essays in Science and Philosophy* (London, 1948), p. 73: "There is not a sentence which adequately states its own meaning. There is always a background of presupposition which defies analysis by reason of its infinitude."

if it is true, would account for the facts; the third in deducing from this hypothesis consequences which can be tested by observation.[59]

Russell is here describing the characteristics of scientific method by which truth is established. Three stages are mentioned in the statement of Russell. The first one deals with the observation of significant facts. Knowing in science has to start with intuition and faith. For a scientist, there are many facts lying around all the time, and it takes imagination and intuition to find out what the problem is and which facts are important and which are not. To recognize a problem is to sense, by a kind of intuition, that there is something to be discovered which has not yet fully revealed itself but of which there are hints. Newbigin explains that

> A good scientist is one who has a sound intuition about where that something lies, and on that basis is able to identify facts which may be significant for searching in that direction. But he has no proof in advance that his intuition is correct. It is a matter of faith, and he has to stake his professional life on it, in the sense that if the intuition is false he may waste years of his life in a futile quest.[60]

Newbigin's point is that this is not a matter of clear and distinct ideas and of things which cannot be doubted. Rather there is a passionate search on the part of the scientist, who exercises

---

[59] Bertrand Russell, *The Scientific Outlook* (London: George Allen & Unwin, 1931), p. 58, quoted by Newbigin, Ibid., p. 30.

[60] Newbigin, *The Gospel in a Pluralist Society*, p. 31.

intuition[61] and 'faith', for facts which are significant for establishing scientific knowledge. To support his argument, he quotes from Albert Einstein's discourse on the 'Principles of Research.'[62] The physicist's daily effort comes from no "deliberate intention or programme, but straight from the heart."[63] Einstein goes on to add: "The supreme task of the physicist is to arrive at those universal elementary laws from which the cosmos can be built by pure deduction. There is no logical path to these laws; only intuition, resting on sympathetic understanding of experience, can reach them."[64] So the observation of facts is a venture of faith, which believes what one cannot yet see, (*credo ut intelligam*) and without this faith and this "intellectual love," science cannot

---

[61]'Intuition', which plays a vital role in the art of personal knowledge, should be understood in the same sense as Michael Polanyi understands, namely, the unaccountable apprehension or insight into hidden coherences or intelligible order. The prevailing conception of natural science in our culture as a set of objective statements based on observation will be shattered, argues Polanyi, "if the intuition of rationality in nature had to be acknowledged as a justifiable and indeed essential part of scientific theory." See *Personal Knowledge*, p. 16.

[62]Albert Einstein, *The World As I See It* (New York: Covici, Friede, Inc., 1934),
p. 22. The state of the mind of a physicist in accomplishing his work is compared to that of a 'religious worshipper' or the 'lover'. It may not always ensue from "extraordinary will-power and discipline." See p. 23. Cf. *The Gospel in a Pluralist Society*, p. 31.

[63]Ibid., p. 23.

[64]Ibid., p. 22.

begin.[65]

The second stage identified by Russell is the stage of framing a hypothesis. Newbigin spurns this analysis of method, because, as he argues from the history of science, it is not always a step-by-step logical procedure. It ignores the possibility of the scientist's imagination and intuition. There are no set rules for framing a hypothesis. Some new theories have been the result of a vision or a dream. The immensely creative generalizations first formulated by Newton or Einstein were in no sense the result of a process which could be described in terms of rules or fixed procedures. They are also the achievements of the human imagination and insight which are common in the work of a poet. Einstein once had this to say to the poet St. John Perse, who spoke to him of the importance of intuition in poetry:

> The mechanics of discovery are neither logical nor intellectual. It's a sudden illumination, almost a rapture. Later, to be sure, intelligence analyzes and experiments confirm (or invalidate) the intuition. But initially there is a great forward leap of the imagination.[66]

Without these elements, argues Newbigin, scientific discovery

---

[65] *The Gospel in a Pluralist Society*, p. 31. Mention should be made that Newbigin is here following the argument of Drusilla Scott, *Everyman Revived: The Commonsense of Michael Polanyi* (Lewes, Sussex: Book Guild, 1985). 1987 Printing.

[66] Reported in John D. Crossan, *The Dark Interval: Towards a Theology of Story* (Niles, Illinois: Argus Communications, 1975), p. 31. Cf. Newbigin, Ibid., p. 31. Note that certain words are not accurately quoted by Newbigin, but there is no change in the overall meaning of the text.

would never happen.

Verification, which Russell describes as the final step in scientific method, is an oversimplification, argues Newbigin. A true hypothesis will prove itself true in many kinds of unexpected ways. A hypothesis is continually tested until more reliable results are obtained. There might be debates until then among the scientists. However, until a better theory has been set forth, the present one would be retained. Russell's account of how science works is open to criticism, for it proceeds in the same line of the popular, objective misconception of what is called science. In this respect, Newbigin affirms that

> There are no two separate avenues to understanding, one marked "knowledge" and the other marked "faith." There is no knowing without believing, and believing is the way to knowing. The quest for certainty through universal doubt is a blind alley. The program of universal doubt, the proposal that every belief should be doubted until it could be validated by evidence and arguments not open to doubt, can in the end only lead- as it has led - to universal scepticism and nihilism, to the world which Nietzsche foresaw and which Allan Bloom and other contemporary writers describe.[67]

It is true that our eyes can deceive us and it is true that what "seems to be" is not necessarily the same as "is." Newbigin's concern is to find the clue to get out of this predicament. For this he invokes the Polanyian insights of perception offered through 'tactual image.'[68]

---

[67] *The Gospel in a Pluralist Society*, p. 33.
[68] Ibid.

In all knowing, there is an indwelling, in which a person indwells clues as a surgeon uses his probe in examining a cavity. Indwelling is the act of knowing in which one gains new meaning in the human as well as natural sciences. According to Thomas F. Torrance's definition, indwelling, as an activity of knowing, helps the mind, when it dwells in a coherence or integration latent in some object, to interiorise it until there is a structural kinship between the knowing subject and the object known.[69] There is a tacit dimension and a focal dimension in all knowing, as Polanyi has delineated. It is the unaccountable, inarticulate component in perception and knowledge. One always knows more than one can tell. In Polanyi's view, the structure of tacit knowing shows that "all thought contains components of which we are subsidiarily aware in the focal content of our thinking, and that all thought dwells in its subsidiaries, as if they were part of our body."[70] Tacit knowing is the fundamental power of the mind which creates explicit knowing and lends meaning to and controls its use. All skills, explicit thought, formal reasoning, and articulate knowing and communication, rely on this dimension. It is only by relying on them that formal systems of thought can operate meaningfully. Tacit knowledge and explicit knowledge are opposed to one another but there is no sharp division between them. Tacit knowledge can be possessed by itself, but explicit knowledge must rely on being tacitly understood and applied. Newbigin utilizes these concepts well.

There are words, languages and concepts which are tools in human knowing. The knower tacitly relies on these tools while focally attending to the meanings the knower has to grasp or to communicate. This can be a "risky business." Knowing things as

---

[69]Thomas F. Torrance, ed., *Belief in Science and in Christian Life: The Relevance of Michael Polanyi's Thought for Christian Faith and Life* (Edinburgh: The Handsel Press, 1980), p. 139.

[70]Michael Polanyi, *The Tacit Dimension*, p. x.

they are is not automatic or free of failure. At every stage of knowing there is a personal commitment of the knower to probe, and to explore. Newbigin adds that

> The commitment is a personal matter; it has to be *my* commitment. In that sense it is subjective. But it is a commitment which has an objective reference. It is, as Polanyi puts it, a commitment "with universal intent." It looks for confirmation by further experience. The test of its validity will be that it opens the way for new (and often unexpected) discovery. It has to be published, shared so that it may be questioned and checked by the experience of others.[71]

Newbigin concludes by asking why, if this is what is involved in knowing, there is in the Western culture a dichotomy between what purports to be "factual knowledge, public truth which everyone is expected to accept, and the world of beliefs and values" which is a matter of personal choice or opinion. This question should lead one to challenge one's own cultural assumptions.

This dichotomy between knowledge and belief has consequences for the culture. Prior to the development of the modern scientific worldview, European people saw the world as a unified cosmos. God was very much a part of human knowledge and thinking and also there was a consensus about what was proper human behaviour. But the new worldview created a new vision of the cosmos from which God was displaced. A new way of understanding has emerged. The way to "explain" things is to analyze them into their smallest parts and show how everything that happens is ultimately governed by the laws of physics and

---

[71] *The Gospel in a Pluralist Society*, p. 35.

mathematics. Things are explained in terms of causes, of what makes them happen. All happenings have causes and all causes are adequate to the effects they produce. In short,

> The ultimate goal is to understand everything in terms of the physics and chemistry of its constituent parts. Human life is ultimately to be understood as the product of an endless series of random happenings in the physical world. Chance and causality are the sufficient "explanation" of all that is and all that happens. The main intellectual drive of our culture is in this direction - to understand everything in terms of the fundamental laws of physics.[72]

Nevertheless, Newbigin believes that the development of science in the present century has called this view into question. For example, the advance of particle physics shows that the ultimate elements of what we call matter are not material. In the atomic structure, its ultimate constitution may be described as a pattern of relationships between non-material entities- relationships which can be represented mathematically but cannot be visualized. Furthermore, the development of quantum physics has shown that a picture of the cosmos which excludes the observing subject (as classical physics did) is not a true picture. The scientists are parts of the picture. The concept of a purely mechanical system operating without any place for purpose is mistaken. These new developments in science have changed the picture of the cosmos which dominated the eighteenth and nineteenth centuries. But these developments are not yet assimilated into the thinking of the people. Therefore, most of them still operate with the myths of

---

[72]Ibid., p. 36.

"value-free facts" and a mechanical universe.[73]

If we apply these insights to theological epistemology, we must speak in terms of 'indwelling' the Christian story. The Christian story provides a set of lenses to look <u>through</u> and not to look <u>at</u>. Therefore Newbigin suggests that the Christian community has to indwell the gospel story, tacitly aware of it as shaping the way it understands, but focally attending to the world in which it lives so that it is able confidently, though not infallibly, to increase its understanding of the world and its ability to cope with it.

The dichotomy, then, that relegates religious belief to the private realm is not valid. Against the background of this dichotomy, the Church has to stress that the gospel is just as much a public truth as any other truth. It can also be said that knowledge can be obtained through personal commitment to the object known. Accordingly, thinking, meaning, interpreting, understanding are all personal ventures. Knowledge is never automatically obtained. This, however, does not mean that knowledge is subjective. The reason is that the personal participation of the knower is controlled by impersonal requirements and submission to universal standards which transcend the knower's subjectivity. By holding together the subjective and objective poles of knowledge, Newbigin is trying, following Polanyi, to restore the unity of knowledge and to prevent a false abstraction of one aspect of knowing. The epistemology which he utilizes goes a long way in forging what may be called a 'postmodern Christian apologetics.' This is a commendable exercise against the prevailing skepticism and negation of the status of the Christian Church as a source of true knowledge.

Quite capably, Newbigin emerges as a skillful analyst to expose the false and materialistic conception of science which

---

[73] Ibid., p. 37.

prevails in modern societies. By calling attention to the unaccountable facts of science such as intuition, imagination, etc., which are so integral to scientific activity, Newbigin rejects the misconception of knowledge commonly found among some thinkers. By doing this, he is opening up a method which, not only improves the troubled relationship between theology and science, but also makes it possible to proclaim the gospel as true news.

2. REVELATION AND SCRIPTURE

Revelation and scripture play a key role in the theology of Newbigin. His views of scripture and revelation are congruent with the centrality of Christ. Christ himself is the revelation, and scripture as a whole bears witnesses to him. His theologizing is always and ultimately rooted in the primacy of revelation and scripture.

Revelation is the only way in which one could come to a personal knowledge of the one who is revealed. The central importance attached to revelation in Christianity, according to Newbigin, depends on two beliefs: the belief that the meaning of the world is personal and revelation is the only way by which it can be made known to us, and the meaning of human life is in fellowship.[74] The Old and New Testaments contain the written records of God's action and will for humankind. The New Testament gives a "note of triumphant proclamation" about God's perfect revelation in the fullness of time. It is the "down-reach" of God's grace through Christ. Newbigin does not regard revelation simply as a piece of information, or a lesson in metaphysics, but as the revelation of a purpose and the establishing of a personal

---

[74]Lesslie Newbigin, "Revelation." Unpublished Theology Paper Presented at Westminster College, Cambridge (1936), p. 1.

relation. It is love that discloses its nature and seeks its object.[75] Newbigin sees here the fundamental and unifying fact, namely, the personal nature of God and the human person. Only in the light of this fact, he believes, could one see the inseparable nature of God's self-disclosure and the human person's valuation as parts of one whole relationship. He argues that if the personal will which is revealing itself is also sovereign over the natural world which is the sphere of reason, then the supernatural becomes not the rival but the interpreter of the natural.[76] There is an important link between the spheres of reason and revelation in this scheme of thought. The Anglican triad of Scripture, tradition, and reason as three sources and criteria for the church's faith is in question.

Reason and revelation are not rival criteria of truth, in Newbigin's thought. He argues that the traditional dichotomy, which has played a major role in theology, is based on a misunderstanding. Reason does not operate except within a continuing social tradition, and `revelation' does not mean that reason has been left behind.[77] The true opposition, argues Newbigin, is not between reason and revelation as sources of and criteria for truth, but between two uses to which reason is put. It can be put to the use of an autonomy which refuses to recognize any other personal reality except its own. But it can also be put to the use of an openness which is ready to listen to, be challenged by another personal reality. Newbigin says that what is happening is not that reason is set against something which is unreasonable, but that one tradition of rational argument is being set against another tradition of rational argument which takes as its starting point a moment or moments of divine self-revelation and which will

---

[75]Ibid., p. 35.
[76]Ibid., p. 31.
[77]*The Gospel in a Pluralist Society*, p. 60.

therefore continue to say, `God spoke and acted.'[78] Newbigin asserts that the Christian tradition of rationality takes as its starting point events in which God made himself known to human beings.

The Bible has been regarded as Holy Scripture for a large part of the world's population, though the influence of the Enlightenment has come to challenge its authority. Newbigin records strong disapproval of the distinction between a `scientific approach' and a `confessional approach' to the study of the Bible, a distinction that is the result of the Enlightenment influence. The revelation is the revelation of God to humankind in the person of Christ. The wisdom of the world cannot fully comprehend the revelation with which Scripture is concerned. There is a radical discontinuity between divine revelation and human wisdom.[79] In order to comprehend it, one has to undergo a paradigm shift, which is conversion. The gospel is nonsense to the natural reason and it is conversion that endows the human person to make sense of the gospel.[80] The Bible is to be read as testimony of God's unique and decisive revelation of himself in Jesus Christ, and Newbigin says

---

[78]Ibid., p. 62.
[79]*Foolishness to the Greeks*, p. 51.
[80]Newbigin is not in favour of the medieval saying that grace does not abandon nature but perfects it. Of course grace does perfect nature, but nature does not naturally accept grace. It is also useful to note here that Newbigin does not make a total break between `general revelation' and `special revelation,' because there is continuity between them. But this continuity is discernible only from one side, namely, the total fact of Christ. See Newbigin's " `Going Public' operates with...." Unpublished paper following correspondence with Peter Wright about *Going Public* (London: National Standing Committee of Polytechnic Chaplains, 1985), p. 2.

that it is an integral part of the Christian commitment as a whole.[81]

After examining a number of views that propose a world faith to unite humankind, Newbigin takes up the matter of Christian revelation as unique.[82] The Christian revelation is unique, because at its centre is the person of Christ. The Bible interprets universal history as the history of divine enterprise, creating faithful relationships, covenant relationships between God and his creatures. It sets the human story within the context of the cosmic story. It is based on the life, dying and rising of Jesus, which is an event in the history of the world. It is possible in our present culture to speak with intellectual coherence about biblical authority.

The Authority of Revelation

When the question 'How do you know?' is asked about our faith in Jesus Christ, we can only speak about the authority of God's revelation in him.[83] The Church is to preach the gospel 'In the Name of Jesus' and it is this name alone that gives it authority. Newbigin suggests that it is the person of Jesus himself who is the real issue with which the Christian mission is concerned. It is Jesus himself who presents humankind with its only real crisis.[84]

The only authority for proclaiming the gospel is the authority of Jesus. Humankind has to come face to face with what

---

[81] Lesslie Newbigin, "Text and Context: The Bible in the Church," in *Theological Review* Vol. 5, No. 1 (April 1982), p. 13.

[82] Lesslie Newbigin, *A Faith for this One World?*, pp. 30-55.

[83] Newbigin's thought on the authority of Scripture is similar to what Karl Barth says about the self-authenticating nature of revelation. Cf. *Church Dogmatics*, Vol. 1/2, pp. 484, 490.

[84] *A Faith for this One World?*, p. 57.

Newbigin calls "the total fact of Jesus." Jesus is himself "the ultimate authority" for humankind, an authority not requiring to be ratified by another. The gospels indicate that the question of authority arose from the very beginning. The gospels present him as one who spoke with authority and not as the scribes. The scribes spoke from higher authorities, and they claimed no ultimate authority of their own. But Jesus spoke differently. If he quoted from any prior authority, he could also add: "You have heard that it was said to them of old, but I say unto you.' The standard of his authority was himself. Therefore,

> By the manner of his teaching, by his acts of forgiveness, by his promises to those who followed him, he made it clear that he possessed or believed himself to possess true and final authority in the affairs of men. He was asked to state what his authority was or to give some sign to authenticate his claim, but he declined to do so. He placed those who met him in the position where they had to make a decision about *him*.[85]

Newbigin states that the centre of Christ's teaching was himself. People had to make up their minds about the claim that in him the Kingdom of God had come, that in him the Creator of the world had come to call back his children, that in him light had come into the world and therefore judgment.

Newbigin, by referring to Rev. 1:12-18, says that the question of authority is answered in the presence of one who was dead and is alive and has the keys of death and Hades.[86] Because of the total fact of Jesus Christ, no authority is required to commend

---

[85] Ibid., pp. 57-58.
[86] Ibid., p. 59.

him. However, Jesus places every person in the position where an answer has to be given one way or the other to the question that he asks. It is this fact of Christ that gives authority for Christian mission and witness. The `fact of Christ' is the whole Christ-event. It is the good news of the Kingdom which came in the person of Christ. To understand the total fact of Christ, one has to look back to the scriptures of Old and New Testaments. By looking back to the Old Testament, one is able to grasp what is being fulfilled, and by looking to the New Testament, one is able to see the record of this fact, and commentary upon it.

A comment must be made here with respect to the Bible as containing the written record of the total fact of Christ. The Bible, for Newbigin, is not a series of illustrations of general truths, but "the record of God's saving acts for the redemption of the world."[87] The Old Testament cannot be fully understood without the New Testament and the New Testament cannot be fully understood without the Old Testament. Therefore the Church treats the two as one book with its central theme of God's election of a people to be his own people, and by whom he purposes to save the world. In order to understand what God has done for the salvation of the whole world, one has to study the whole record. The Bible presents the central thread of the history of God's people. Newbigin says,

> And the centre point of the story is the birth, life, death, resurrection and ascension of Jesus and the coming of His Spirit to His disciples. It is from that centre point that we understand the whole Bible, both the Old Testament and the New. Everything in the Bible points towards Him, and then points outward from Him to the end of the world and the

---

[87]Lesslie Newbigin, "Why Study the Old Testament?" *National Christian Council Review*, Vol. 74, (1954: 71-76), pp. 71-72.

ends of the earth.[88]

Newbigin presents, then, a thoroughly Christ-centered understanding of the Bible. Everything in the Bible is to be understood by its reference to Christ. He is the "turning point" of the story. The aim of everything in the Bible is to lead one to Christ, who is at the centre and turning point of actual history.[89]

The belief that the scriptures of the Old and New Testaments are the "locus of reliable truth"[90] has been challenged by modernity. It is quite common to speak of the liberal and fundamentalist approaches to the Bible, and Newbigin rejects both positions. The story of the transmission of biblical texts from the original to the present involves the "interaction of men and women with God" and "human judgment and human fallibility."[91] He certainly does not want to believe that in this long story of transmission a line was drawn before which everything is divine word and after which everything is human judgment. He rejects the kind of Protestant fundamentalism which seeks to affirm the "factual, objective truth of every statement in the Bible and which thinks that if any single factual error were to be admitted, biblical authority would collapse."[92] There is the "unavoidable existence of discrepancies in matters of fact to be found in the Bible," but it is absurd to believe that they occurred only at a date some time after the moment at which the original Hebrew text was written.[93] This arises from a false concept of biblical authority imposed on the Bible.

---

[88]Ibid., p. 76.
[89]Ibid.
[90]Lesslie Newbigin, *Proper Confidence*, p. 79.
[91]Ibid., p. 86.
[92]Ibid., p. 85.
[93]Ibid.

Newbigin maintains that the "doctrine of verbal inerrancy is a direct denial of the way in which God has chosen to make himself known to us as the Father of our Lord Jesus Christ."[94] We must allow the Bible to inform us of what it means to speak of the word of God. The Bible is a new starting point for thought and we have to learn, by the actual practice of living with the Bible, how God speaks.

Newbigin's hermeneutics proposes a "continual twofold movement," which, from within the Christian tradition, tries to understand Jesus in the context of the whole biblical story, and the story in the light of Jesus.[95] This understanding can be aided by a "critical activity" of the mind, which challenges one's old views and assumptions about the story of the Bible. However, this critical activity is perspectivally different from that of the post-Enlightenment in that it reads the Bible from within the Christian community. This activity would result in asking essential questions concerning the variety of biblical materials and would reconcile seemingly irreconcilable texts. An example of these irreconcilable texts is Paul's description of the Roman power as God's servant in Romans 13 and the identification of the same power with the work of Satan in Revelations.[96] The whole story of God's dealing with the people is important for understanding Jesus rightly. No one can understand Jesus rightly except in the context of the Bible as a whole. And to separate Jesus from the Bible is to create a mythical figure.[97]

The work of the Holy Spirit, as a hermeneutical principle, is

---

[94] Ibid., p. 89.
[95] Ibid., p. 88.
[96] Ibid., pp. 87-88.
[97] Ibid., p. 88.

essential to Newbigin. The Spirit of the Father and the Son interprets to the believers the meaning of Jesus' words and deeds and leads them to the truth as a whole.[98] We grow into knowledge of God by allowing the biblical story to awaken and to challenge us. The scriptures of the Old and New Testaments, with the aid of the Holy Spirit, impart to us the knowledge of God. Newbigin is of the opinion that if we do not know the whole story of the Bible and context of Jesus, we cannot truly know Jesus and the Father. It is through the person of Jesus that we are led into a true knowledge of God, because as Jesus said, "no one knows the Father except the Son and those to whom the Son makes him known" (Lk 10:22; John 15:15).

Because of this centrality of Christ which Scripture presents, the Christian revelation as set forth in the Bible is the starting point of thought for Newbigin. This is the major reason for his commendation of Augustine, who found a fresh starting point for thought in the Scriptures. Concerning Augustine, Newbigin comments:

> Revelation, the action of God himself in the events which the Church celebrates, gave him his new starting point. From a new standpoint his massive intellect could see in a wholly new perspective the landscape through which he traveled. As a result he was able to hand on to the following centuries a coherent and rational way of understanding the world and human history which also carried forward much that was precious in classical culture.[99]

The substance of the Scriptures is in the events of God's speaking

---

[98] Ibid., p. 90.
[99] *Truth to Tell*, p. 20.

and acting. In Augustine's time, this understanding of the Scriptures provided reason with new data for thinking. It opened up a new possibility for confident and hopeful living even in the darkness of the invading barbarism.[100] Everything depends on the *arche*, the new starting point offered by the revelation in Christ.

Newbigin reiterates the validity and the truthfulness of revelation for our contemporary cultural crisis. The church which is set within our culture should so present to our culture God's word in scripture that the world can hear and believe. His work is a call back to the affirmation of revelation as the sure source of truth, because it presents the incarnation of truth and knowledge, Jesus Christ. We shall see that his attitude to revelation and Scripture as source of truth is highly determinative for his attitude toward inter-religious dialogue.

3. USING POLANYI'S EPISTEMOLOGY

The trend of Newbigin's theological work which deals with the mission of the Church to modernity has utilized the ideas and concepts in science and sociology. Newbigin is widely knowledgeable in modern and contemporary philosophy, and there are a number of major philosophical thinkers who share his basic epistemological orientation (e.g., Temple, MacMurray, and Buckley). With respect to the philosophy of science, he has great admiration especially for the achievements of Michael Polanyi. As we have already glimpsed in the previous section, he makes substantial and constructive use of Polanyi's scientific concepts and models in order to strengthen a Christian vision of knowledge and truth. A brief diversion into Polanyi's work, so influential in the thought of Newbigin, will help us to appreciate Newbigin's rejection of `pluralist' approaches to inter-religious dialogue, as

---

[100]Ibid., p. 24.

well as his criticism of the relativism and privatization of the Christ of truth.

Polanyi (1891-1976), who was born in Hungary, was a well known physical chemist and social scientist. He could be called one of the greatest scientist-philosophers of our age, his scientific interests taking him into substantially independent fields of research. His contributions to the areas of Adsorption, Plasticity and Strength of Materials, X-ray Analysis, and Reaction Mechanism have received the special attention of the scientific world. He was a great scientist, opposed to scientism. Polanyi's search for truth led him to the rediscovery of basic tenets in science and philosophy which cannot be disregarded without destroying their own foundations. He has worked to restore the relationship between science and faith, illustrating the inner relationship between faith and reason in all scientific activity. In his work he has reconstructed the scientific basis of the human knowledge of the universe in a way that makes room for religious faith. Although this was not his main intention, he was nevertheless aware of doing just this, as an outgrowth of his scientific/philosophical reasoning. Polanyi's position points to the creation of far-reaching change in the relations of science and theology. His thinking in this area shows that theology and science are not opposed to each other, as some might think. Rather, they complement each other in the human understanding about the created universe. As Thomas F. Torrance, who comments on the work of Polanyi, points out,

> Theology and science arise and take shape within the one world which God has made and upon which he has conferred the rational order that makes it accessible to our scientific inquiries. Hence constant dialogue with natural science enabling us to share in its remarkable discoveries of God's handiwork can only be helpful to us in developing our knowledge

of God, even when we allow our minds, as we surely must, to be lifted above the world of nature that they may acquire patterns of belief and thought really appropriate to God under the transforming impact of his self-communication to us in Jesus Christ.[101]

I shall, in this section, discuss some important Polanyian ideas which are extensively and creatively used by Newbigin. What is central to this section is Polanyi's vision of knowledge which Newbigin ardently follows and develops in his epistemology. This is the major reason for the term 'philosophical mentor'. For his theological explorations, Newbigin draws upon Polanyi's scientific/philosophical analysis. I shall highlight in this section three areas of his work which are essential to an understanding of Newbigin.

a. The Need for a Fresh Starting Point for Thought

Polanyi draws parallels between St. Augustine's time and modern Western culture, which Newbigin believes to be an accurate description.[102] In Polanyi Newbigin finds an intellectual ally who determines the situation of the post-Enlightenment Western culture which is given to skepticism and relativism. Modern scientism, a form of reductionism in which knowledge of things at all levels is reductively redefined in terms of a limited, objectivist and mechanistic understanding of nature, has cruelly fettered human thought. This is because it eliminates all beliefs and traditionally guiding ideas and destroys the creative symbiosis

---

[101] Thomas F. Torrance, ed., *Belief in Science and in Christian Life: The Relevance of Michael Polanyi's Thought for Christian Faith and Life*, p. xvii.

[102] Lesslie Newbigin, *Truth to Tell*, p. 19.

between science and faith.[103] Scientism, in Polanyi's opinion, provides "no scope for our most vital beliefs and it forces us to disguise them in farcically inadequate terms."[104] He draws a comparison between the medieval cosmos and the past four or five hundred years. Thus Polanyi concludes,

> The past four or five centuries, which have gradually destroyed or overshadowed the whole medieval cosmos, have enriched us mentally and morally to an extent unrivalled by any period of similar duration. But its incandescence had fed on the combustion of the Christian heritage in the oxygen of Greek rationalism, and when this fuel was exhausted the critical framework itself burnt away.[105]

Following Polanyi's observation, Newbigin points out that classical thought, for all its splendid achievements, had been unable to overcome dichotomies between being and becoming, between reason and will, between the intelligible or spiritual world and the material world known by the senses.[106] This, he says, led to an

---

[103] *Personal Knowledge*, p. 265.

[104] Ibid.

[105] Ibid., pp. 265-256.

[106] Here Newbigin refers to the work of Charles N. Cochrane, *Christianity and Classical Culture: A Study of Thought and Action from Augustus to Augustine* (New York: Oxford University Press, 1957), First Published in 1940. This book, by an Oxford classicist, has been of "crucial importance" in Newbigin's thinking. The author traces the movement of thought from Augustus to Augustine, from the time when classical thought was at the height of its glory to the time when it had disintegrated into nihilism and skepticism. See Newbigin's *Truth to Tell*, p. 15.

"unending struggle of virtue against fortune, of the skill and courage and cunning of human will against the blind power of fate which would - in the end - always prevail."[107] As a result, truth was ultimately unknowable. All religions were equally valid to the people. The spiritual decay of this situation together with other disasters caused the disintegration of classical civilization.

One should compare the classical period with that of Augustine, who was himself one of its products, to see how he offered a fresh starting point for thought in his theology. Even pre-Augustinian Christian thinkers, who were well-versed in classical thought, as Newbigin says, struggled to express in their own terms the trinitarian faith found in Matthew's gospel, and articulated in the Nicene Creed. Trained in classical thought, Augustine did not discard all what he had learned from it, but made a fresh assessment of it after his conversion, carrying over whatever was good in the old culture to the new. He was introduced to the Christian faith and to the Church by Ambrose. Thus the trinitarian faith became a new starting point for thought, although modern Western culture might consider it nonsense.[108] This new starting point helped overcome ancient dichotomies by offering a new framework. The old dichotomy of matter and spirit, for example, was overcome in the fact that God took human flesh and became incarnate in Jesus Christ.

Both Polanyi and Newbigin believe that Augustine has important lessons for the Church in its present transcultural journey. The brilliance of the past three hundred years was produced by the "combustion of a thousand years' deposit of the Christian heritage in the Oxygen of Greek rationalism." Now, the fuel is burned up and pumping up more oxygen does not yield

---

[107] *Truth to Tell*, p. 16.
[108] Ibid., p. 17.

fresh light. What is now needed is a renewal of the material on which critical reason should work. Augustine articulated a new vision based on the new data of the Scripture. Polanyi suggests that "we must go back to Augustine to restore the balance of our cognitive powers." He adds,

> In the fourth century A.D., St. Augustine brought the history of Greek philosophy to a close by inaugurating for the first time a post-critical philosophy. He taught that all knowledge was a gift of grace, for which we must strive under the guidance of antecedent belief: *nisi credideritis, non intelligitis.*[109] His doctrine ruled the mind of Christians scholars for a thousand years.[110]

The problem began to set in when faith declined and "demonstrable knowledge" gained superiority over it. An example of this from the end of the seventeenth century is John Locke, who distinguished between faith and knowledge.[111] Locke says,

> How well-grounded and great soever the assurance of faith may be wherewith it is received; but faith it

---

[109]St. Augustine, *De libero arbitrio*, Book I, par. 4: "Unless ye believe, ye shall not understand," and *Credo ut intelligam* (I believe in order to understand) based on [Isaiah 7:9 Septuagint]. See also Augustine's *On Free Choice of the Will*, Trans. Anna S. Benjamin and L. H. Hackstaff (New York: Bobbs-Merrill, 1964), pp. 5, 39.

[110]*Personal Knowledge*, p. 266.

[111]*Truth to Tell*, p. 30. For this distinction, see Locke's *A Third Letter for Toleration* (London: Awnsham and John Churchill, 1692), chapter 1, p. 2, where he says: "...where vision, knowledge and certainty is, there faith is done away."

is still and not knowledge; persuasion, and not certainty. This is the highest the nature of the thing will permit us to go in matters of revealed religion, which are therefore called matters of faith: A persuasion of our own minds, short of knowledge, is the last result that determines us in such truths.[112]

Locke's definition of faith runs against Augustine's antecedent belief: *Credo ut intelligam* (I believe in order to understand). According to Locke's definition, belief is no longer a higher power that reveals to us knowledge lying beyond the range of observation and reason, but a mere "personal acceptance which falls short of empirical and rational demonstrability."[113]

Newbigin is in complete agreement with Polanyi, who says that the distinction between faith and knowledge has "reduced all belief to the status of subjectivity: to that of an imperfection by which knowledge fell short of universality."[114] Against this, Polanyi asserts that belief must once more be recognized as the source of all knowledge. This assertion is both right and important as Polanyi finds the element of faith and commitment underlying all of our culture, from the most objective science to the implicit values of a free society. He declares:

> Tacit assent and intellectual passions, the sharing of an idiom and of a cultural heritage, affiliation to a like-minded community: such are the impulses which shape our vision of the nature of things on which we rely for our mastery of things. No

---

[112]*A Third Letter for Toleration*, chapter 1, p. 3. Also quoted by Michael Polanyi, *Personal Knowledge*, p. 266.
[113]*Personal Knowledge*, p. 266.
[114]Ibid.

intelligence, however critical or original, can operate outside such a fiduciary framework.[115]

Polanyi's epistemology and his critical analysis of Western culture are fully followed by Newbigin, who sees both "originality and power" in Polanyi's attack on the scientism and false objectivism that stems from this belief.[116] The very heart of the problem is epistemological and Newbigin recognizes it. He, by following Polanyi, is reiterating the need for accepting the revelation of God in Jesus Christ, articulated in the trinitarian faith, as a starting point for understanding the gospel. This trinitarian faith is also crucial to inter-religious dialogue. "Faith," says Newbigin "is not a terminus but a starting point from which understanding can begin."[117] What Polanyi draws from the Augustinian work must be an acceptable model for the modern Western cultural context. Newbigin believes that Christian dialogue with modern culture will also be a dialogue with the natural scientists.

b. **The Republic of Science**

Polanyi's 'Republic of Science'[118] is a concept which is well used by Newbigin as a tool in his explanation of what he calls,

---

[115] Ibid.

[116] *Truth to Tell*, p. 30.

[117] Lesslie Newbigin, *The Other Side of 1984: Questions for the Churches* (Geneva: World Council of Churches, 1983), p. 24.

[118] This phrase deals with the structure and nature of the 'community of scientists', a concept which Polanyi explains in his work *Science, Faith and Society* (Chicago and London: The University of Chicago Press, 1946), pp. 29-51. For the same subject, see Polanyi's *Personal Knowledge*, pp. 163, 217, etc.

`Committed Pluralism.'[119] Members of the Republic of Science or the community of scientists, according to Polanyi, are committed to a common goal. The membership in this community is not readily granted as in a civil society, where one becomes a citizen by mere birth. According to Polanyi, there are roughly three stages in the process of learning the premises of science.[120] Starting at school one must acquire a facility in using scientific terms "to indicate the established doctrine, the dead letter of science". Then at the second stage the university imparts scientific judgment by teaching the practice of experimental proof and giving a first experience in routine research. The student graduates from the university with a degree, which in a way is passing a means test. The student's prolonged application of will and some gifts makes him or her successful in the process of scientific education. The insufficiently willing and the insufficiently gifted are weeded out by the system of education. The successful candidate is still not a part of the community of scientists until he or she has been initiated into the community and worked under the supervision of mature scientists. The most vital premises of scientific discovery are fostered in the great schools of research. On this level of initiation and experience, Polanyi has this to say:

> A master's daily labours will reveal these to the intelligent student and impart to him also some of the master's personal intuitions by which his work is guided. The way he chooses problems, selects a technique, reacts to new clues and to unforeseen difficulties, discusses other scientists' works, and keeps speculating all the time about a hundred possibilities which are never to materialize, may

---

[119] Lesslie Newbigin, *Truth to Tell: The Gospel As Public Truth*, pp. 55-56.
[120] *Science, Faith and Society*, Op. cit., p. 43.

transmit a reflection at least of his essential visions.[121]

In Polanyi's understanding, in the Republic of Science there is a commitment to a common `faith'. Polanyi[122] considers this model to be valid beyond the case of the community of scientists and it is this validity that Newbigin develops in his assertion of truth. Again, in the words of Polanyi,

> Scientific society is not and cannot be formed by a group of persons taking first the decision of binding themselves to a General Will and then choosing to direct their general will to the advancement of science. Scientific life illustrates on the contrary how the general acceptance of a *definite* set of principles brings forth a community governed by these principles - a community which would automatically dissolve the moment its constitutive principles were repudiated. The General Will appears then as a rather misleading fiction; <u>the truth being (if the case of science be a guide) that voluntary submission to certain principles necessarily generates a communal life governed by these principles, and that ultimate sovereignty then rests safely with each generation of individuals who, in their devotion to these principles, conscientiously interpret and apply them to the issues of the period.</u>[123]

This model of the dedicated company can with proper alteration be

---

[121]Ibid., pp. 43-44.
[122]Ibid., p. 64.
[123]Ibid. Emphasis added.

used for civil society, as Polanyi seems to suggest and Newbigin certainly agrees.

In the Republic of Science, what brings and keeps scientists together is their pursuit of knowledge. If one loses the appetite for scientific discovery, one would lose his or her partnership. In the Republic, there is no validity for the `live and let live' maxim. There are rigorous standards to be maintained in not only one's own work but also in one's judgment of other works. There is a natural and necessary censor[124] and an internal system of cross-checks. The works of the scientists are subject to verification within the community and the consensus of scientific opinion goes far beyond an agreement concerning a common experience. Polanyi calls their work a "joint appraisal of an intellectual domain."[125] The underlying principle of this internal cross-check is this:

> Each scientist watches over an area comprising his own field and some adjoining strips of territory, over which neighbouring specialists can also form reliable first-hand judgments. Suppose now that work done on the specialty of B can be reliably

---

[124] When Polanyi speaks of `censorship' he does not mean it in the modern sense of shutting people's mouths. As one commentator on Polanyi says, he uses it with the meaning attached to the word in Greek and Roman Republics, where censoring meant "putting people in the place which they deserved, or downgrading them if their conduct called for this." See Bertrand de Jouvenel, "The Republic of Science," in *The Logic of Personal Knowledge: Essays Presented to Michael Polanyi on his Seventieth Birthday*, Names of editors unlisted (London: Routledge & Kegan Paul, 1961), p. 140.

[125] Michael Polanyi, *Personal Knowledge*, p. 217.

judged by A and C; that of C by B and D; that of D by C and E; and so on. If then each of these groups of neighbours agrees in respect to their standards, then the standards on which A, B and C agree will be the same on which B, C and D agree, and on which also C, D and E agree, and so on, throughout the whole realm of science.[126]

The mutual adjustment of standards occurs in this way. The consensus in the community forms a continuous line of critics whose scrutiny upholds the same minimum level of scientific value in all publications accredited by scientists. The scrutiny of one member's work by another measured by equivalent standards throughout the various branches of science, ensures the highest degree of scientific excellence.

A point that is to be kept in mind about the Republic of Science is the absence of a central supreme authority. If freedom of opinion is meant to imply the opportunity to express publicly whatever one would like to say, then there is no such freedom in the community of scientists. This might be a point of surprise for one who thinks that the small number of senior scientists control all avenues of research. Jouvenel finds it strange that the internal constitution of the Republic of Science should present traits so similar to those which scientists ardently denounce in the body politic whenever they utter political opinions.[127] Polanyi does not draw attention to the dangers of the structure of power, but to its efficiency. Familiar with the world of science, he would denounce such evils, should occasions arise.

Newbigin draws upon the idea of the Republic of Science

---

[126]Ibid.
[127]Op. cit., p. 140.

and applies this to Western pluralistic societies. The recent collapse of communism in Eastern Europe has given rise to a mood of euphoria in the Western countries about the benefits of a free society. Pluralism is contrasted with totalitarianism as light with darkness. However, Newbigin contends that total pluralism has led Western society to a state of anomie, to lostness, to meaningless life in a meaningless world.[128] Total pluralism offers no criteria to judge different life-styles and provides no cultural norms. The censorship which is part of the scientific community is not found in these societies, and as a result, there is no truth, but only "what seems meaningful for me."

To transpose this situation to politics, Marxism claimed to be a scientific account of human affairs, objectively true apart from any value judgments or moral passions. As such it claimed the right to impose itself as public doctrine controlling all aspects of life. Marxism had strong appeal to moral passions for justice and equity, claiming to be true without reference to the moral passions which it despised. Newbigin criticizes its claim to be the objective truth. This doctrine produced disastrous consequences for the intellectual and political life of the world. With the fall of communist regimes, the most desirable alternative appears to be the society where pluralism reigns. However, the essential mark of a pluralist society is subjectivism, which carries the disastrous consequence of a false objectivism (as was seen in Marxism). Unlike the case of the community of scientists, here freedom means saying whatever a person wants to say without being censored. Thus there are no rigorous standards of judgment or criteria of truth. This, in Newbigin's view, is not freedom at all.

Newbigin offers, at this point, a distinction between

---

[128]*Truth to Tell*, p. 55.

'Agnostic Pluralism' and 'Committed Pluralism.'[129] According to Agnostic Pluralism, truth is unknowable. It offers no criteria whatever to judge different kinds of belief and behaviour. This kind of pluralism is increasingly maintained in what are called "free" societies. Committed Pluralism, which is neither purely objective nor purely subjective, is in line with Polanyi's vision of knowledge in the scientific community. It is the characteristic of a person who is committed to seeking the truth and openly stating it. Newbigin views Polanyi's vision of the scientific community to be a pluralist community which is not controlled or directed from one centre. According to this Committed Pluralism, scientists are free to pursue their own line of research and investigation. The have the freedom to differ from one another and to argue with one another. The scientific community operates within the tradition which respects the past members of the Republic. The tradition is not infallible nor incorrigible. On the contrary, it is being changed and modified constantly by new discoveries. Nevertheless, it offers a reliable framework for research. Scientists have freedom, but not anarchy. There are norms to carry out research. Newbigin adds:

> Long established views are not cast aside without a very great deal of experimental work, and in any case - not until a more viable theory has become available. Freedom of thought and speculation is limited by what has already been well established as truth.[130]

The presupposition of all this is the understanding that there is reality out there to be known, even if knowledge in the present is partial. Differences of opinion are not allowed to co-exist in a scientific community as the glory of pluralism. Newbigin sees

---

[129]Ibid., p. 56.
[130]Ibid., p. 57.

them as subjects of debate, scrutiny, testing, argument, and fresh research until either one view prevails over the other as more true, or some fresh ways of seeing things enables the two views to be reconciled as two ways of seeing one reality.[131]

Newbigin wants to apply the same principle to contemporary culture and the search for truth in the culture. This is especially important when we see that the scientific part of the culture is by far the most dynamic part. Why should there be a gap between the natural sciences and other disciplines? He wants to see the model of the Republic of Science aiding in the search for truth in the contemporary pluralist culture. This would be pluralism, neither agnostic nor anarchic, but committed and responsible, in the search for truth.[132]

This has certain implications for the life of the Church. Polanyi's idea of a society of responsible personal knowledge should be a guideline for the Church. In Newbigin's words,

> Clearly the Christian Church ought to be the model and nursery of such a society. It can be so only if we can extricate ourselves from the false dichotomy of objective and subjective, which is reflected in the battle between liberals and fundamentalists, and the key lies in the acceptance of personal responsibility for seeking to know the truth and publishing what we know. Both objectivism and subjectivism are ways of evading personal responsibility for knowing the truth.[133]

---

[131] Ibid., p. 58.
[132] Ibid.
[133] Ibid., p. 59.

This means that the Church is to enter vigorously into the struggle for truth in public life. The Christian faith, in accordance with this, has to be brought into the public arena, to publish it, to put it at risk in the encounter with other faiths and ideologies in open debate and argument, and in the risky business of discovering the meaning of Christian obedience in radically new circumstances and in radically new human cultures.

So Polanyi's concept strengthens Newbigin's argument against agnostic pluralism which, in his view, confuses the normal with the normative. In the case of inter-religious dialogue, the supposition that the unity of humankind can be achieved by raising no question of ultimate truth would make unity an end in itself. It denies the centrality of Christ in the gospel, which alone is the centre around which alienated human beings can be drawn together in a reconciled fellowship. Therefore the gospel has to be proclaimed as truth and as public truth. It has to be proclaimed, "not as a package of estimable values but as the truth about what is the case."[134]

c. Fiduciary Act in Intellectual Inquiry

In the thought of Polanyi, fiduciary act[135] is present in every intellectual inquiry, whether scientific or religious. By this personal commitment or fiduciary act, the scientist relies on the coherence and meaning of that which is believed to exist. Only the person who discerns a coherent pattern in nature can use it as a clue to

---

[134] Ibid., p. 64.

[135] An act of faith which relies upon coherence and meaning in that which one believes to exist. See for an explication of this theme in scientific inquiry in Michael Polanyi, *Personal Knowledge*, pp. 264-268.

active inquiry. Scientific investigation depends upon firm beliefs grounded in reality and grounded in personal involvement. The scientist's inquiry is a personal choice, seeking and eventually accepting something believed to be given. This is what Polanyi calls the `fiduciary act', because it is an act of faith. Belief is the source of all knowledge.[136] In a fiduciary act a person's mind is submitted both personally and responsibly to the requisite of a reality independent of it. This is related to what Polanyi speaks of as personal knowledge, which involves the personal participation of the knower. Without the fiduciary act, no scientific inquiry can take place. Newbigin, following Polanyi's theory of knowledge, attacks a materialistic conception of science which negates the subjective elements involved in it.

Contrary to popular belief, social factors are operative in scientific work, such as the tradition of scientific work into which young scientists are apprenticed, which establishes guidelines and sets limits, which provides the concepts, methods, and tools with which scientists do their work. Also there are personal elements such as intuition, imagination, judgment, courage to take risks, and sheer pertinacity without which, Newbigin says, great scientific work is not done.[137] It is absurd to ignore all of this and treat scientific work as though the scientist does not exist, as though the "findings of science were simply a transcript of reality" in which the human subject has no place.[138] Contrary to this detached and purely objective view of science, Newbigin points out that

> The effort to know the truth involves struggle, groping, feeling one's way. It is true that there are also moments of sudden illumination, but these

---

[136]Ibid., p. 266.
[137]*Truth to Tell*, p. 31.
[138]Ibid.

come only to those who have accepted the discipline of patient groping, of trying out different possibilities, of sustained reflection.[139]

The nature of the process implies that one has to start out as a disciple or pupil. One has to learn a language to express what one has learned and the language is itself the form of one's knowing. Then one has to go on to struggle with the concepts and models used in the particular field of research until they become part of one's mind, and one ceases to think about them just as one ceases to think about the words he is using. What is fundamental to this process of grasping the truth is the faith that those who have gone ahead can guide the learner. One has to believe in the available clues. Personal commitment in faith and personal judgment about evidence are required at every level. This means there is no absolute separation of faith and knowledge. All knowing involves a personal commitment. In this respect Newbigin admires Polanyi's post-critical philosophy as a "massive attempt to demonstrate that all knowledge of reality rests upon faith commitments which cannot be demonstrated but are held by communities whose "conviviality"[140] is a necessary factor in the enterprise of knowing."[141] Fiduciary act is applicable not only to the scientist but also to the Christian believer. No fiduciary framework can exist except as it is held by a community. Newbigin calls the community of scientists the confraternity of scholars, who share the same basic

---

[139]Ibid., p. 32.

[140]In Polanyi's thought it denotes the interpersonal relations of a community in tacit sharing of basic convictions which underlie all articulate consensus and communication. It implies a common frame of mind in experience and knowing.

[141]Lesslie Newbigin, *The Other Side of 1984: Questions for the Churches*, Op. cit., p. 23.

framework of thought. He makes the point that no systematic scientific work is possible except where there is some kind of community which sustains and protects the fiduciary framework for research and discussion.[142]

Newbigin joins forces with Polanyi in the criticism of the materialistic conception of science, tracing this conception to certain elements of Greek thought.[143] The materialistic conception of science has been set forth by many as self-evident, positive, and demonstrable. This is a knowledge that is based exclusively on recorded observations. Such a conception of science necessarily involves the rejection of anything that cannot be proved or disproved by scientific experiments. The major consequence is that all personal beliefs, which cannot be proved or disproved scientifically, are to be abolished. The Bible is studied critically within the fiduciary framework of the Enlightenment. One cannot lay any claim to truth if it cannot be demonstrated by scientific methods. Resultantly, it poses a threat to religious and moral truths. Modern scientific minds dismiss such religious and moral statements as subjective, a form of personal bias. This, as Alexander Thomson observes, leads us to an epistemological problem where

> All human beliefs accepted on the grounds of authority or tradition were regarded as being purely subjective and had to be discarded in order to achieve a proper scientific detachment and a truly objective approach to the world. Faith and belief fell short of knowledge in that they fell short of

---

[142]Ibid., p. 30.
[143]*Personal Knowledge*, pp. 6-8.

empirical and rational demonstration.[144]

Newbigin affirms that this false conception of science challenges the question of truth in religion. Therefore, he tries to restore the balance of the act of knowing by emphasizing its fiduciary act and subjective and objective elements. This fiduciary act is found in every intellectual inquiry, whether scientific or religious.

Newbigin does not stop his analysis at this point, but he goes on to say that there are different fiduciary frameworks co-existing in modern Western culture.[145] For Polanyi, the process of examining any topic involves an "exploration of the topic" and an "exegesis of our fundamental beliefs," and it is a "dialectical combination of exploration and exegesis."[146] "Our fundamental beliefs are," says Polanyi, "continuously reconsidered in the course of such a process, but only within the scope of their own basic premises."[147] Here Newbigin wants to go even beyond Polanyi to speak about the Christian mission and the need for "acting out of a fundamental belief" in every sector of human affairs and "in dialogue with every other pattern of thought by which men and women seek to make sense of their lives."[148] To acknowledge the fiduciary framework is the starting point, not the cut-off point for exploration and questioning. Here arises the need for genuine dialogue with other fiduciary frameworks. Newbigin's question is whether the different frameworks should co-exist merely in mutual

---

[144]*Tradition and Authority in Science and Theology With Reference to the Thought of Michael Polanyi* (Edinburgh: Scottish Academic Press, 1987), p. 3.
[145]*The Other Side of 1984*, p. 30.
[146]*Personal Knowledge*, p. 267.
[147]Ibid.
[148]*The Open Secret* (1978), p. 31.

toleration or in dialogue.[149]

Genuine dialogue should take Christians to the place where the fiduciary framework itself is questioned. There are those who praise the virtues of dialogue, who believe that their fiduciary framework is safe from fundamental questioning and that inter-religious dialogue can be conducted within this framework. Newbigin's suggestion is to have open and genuine dialogue not only with people of other religions, but also with people who live by other fiduciary frameworks.[150] This is done by the Christian community on the basis of its own fiduciary framework which is quite different from other frameworks. The centre of this framework is an appeal of love which can only be answered in faith, love and obedience. This is the love of God which was manifested in the cross of Christ.[151]

4. INTERACTION WITH PETER L. BERGER

Newbigin's attention turns not only to the philosophy of science but also to sociology of knowledge. In this section, I shall deal with Newbigin's interactions with Peter Berger's sociology of knowledge. Newbigin shows great interest in Berger's sociological concepts, because they enable him to reach a clear perception of modern Western culture. Although Newbigin uses these concepts as analytical tools, he does not adopt them uncritically. He uses them to the extent they sustain his investigation of truth and religious authority in modern culture. Certain concepts here too are relevant to his approach to inter-religious dialogue.

---

[149] *The Other Side of 1984*, p. 30.
[150] Ibid., p. 31.
[151] Ibid., p. 54.

a. Plausibility Structure

A major concept of Berger's sociology to which Newbigin turns is called `plausibility structure.' Berger gives a comprehensive treatment of this concept in his work *The Heretical Imperative: Contemporary Possibilities of Religious Affirmation.*[152] A plausibility structure "represents a central concept for an understanding of the relationship between society and consciousness."[153] Berger points out that, except for a few areas of direct personal experience, human beings require what is called `social confirmation' for their beliefs about reality. He says that, for example, morality requires particular `social circumstances' in order to become and remain plausible to the individual. These social circumstances constitute the plausibility structure for the morality at issue.[154] As Newbigin comments on this, it is a "social structure of ideas and practices that create the conditions determining what beliefs are plausible within the society in question."[155]

Peter Berger sees a plurality of world views in modern society. As a result, the modern person is confronted not only by "multiple options of possible courses of actions but also by

---

[152](Garden City, New York: Anchor Press/Double Day, 1979). The central concern of this book is modernity and the choice one has to make in a pluralist society. Berger is concerned to explore the possibilities of religious affirmations, to statements about the world that can plausibly be prefaced by the words, "I believe." He proposes that the heretical imperative can be turned from an obstacle to an aid both to religious faith and to reflection about it. See p. 36.
[153]Ibid., p. 17.
[154]Ibid., p. 18.
[155]*Foolishness to the Greeks*, p. 10.

multiple options of possible ways of thinking about the world."[156] In modernized American culture, this option means that the individual may choose his *weltanschauung* very much as he or she chooses most other aspects of private existence. There is a smooth continuity between consumer choices in different areas of life and a decision to settle for a particular `religious preference.' Berger contends that this situation results from what he calls `modernity,' which pluralizes both institutions and plausibility structures.[157] He draws a contrasting picture of traditional and modern societies. In a traditional society, there are highly reliable plausibility structures, while modern societies are characterized by unreliable, unstable, incohesive plausibility structures. The modern world is a world of choice, contrary to the `world of fate' inhabited by traditional human beings. In the traditional society, one must choose in innumerable ways which reach into the areas of beliefs, values and world-views. An adverse effect of this situation upon a human individual is a new measure of complexity in the individual's experience of himself or herself. Modernity, argues Berger, brought with it a subjective side to human existence. According to him, `modernization and subjectivization are cognate processes'.[158]

Berger observes that premodern times was characterized by religious certainty, and by sharp contrast, modern society is a world of religious uncertainty. The modern individual is faced with the necessity to make choices as to what to believe. This fact constitutes what he calls `the heretical imperative' in the

---

[156]*Heretical Imperative*, p. 17.
[157]Ibid.
[158]Ibid., p. 20.

contemporary situation. Thus 'heresy[159],' once the occupation of marginal and eccentric types, has become a much more general condition, and indeed, has become universalized. Berger, who looks at the original connotation of this word in the context of a presupposed religious authority, goes on to say that the heretic denied this authority, refusing to accept the tradition *in toto*.[160] Instead, there was a picking and choosing which constructed the heretic's own deviant view. As there have always been rebels and innovators in human societies, argues Berger, the possibility of heresy has always existed. By drawing a contrast between the premodern and modern societies, Berger points out that

> *In premodern situations there is a world of religious certainty, occasionally ruptured by heretical deviations. By contrast, the modern situation is a world of religious uncertainty, occasionally staved off by more or less precarious constructions of religious affirmation.* Indeed, one could put this change even more sharply: *For premodern man, heresy is a possibility -usually a rather remote one; for modern man, heresy typically becomes a*

---

[159]Etymologically, the word comes from the Greek verb *hairein*, which means 'to choose.' Peter Berger explains that, originally it simply meant the making of a choice. In the New Testament, in the Pauline epistles, the word already has a specifically religious connotation - that of a faction or party within the wider religious community. It refers to the particular religious opinion that its members have chosen. Thus, in Galatians 5:20 the apostle Paul lists *hairesis* or 'party spirit' along with such evils as 'strife, selfishness, envy,' etc. The point which Berger makes here is that, for this notion of heresy to have any meaning at all, the authority of a religious tradition was presupposed. See p. 27.

[160]Ibid., p. 28.

necessity.[161]

Berger suggests that with the coming of modernity, the picking and choosing becomes imperative. As a result, heresy does not now stand against a clear background of an authoritative tradition. The background has become dim or even has disappeared. Berger affirms that the modern situation is not conducive to the plausibility of religious authority. There is a pluralism which has plunged religion as a whole into crisis. The peculiarity of this pluralism may be manifested in the well-known American phrase `religious preference.'

According to Berger, choices are multiplied by modernity and in the matter of religion, as in other areas of life and thought, this means that the modern individual is faced not just with opportunity but with the necessity of making choices as to his beliefs. This fact forms the heretical imperative in modern society.[162] In the modern society, the religious thinker experiences what Berger calls the `cognitive pressure' from modernity, with its closely related aspects of pluralism and secularization. As long as the secular worldview exists in the social context of the modern person, the religious thinker is pressured "to softpedal if not to abandon altogether the supernatural elements of his tradition."[163]

What is relevant to the present discussion is the modern pluralist situation which Berger points out to be difficult for religious affirmation. Newbigin follows Berger to a certain extent in exposing this situation. A genuine encounter of the gospel with this Western cultural situation, a voice that can challenge it on its own terms, is what Newbigin is most concerned about. `How does

---

[161]Ibid. Italics original.
[162]Ibid., p. 30.
[163]Ibid., p. 54.

or can the Bible function in the confrontation of modern western culture with the gospel?' is the question that Newbigin is trying to answer.[164] Since the time of the Enlightenment, it has been impossible to speak of the Bible simply as the word of God in the manner earlier ages did. In the present, affirming Scripture as God's word will be viewed as a personal decision, one of a number of possible decisions.

It is in this context that Newbigin refers to Berger as one among those who have written extensively about the possibility of Christian affirmation. He examines the three possibilities for affirmation which Berger calls `deductive,' `reductive,' and `inductive.'[165] The deductive possibility simply reasserts the authority of a religious tradition in the secularized society. The reductive option is to reinterpret the tradition in terms of modern secularity, which in turn is taken to be a compelling necessity of participating in modern consciousness. The third option turns to experience as the ground of all religious affirmations, either one's own experience or the experience embodied in a particular range of traditions. The inductive option is rooted in the modern situation and its heretical imperative.

Berger, following Schleiermacher, favours the inductive option which takes the human religious experience (or `signals of transcendence') as the presupposition of all theologies as the clue to the human situation. But Newbigin raises a legitimate criticism as to how, among the many signals of transcendence, one distinguishes the true signal from the false. To answer this question, Berger depends on the Muslim theologian and mystic, al-Ghazali, according to whom they must all be weighed on "the scale

---

[164] *Foolishness to the Greeks*, p. 10.
[165] *The Heretical Imperative*, pp. 60-63. Cf. *Foolishness to the Greeks*, p. 11.

of reason." Newbigin recognizes that Berger defends himself against any surrender to the rationalism in the Enlightenment style. Nevertheless, he defends his `sober rational assessment' as the only way to distinguish between true and false religious experience. But, what is the basis on which Berger describes, or even accepts the criteria for this rational assessment? This is a critical question for Berger. Newbigin's analysis of al-Ghazali's scale of reason and Berger's sober rational assessment moves him to conclude: "Berger's own formulation that religious certainty is located only within the enclave of religious experience itself, and cannot be had - except `precariously in recollection' -in the ordinary life of the world."[166] Newbigin views Berger's `sober rationality' with suspicion, as it "does not appear to belong to the enclave but to the public world outside."[167] Therefore, Newbigin remarks,

> It is not a kind of rationality that derives from the religious experience itself but one that judges this experience. And it is not difficult to see that it is in fact the rationality that rests on the assumption of our culture.[168]

b. Newbigin's Critique of Berger

Newbigin agrees with Berger's observations about the modern situation, but is not willing to accept his solutions. Rather he disagrees strongly:

> My point here is simply this: while Berger correctly shows how the traditional plausibility structures are dissolved by contact with this modern world-view,

---

[166] *Foolishness to the Greeks*, p. 13.
[167] Ibid.
[168] Ibid.

and while he correctly reminds us that the prevalence and power of this world-view gives no ground for believing it to be true, he does not seem to allow for the fact that it is itself a plausibility structure and functions as such.[169]

When Berger makes the observation that the modern situation is not conducive to the plausibility of religious authority, Newbigin makes the point that the existing situation *is* the plausibility structure according to which individuals are to make choices. He moves a step further by adding that Berger's inductive method, which tries to deal with this situation, is itself part of this plausibility structure.[170] The public world, which he contrasts with the private enclaves, is the world governed by the assumptions of this scientific world-view developed from the time of Bacon and Galileo.

Looking at the scientific world view from the point of view of the Christian revelation, Newbigin sees the validity of the inductive method as both real and limited.[171] It is a valid way of coming to the truth, because the created world is both rational (because it is the creation of God, who is light and not darkness) and contingent (because it is not an emanation of God but the creation of God, endowed by its Creator with a measure of autonomy). As a result, through the study of things and happenings in the created world, we can arrive at a true understanding of them. This is the foundation on which true science rests. However, this inductive method has a limited validity in that it cannot decide the question, namely, `By whom and for what purpose was this whole world created?' The answer to this question cannot be given by any

---

[169]Ibid., pp. 13-14.
[170]Ibid., p. 14.
[171]Ibid.

method of induction until history reaches its end. Until such a time, the full data of induction are lacking.[172] In continuing his attack on Berger's proposed method, Newbigin charges that

> Berger is a true follower of Schleiermacher in commending religion to its cultured despisers, and in seeking to show that there is a proper place for religious affirmation within the plausibility structure of the modern scientific world-view. But all of this procedure leaves that world-view unchallenged. The autonomous human being is still in the center - with total freedom of choice.[173]

This whole method of inquiry and discussion excludes the possibility that it might actually be the case that the God who created and sustains the universe has revealed himself in the history of the world. Any possibility of Christian affirmation has been treated as something that has happened in a private enclave where religious experience took place. Therefore the critics of the gospel feel the need of bringing it out of the enclave into the public world, to be weighed in the scale of reason along with other varieties of religious experience. Newbigin agrees with Berger's comment that in Western societies we all are under the heretical imperative. It is true, as Berger points out, that in Western culture, the ideology of pluralism reigns.

    The central core of Western culture, as Newbigin recognizes, is an ideal of knowledge of what are called 'the

---

[172] Ibid.
[173] Ibid., p. 15.

facts'[174], a knowledge that is supposed to be independent of the personal commitment of the knower. While rejecting this ideal, he invokes the twin dogmas of Incarnation and Trinity that show the way to understanding reality as a whole. At the centre of the divine disclosure is the cross of Christ which provides the clue to understanding the whole rational and contingent universe.[175] Because God has spoken we are able to know God and know the truth as it is in Jesus. The gospel gives rise to a new plausibility structure, a radically different view of reality from those that shape all human cultures. There is a criterion of truth. Newbigin's view of knowledge and truth, which is centred on the vision of Christ, challenges the central core of Western culture. That challenge leads us to the theme of the next chapter.

Concluding Critical Comment

This writer is appreciative of Newbigin's creative use of the Polanyian concepts. He is often seen to be drawing an analogy between science and Christian faith with its emphasis on the role of `faith'. While he is right that all significant knowledge involves a `fiduciary framework,' and a kind of `faith' is operative even in the sciences, has he not underestimated the `radically given' character of Christian faith as a gift of the Holy Spirit? In insisting, quite rightly, on the `rational' character of faith, has he not drawn `faith' and `reason' too close as though every rational person must believe in Jesus Christ? Can the `fact of Christ,' including the resurrection of Jesus, be spoken of as though it were an assured piece of

---

[174]Newbigin is in agreement with Alasdair MacIntyre, who says that fact in modern culture is a "folk-concept with an aristocratic ancestry." See MacIntyre, *After Virtue*, 2nd. ed. (Notre Dame, Indiana: Notre Dame University Press, 1984), p. 76. Cf. *Foolishness to the Greeks*, p. 76.

[175]*Foolishness to the Greeks*, p. 90.

empirical knowledge? Also, Newbigin might be considered vulnerable in the very positive believing attitude he takes to the Bible. Many scholars and theologians would argue that he is far too uncritical and has not really heard or felt the force of biblical criticism, critique of the canon, ideological critique of biblical materials, etc. He often resorts to his own subjective

experience of God to answer the question, 'How do we know?', a 'fideism' he wants to avoid.

Newbigin has argued persuasively, with the help of Polanyi, that it is possible to have knowledge of ultimate truth. He clearly shows that the church, as the bearer of the gospel, inhabits a new plausibility structure which is at variance with all other plausibility structures including those of modern Western culture, to his discussion of which we shall now turn.

CHAPTER 4

CHRIST AND CULTURE
A CRITIQUE OF CONTEMPORARY CULTURE

A lifetime of crosscultural experience and a consistent reliance on the biblical revelation have made Bishop Newbigin a keen and penetrating cultural analyst. `Christ and Culture,' an important theme in Christian thinking, especially with reference to Western culture, has been brought to our immediate attention by Newbigin's recent writings. They offer an analysis of modern Western culture, which he believes finds itself in profound crisis, and offer an exploration of the ways in which the church should relate to this crisis. Because Jesus Christ is Lord, Christ is, once again `central' to any critique of culture. Moreover, since religion and cultures are inseparable, it is essential to understand Newbigin's attitude to culture, if we are to appreciate his approach to inter-religious dialogue. Modern Western secular culture, he holds, is also `religious', and is therefore one of the major dialogue partners for Christian believers. Inter-religious dialogue, therefore, is inevitably also inter-cultural dialogue. Communication with people of various cultural contexts, therefore, is essential to our inquiry.

The main thrust of this chapter is the study of Newbigin's interpretation of modern culture, with special attention to his reading of Western culture and its challenges to the Christian faith. I propose to begin by presenting his definition of human culture, and his understanding of the relationship between culture and religion. He views culture from the standpoint of the Christian revelation, which furnishes him with an analytical framework to call every cultural and religious assumption into question. I shall show in this chapter how Newbigin interprets the highly secularized modern European culture as one which is devoid of hope and therefore needs to be brought into an encounter with the gospel.

Definition of `Culture'

There are many different definitions of culture given by theologians and anthropologists. The encounter of the gospel with any given culture raises many questions about the gospel as well as the culture. Many authors have dealt with the problem of various cultural systems. For example, in one of his essays[1], Carl F. Starkloff, who utilizes Clifford Geertz's "cultural system" as a primary source, demonstrates the complexity of the discussion around this theme. Culture, in Geertz' terms, is a "system of inherited conceptions expressed in symbolic forms by means of which men communicate, perpetuate, and develop their knowledge about and attitudes toward life."[2] The mental basis of culture is often stressed in certain definitions like the one offered by Geertz. This is because individuals interact with one another according to preconceived mental patterns.[3] Culture, as A. Shorter points out, is not simply about behaviour; it is also about ideas.[4] Thus, culture is about transmitted patterns of meaning, embodied in symbols. It follows that if religion is a human phenomenon or activity, it must affect, and be affected by culture. Newbigin's definition of culture shares common elements of the above definitions.

---

[1]"Inculturation and Cultural Systems," Part 1, in *Theological Studies*, Vol. 55, No. 1 (March 1994), p. 66.
[2]Clifford Geertz, "Religion as a Cultural System," in *The Interpretation of Cultures* (New York: Basic Books, 1973), p. 89.
[3]Aylward Shorter, *Toward a Theology of Inculturation* (Maryknoll: Orbis, 1988), p. 4.
[4]Ibid.

"Culture," says Newbigin "is the cultivation of those capabilities which constitute human excellence."[5] It is "simply the way in which human societies order their corporate life, and as such it is corrupted by sin."[6] In an earlier work, Newbigin defines culture in its broadest sense as "the sum total of ways of living which shape (and also are shaped by) the continuing life of a group of human beings from generation to generation."[7] The sum total of ways, according to this definition, would include cultural elements such as language, law, custom, and forms of social organization, including marriage, family, and nation, and also art, science, technology, agriculture, and social and political organization. These elements are given as part of the tradition into which a person is born and socialized. While these are shaped, modified, and developed by members of the society from generation to generation, they also in turn shape the members of the society. So, culture is human behaviour in its corporate or social aspect. According to Newbigin, the "most fundamental element" in culture is language. It is by means of language that each member of the society is able to "grasp, conceptualize, and communicate" the reality in the individual's world.[8] The event of Pentecost is a "biblical warrant" for saying that God accepts and approves human languages. How is it possible to say who Jesus is without a language? Newbigin's definition of culture has four elements.[9] First, it is a product of human initiative, not an unchangeable datum. Second, it is a social product created, valued, and

---

[5] Lesslie Newbigin, "Culture and Culture," in Alister E. McGrath, ed., *The Blackwell Encyclopedia of Modern Christian Thought* (Cambridge, MA.: Blackwell Publishers, 1993), p. 98.

[6] *The Gospel in a Pluralist Society*, p. 185.

[7] Lesslie Newbigin, *The Open Secret*, p. 159.

[8] Ibid.

[9] Lesslie Newbigin, "Christ and the Cultures," in *The Scottish Journal of Theology*, Vol. 31 (1978), p. 9.

transmitted by a group. Third, it exists in transmission, and fourth, it is the sum total of a vast variety of human ways of living, including verbal and non-verbal communication. To speak of culture in the course of a theological discussion is to speak about humanity in its public, social, and historical aspect.[10]

Since human culture is "corrupted by sin", it is not free from evil.[11] But this corruption due to sin does not mean that the distinctions between good people and bad people, between just causes and unjust causes, are eliminated. Rather they are felt with the deepest intensity. Newbigin wants to stress the reality of sin and the divine sentence which has been passed over all humanity and over all its works for its rebellion against God.[12] Therefore, he does not view culture as an innocent, ethically neutral entity. The inherent corruption of human culture may express itself in various forms, such as cannibalism, polygamy, slavery, and the ancient practice of *sati* among certain Hindus of India. Because culture is corporate human behaviour, to discuss it as an entity quite apart from 'religion' is not a viable scheme.

Concept of Christ

Newbigin speaks of Jesus Christ as the one whom he knows and confesses as Lord of all that is, whom he knows through the witness of Christian tradition primarily embodied in the canonical

---

[10]Ibid.

[11]Lesslie Newbigin, "The Duty and Authority of the Church to Preach the Gospel," in *The Church's Witness to God's Design*, Amsterdam Assembly Series, Vol. II (New York: Harper & Brothers, 1948), p. 26.

[12]Ibid.

Scriptures.[13] The question "Who is Jesus Christ?" can be fully answered only when the fullness of humankind has been gathered into the confession of his name. In the confession 'Jesus is Lord,' the meaning of the word 'Lord' can only be shaped by and be limited by the culture of the person who speaks. From this perspective, argues Newbigin, a faithful Christology has to be done in the openness of dialogue with the varied cultures, in the openness of learning within the ecumenical fellowship of all Christians, and in faithful adherence to the given tradition.[14]

H. Richard Niebuhr, in his classic entitled *Christ and Culture*[15], makes a broad attempt to define the complex terms 'Christ' and 'Culture'[16]. For both Niebuhr and Newbigin, 'Christ' has to be defined utilizing the whole biblical story. Newbigin sees Jesus Christ, the incarnate Son of God, to be the "central substance" of the Christian message, which the Church is called to preach. His proper name 'Jesus' implies that he was a man living in Palestine during the reign of Herod, and his title 'Christ' indicates that he is honoured much more than any other figure of history - indeed as eternal Lord.[17] To confess the Lordship of Jesus Christ is to acknowledge that he alone is to be obeyed here and now. This obedience to him is to be evident in the Christian's small circle of home or in the vaster worlds of political, economical and cultural

---

[13]"Christ and the Cultures," Op. cit., pp. 9-10.

[14]Ibid., p. 10.

[15](New York: Harper & Brothers, 1951).

[16]pp. 11-19.

[17]Lesslie Newbigin, "Jesus Christ," in Stephen Neill, Gerald Anderson and John Goodwin, eds., *Concise Dictionary of the Christian World Mission* (Nashville and New York: Abingdon Press, 1971), p. 308.

life.[18] To speak of Jesus is to speak of what the New Testament says of him.[19] His coming is the coming of the reign of God. It teaches (Acts 10:37-41) that Jesus went about doing good and he made friends of the outcast. He forgave sins and spoke with authority.

It is true that images of Christ can vary in various cultures, but for Newbigin, Christ is the historical person, who was crucified, died, and risen. By his resurrection, all authority in heaven and earth is given to him to reign over all cultures and nations. He is also the one who will consummate history and reveal its meaning in the light of his eternal purpose. It is this New Testament picture of Christ that Newbigin is portraying here in relation to the concept of human culture.

1. RELATIONSHIP BETWEEN RELIGION AND CULTURE

a. Their Inseparability

Culture and religion are distinguishable, but not separable from each other. Neither can they be discussed as though separable from the entire life of human communities. Newbigin notes that, from a sociological perspective, religion is part of culture, and no religious belief is without implications for culture.[20] We have already in the introduction of this chapter discussed what Newbigin means by `culture'. `Religion' is a "notoriously difficult" word to

---

[18]Lesslie Newbigin, "Can Churches Give a Common Message to the World?" in *Theology Today*, Vol. 9 (1953), p. 516.

[19]Lesslie Newbigin, *Journey into Joy* (Grand Rapids: Wm. B. Eerdmans, 1972), pp. 40, 41, 42, 43.

[20]*The Gospel in a Pluralist Society*, p. 184.

define. There are two common ways in which this word is used. Sometimes it is used to describe any system of belief and practice which suggests some sort of transcendence of the experience of the senses. In this sense, Newbigin finds it too vague to be useful. Sometimes, it is used as if it referred to beliefs and practices concerning God and the immortal soul, in which case it is a too narrow usage, as it "excludes the original message of the Buddha."[21] So he uses the word religion to refer to

> that which has final authority for a believer or society, both in the sense that it determines his scale of values and in the sense that it provides the models, the basic patterns through which the believer grasps and organizes his experience. When the word is used in this way it follows that it will include ideologies as well as what are usually called religions.[22]

A very interesting insight that Newbigin brings to this discussion is the distinction that he makes between a person's implicit religion and explicit religion. What a person calls his 'religion' may in fact be other than the ultimately authoritative factor in his or her thinking and acting. For example, people may call themselves Christians and yet limit the operation of their Christian commitment to a restricted, private area of life, while their ultimate commitment may be to some other way of understanding and judging experience, such as the modern scientific worldview. Consequently, this commitment to Christ will be conditioned by the commitment to the "overriding myth" which may be the real 'religion' of the person.

---

[21] *The Open Secret*, pp. 181-182.
[22] Ibid, p. 182.

It is this concern for ultimate commitments which turns Newbigin away from approaching religion from the "enterprise" of what is known as *Religionswissenschaft*, as defined by one of its pioneers, Max Müller.[23] Newbigin does not favour this approach to religion which is based on scientific comparison, because it does not foresee the "possibility of the meeting of different ultimate commitments." Its ultimate commitment is to the scientific method as the clue to the apprehension of truth. It is a weak approach, because it ignores the fact that the very foundations of what Müller calls "true science" can be called into question by one of the religions so studied.[24]

Newbigin shows that religion is an integral part of human culture. In a more recent work, *Foolishness to the Greeks*, he complements his earlier definition of culture by saying that fundamental to any culture is "a set of beliefs, experiences, and practices that seek to grasp and express the ultimate nature of things, that which gives shape and meaning to life, that which claims final loyalty." Christianity as a religion has also been included in this definition.[25]

Since the relationship between `religion' and `culture' is so integral, in using the word `religion', one is making several unacknowledged assumptions which need to be closely scrutinized.

---

[23]Ibid., p. 182. Here reference has been made to Müller's *Introduction to the Science of Religion* (1873), quoted by Eric Sharpe, *Comparative Religion* (London: Duckworth, 1975), p. xi.
[24]*The Open Secret*, p. 183.
[25]Ibid., p. 3.

'Religion' is not a separate activity set apart from the rest of life.[26] Human culture is a "seamless texture."[27] Newbigin's view is right in that the cultural life of a society is permeated by religious belief. Here his thought is similar to that of a Dutch theologian J. H. Bavinck, who says that, although there is a strictly personal element in religion, the great religions of the world have been and still are great social powers.[28] Religion appears to be a social phenomenon, because human beings act collectively, especially when they respond to what is called the deepest realities of life.[29] The sharp line that has been drawn in Western culture between 'religious affairs' and 'secular affairs' should be seen as a forced separation, according to Newbigin's view. This is a false dichotomy. He also says that the contemporary debate about Christianity and the religions of the world is often carried out with the unspoken assumption that 'religion' is the primary medium of human contact with the divine.[30] This assumption has to be questioned.

b. 'Gospel' and the Criticism of Culture

---

[26] *The Gospel in a Pluralist Society*, p. 172. The integral relationship between religion and culture increases the complexity of the word 'religion' and the task of its precise definition. Clifford Geertz expressed the same opinion when he speaks of the sociological nature of religion. He points out that 'religion' describes social order to a great extent, and it has a direct bearing on a people's secular life. See his essay, "Religion As a Cultural System," in *The Interpretation of Cultures* (New York: Basic Books, Inc., 1973), pp. 119, 124.
[27] *The Gospel in a Pluralist Society*, p. 195.
[28] *The Church Between Temple and Mosque* (Grand Rapids, Michigan: Wm. B. Eerdmans Publishing Co., 1967), p. 19.
[29] Ibid.
[30] *The Gospel in a Pluralist Society*, p. 172.

The criterion that Newbigin uses in the critique of culture is 'the gospel'. This criterion might sound inadequate and therefore problematic in light of the fact that the gospel is shrouded in cultural elements such as language and concepts, and there are many differing ideas about what the 'gospel' is, in many different theologies. But for Newbigin, 'the gospel' is news about a man called Jesus, "and there were witnesses who had known him, seen him, heard him speak, and touched him (1 Jn 1:1)."[31] The gospel is the story of "God's decisive acts" (Heb 1:1-4; Lk 20: 9-18; Jn 3:16-18). The fact of Jesus' death has a central place in the gospel. Peter's gospel proclamation in Acts 2:22-36, which Newbigin uses as a reference point, makes clear that it contains implied views as to the nature of God and the well-known facts about Jesus' life (v.22). It speaks about his death (v. 23), and resurrection (v. 24), about who Jesus is (v. 25-32, 34-36), and about the new powers that follow (v.33).[32] In short, we find in the gospel the record of Jesus' teaching, acts, death, resurrection and ascension, and of the coming of the Holy Spirit. It contains a series of events in history decisive for human history and for every person. The gospel, which is the revelation of the meaning and end of history as a whole, is the revelation of God's age-long secret, his purpose to sum up all things in Christ (Eph 1: 10).[33]

In *The Gospel in a Pluralist Society*, Newbigin observes that "all of us judge some elements of culture to be good and some bad," but "no one is willing to accept a total relativism about

---

[31] Lesslie Newbigin, *The Light Has Come*, p. 1.
[32] Lesslie Newbigin, *What is the Gospel?* (Madras: CLS, 1942), p. 3. Space does not permit us to go into a detailed account of this study on the theme of the gospel.
[33] "The Duty and Authority of the Church to Preach the Gospel," in *The Church's Witness to God's Design*, Op. cit., pp. 23, 31, 34.

culture."³⁴ There are certain examples of cultural practices such as *sati*, slavery, and polygamy, which are almost universally condemned. There are some who might still be defending some of these practices. On what does a person's judgment of culture rest? Does the judgment arise from the gospel itself or from the cultural presuppositions of the person who judges? These are questions of criteria which become useful tools in the discussion of the present topic. If the judgment ought to be made only on the basis of the gospel itself, then it is to be pointed out that there is no such thing as a gospel which is not already culturally shaped. An illustration offered to bring out this difficulty is the caste system in India, which is a fundamental element of its culture. The European Christian missionaries of the eighteenth century regarded the caste system as a social arrangement similar to the hierarchical social structure which was normal at that time in Europe. Indian Christians were not asked to drop their caste identity and they could add their caste name to the personal name without any embarrassment. But this view of caste changed with the new European missionaries who came in the nineteenth century, filled with the egalitarian ideas of the French revolution. They criticized the older generation of missionaries for compromising the gospel and perpetuating the horror of casteism. The point that Newbigin makes about this is that the same cultural element was differently judged by different groups of missionaries. This situation, therefore, gives rise to a complex question of how the gospel can have a critical relation to culture if the gospel is always and everywhere culturally embodied - in a particular language and particular life-style.³⁵ To transpose this question into the Western cultural milieu, one has to ask as to how a Christian, who is also the product of a post-Enlightenment culture, can find a stance from which to criticize his/her own culture? Newbigin acknowledges the

---

[34] p. 186.
[35] Ibid., p. 191.

difficulty of understanding the Bible except through the "concepts and categories of thought" with which one has been equipped through one's intellectual formation from childhood.[36] How shall one take a stance quite apart from the cultural understanding of the gospel? Of course it is impossible to do this in any infallible way. All our theological efforts will be human, fallible, and flawed.

Nevertheless, Newbigin offers as a clue the fact that "the Bible speaks of things which are not simply products of human culture." They are "words and deeds of God", who is creator and sustainer of all that is.[37] This is the only stance from which a Christian can interpret and critique a culture. Basing a critique of culture in Christ is an aspect of the Christian's fiduciary framework. If we do not base ourselves in Christ, we will inevitably use some other `faith' stance as a criterion of judgment. The appeal to the words and deeds of God might be open to attack. One might charge that the biblical stories are objectified representations of the religious experiences of the peoples of Israel and of the Eastern Mediterranean. Newbigin suggests that one may attempt to verify beliefs by "making perceptions public," "discussing with others," "comparing different perceptions and checking their reliability against those of others."[38] In the last analysis, one has to take `personal responsibility' for what one claims to know. Still, because faith claims are made out of contact with reality beyond oneself, they are to be held "with universal intent."[39]

Newbigin knows that one's understanding of the gospel and the whole biblical story is shaped by one's culture. It is this cultural

---

[36] Ibid., p. 192.
[37] Ibid.
[38] Ibid.
[39] Ibid., p. 192.

shaping that has portrayed Jesus in many different ways down through the centuries, such as the `Byzantine Pantocrator', the `medieval crucifix and Jesus of the sacred heart', the `blue-eyed blonde' of the American protestantism, and the `Che Guevara freedom fighter' of liberation theology. But the New Testament is clear that Jesus is not a name to which one can attach any character one likes to imagine. There are four Gospels in the church's canon. Although each gives a rather different picture of Jesus, there is one Lord Jesus.[40] Their perceptions are to be verified in the same way that all other claims to perceive reality have to be verified.

Is this method of verification which Newbigin outlines reliable? The experience of Jesus as risen Lord is limited to the community of Christian believers, while the experiences of the senses, for example, are shared universally. Here Newbigin introduces the biblical doctrine of election and the calling of the Christian community to be the bearer of the gospel for all communities. If Newbigin is to be pressed further about his method of verification, he can only say that the Christian community's faith cannot be shown to be valid by reference to some more ultimate belief, just as other "fiduciary frameworks" cannot be proved from beyond themselves.[41] As God's community and the bearer of the gospel, Christians belong to two `cultures.' While they live in this world as citizens of this world, as Paul teaches (Phil 3:20), they are also citizens of heaven.

The critique of human culture, in the light of the biblical events of the crucifixion and resurrection of Christ, is a major thrust in Newbigin's analysis.[42] He calls it the "double event of Jesus' death and resurrection." On the cross Jesus was "rejected and

---

[40]Ibid., p. 193,
[41]Ibid., p. 197.
[42]*The Gospel in a Pluralist Society*, p. 194.

cast out by the representatives of human cultures in religion, politics, law, and morals." This would imply for Christians a rejection by the culture in which they live. However, God's last word is not the cross but the resurrection of Jesus. It offers the "pledge and the foretaste of his unconquerable kindness and patience toward the world."[43] It is the reaffirmation of the "original covenant with creation and with all human life, the covenant with Noah and his descendants." The Christian believer has to hold two realities at the same time, namely, the rejection of God by human culture and God's judgment of culture. Although human culture rejects God, God still sustains the created world and the world of human culture. This gives it time and space for repentance and for the coming into being of the new creation within the womb of the old. Newbigin says,

> God still cherishes and sustains the world of creation and of culture, in spite of its subjection to illusion and vanity. The covenant with Noah and its rainbow sign refer explicitly to one of the most basic elements in human culture, namely the work of the farmer who cultivates the wilderness in order that it may bring forth food for human beings (Gen. 8:22). Here the interdependence of human beings and nature, and the dependence of both on the grace of God, are at their most manifest. God's promise that while earth remains seedtime and harvest shall not cease stands over the entire story of human culture.[44]

God's covenant with Noah serves as a pattern and motivation for Christians to cherish the culture and care for the creation. They

---

[43]Ibid.
[44]Ibid.

must acknowledge a gracious God who sustains and cares for the whole creation.

Newbigin is helpful in understanding a model that would critique human culture on the basis of the gospel and not vice versa. The Bible provides a vision that runs counter to the plausibility structure of the Western culture. The gospel provides the stance from which every culture is to be evaluated. While this model is not anti-cultural, it challenges the culture by calling it to conversion.

c. The Role of the Church in Cultural Criticism

Given the lordship of Christ over all creation and cultures, what is the church's role in relation to culture? The church's path within its culture has to be defined with care so as to avoid two extremes. On the one hand, the church may so conform its life and teaching to the culture that it no longer functions as the bearer of God's judgment and promise. This is dangerous, because it becomes the "guardian and guarantor" of the culture. It would lose its capacity to challenge it. And on the other hand, if the language and life-style of the church is so strange and foreign that it makes no contact with the culture, it will become nothing but an irrelevant ghetto. Between these two extremes, Newbigin sees "a wide spectrum of possibilities."[45]

---

[45] *The Open Secret*, p. 164. Here Newbigin recognizes the "classic work" of H. Richard Niebuhr, *Christ and Culture* (New York: Harper & Row, 1951) where these possibilities are explored. But his main criticism of this work is that it deals with the relation of church and culture within a single culture. It does not raise the "difficult and complicated questions" which arise in the cross-cultural communication of the gospel.

But the difficult question is: How shall we find the discernment for judging what is to be accepted and what is to be rejected in existing cultures? The question is difficult, because to a large extent, we are what our culture has made us. The example he uses for finding an answer to this question is the experience of European churches during the First World War.[46] The churches on both sides identified the cause of Christ with the cause of their own nation. What triggered a change was a fresh and more humble listening to the Bible. One of the results of this was the ecumenical developments of the 1930s and 40s. The blasphemies of the First World War were not repeated in the Second World War, at least on the same scale. Spiritual bonds remained through the years of conflict which caused the churches on both sides, after the war, to pray and work together for a new form of Christian presence in Europe. Newbigin's point is that churches in the post-war era were not content, at least not always, to be "domestic chaplains" to their nations. The need for a "supranational entity", to express the "supranational and supracultural character of the gospel" was strongly felt. This need was given concrete form at Amsterdam in 1948 when churches whose nations had been at war with each other pledged to be faithful to one another and to receive correction from one another.

The principle of mutual correction among Christians of different cultures is often reiterated in Newbigin's writings. This is because one's reading of the Bible and Christian discipleship are necessarily shaped by one's culture. In Newbigin's opinion, various aspects of modern European culture, for example, nation, science, technology, progress, etc., over the past four hundred years have taken the place of God, as supreme realities, calling for absolute and total devotion. In a situation of such powerful and idolatrous cultural conditioning, the principle of mutual correction would help

---

[46]*The Gospel in a Pluralist Society*, p. 196.

tremendously in maintaining that supranational and supracultural character of the gospel. Moreover, in a transcultural situation, Newbigin finds a `three-cornered relationship,' involving the traditional culture, the Christianity of the missionary, and the Bible.[47] The message of the missionary is culturally conditioned. In this set up, ecumenical fellowships and openness among Christians of other cultures can provide a continual critique of the ways in which the church within any culture is related to that culture. The witness of those who read the Bible with minds shaped by other cultures could challenge other culturally conditioned interpretations of the gospel.[48] Here there is a need for seeing the entire global church as a company that lives only by the grace of God to sinners. It gives the possibility of radical mutual criticism which depends absolutely on the centrality of Christ and his atoning deed.[49] To carry out this task, Christians have to be faithful participants in a supranational multicultural family of churches. It is in this way that they find resources to be at the same time sustainers and critics of human cultures. Newbigin believes that the gospel "endorses an immensely wide diversity among human cultures,"[50] but it does not support a total relativism. There are ongoing developments that are either creative or destructive, either in line with God's purpose as revealed in Christ for all human

---

[47] *The Open Secret*, p. 166.

[48] Ibid., pp. 196, 197. See also Newbigin's "The Enduring Validity of Cross-Cultural Mission," in *International Bulletin of Missionary Research*, Vol. 12 (April 1988), p. 50, where he speaks of the way in which the gospel can come back to question Western culture in the idiom of other cultures. This thought, I believe, is very important for forging a global, reciprocal understanding of missions.

[49] Lesslie Newbigin, "Ecumenical Amnesia," in *International Bulletin of Missionary Research*, Vol. 18, (January 1994), p. 4.

[50] *The Gospel in a Pluralist Society*, p. 197.

beings, or in opposition to it.

The criteria for critique of other cultures cannot arise from one culture only, which is the familiar mistake of cultural imperialism. The criteria can come only from God's revealed will in Christ. If this is denied, then one remains with no valid criteria to assess the positive and negative developments in a given culture. For Newbigin,

> [T]he content of the revelation in Christ, defined crucially by the twin events of cross and resurrection, provides a basis on which the great diversity of cultures can be welcomed and cherished and the claim of any one culture to dominance can be resisted.[51]

Newbigin's call for exposing the ideologies and anti-gospel assumptions of Western society arises from this understanding of the gospel, which offers an alternative vision of reality. It challenges the dogma that calls us to live our lives in competing plausibility structures. The church must not be carried along by the culture. Instead, it must examine and challenge the root paradigms of the culture on the basis of the gospel.

d. The Question of Contextualization

The whole vast debate about contextualization has been carried on especially by those who are involved in crosscultural missionary activities. But Newbigin shows that this question is not limited to a foreign culture; it is pertinent in any given culture in which the need for gospel communication arises. Christian theology is a "form of rational discourse developed within the

---

[51]Ibid.

community" which accepts the primacy of the gospel.[52] It can fail, on the one hand, by failing to understand and take seriously the context in which it is placed. The result is that the gospel remains incomprehensible. On the other hand, it can fail by allowing the world to dictate the issues and terms of the meeting. The result is that the context is not challenged at its depth but rather absorbs and domesticates the gospel.[53] When the Christian message has to be communicated to a foreign cultural context which is outside the periphery of the 'Christian culture' or influence, the question is an obvious and lively one. Out of his rich and varied experience of cultures around the world, Newbigin brings valuable insights into the debate about contextualization. I shall here gather together those insights which I believe are relevant to the question of dialogue with people of one's own, or other cultures.

First let us note the way in which Newbigin uses the word 'contextualization.' The communication of the gospel takes place with the aim of appealing to the minds and hearts and consciences of the hearers. In order for them to respond to the message, they need to understand it. People can understand the gospel only if it is communicated in terms of the language, custom, institution and ways of life of their culture. As Newbigin points out, the gospel has to be "clothed in symbols which are meaningful to them."[54] This is because the gospel is not a "disembodied message," but it is the message of a community which claims to live by the message. Therefore, the purpose of contextualization is to "make sense" or to make the message "come alive," and as a result, the receptor should be able to say, "Yes, I see. This is true for me, for my situation." Newbigin suggests that the hearer, as a result of the communication, must have the "real gospel and not a product

---

[52]*The Gospel in a Pluralist Society*, p. 142.
[53]Ibid., p. 152.
[54]Ibid., p. 141.

shaped by the mind of the hearer."⁵⁵ The most important aim of contextualization, according to Newbigin, is for the gospel to "come alive" in different cultural contexts, while yet remaining the same authentic gospel.

Contextualization is a more recent term than 'indigenization', 'adaptation', or 'accommodation.' The concept of 'Inculturation,' which was developed from 1970 onwards, found its theological authorization in the incarnation itself. Newbigin does not discuss 'Inculturation' in detail but says that it has brought important new insights from various cultures to enrich the life of the church.⁵⁶ While indigenization was generally a Protestant usage, Roman Catholics have often used the word adaptation, though this term is no longer favoured. Newbigin finds both concepts inadequate. Indigenization used the traditional styles of culture such as words, concepts, liturgy, architecture, music, visual art, etc., to communicate the gospel, but tended to be superficial in that it does not connect to the foreign culture in depth. The concept of 'adaptation' also implies some superficial relationship to the culture, and also tends to give the impression thatwhat the missionary brings to a foreign culture is a pure, unadapted gospel.⁵⁷ Thus adaptation was a kind of concession to those who had not the advantage of being brought up in a Christian culture. Newbigin

---

⁵⁵Ibid.

⁵⁶Lesslie Newbigin, "Culture and Theology," in Alister McGrath, ed., *The Blackwell Encyclopedia of Modern Christian Thought*, Op. cit., p. 99.

⁵⁷'Incarnation' is another model of doing theology, an attempt to relate the gospel more profoundly to a culture. This model, which is centred on the pre-existent Logos becoming flesh, has many implications. For a discussion of this model, see Aylward Shorter, *Toward a Theology of Inculturation* (Maryknoll: Orbis Books, 1988), p. 81.

affirms that what a missionary brings to a foreign culture is not an unadapted gospel, but a gospel that was shaped by the missionary's own culture. This approach of the "pure, unadapted gospel," says Newbigin, blinds the missionary to the fact that a true missionary encounter will always confront both the missionary and the people who are to receive the message. This may be illustrated by the story of the encounter of Peter with the household of Cornelius (Acts 10), a true missionary encounter which profoundly changed both the missionary and the receptor community. Further, both `indigenization' and `adaptation' have a tendency to relate the gospel to past traditions and to underestimate the forces in every society which are making for change. By following the path of indigenization, the missionary is allying himself with the conservative elements (those least open to change) in a culture and alienates the radicals who are looking for something new. He thinks that it is the inadequacy of these two terms that resulted in the introduction of the new term `contextualization'. It seeks to avoid both these dangers conveyed by the older terms. It directs one's "attention to the need so to communicate the gospel that it speaks God's word to the total context in which people are now living and in which they now have to make their decisions."[58]

Even the term `contextualization' is not a perfect term for Newbigin. He calls it a "dreadful" word, and a "monster," but a "useful" one.[59] It is useful because it acknowledges the need to address the real context of the hearers. It speaks to the people where they are at now, where they face fundamental issues of life. A "biblical paradigm" which Newbigin uses as an illustration is the story in Acts 26:14 where Paul, who was a man of two worlds and two cultures, explains a speech in Greek to tell King Agrippa that

---

[58]*The Gospel in a Pluralist Society*, p. 142.
[59]Lesslie Newbigin, "The Bible and Our Contemporary Mission" in *The Clergy Review*, Vol. LXIX (January 1984), p. 10.

God spoke Hebrew. He was at home in the imperial, metropolitan world of which Greek was the language. He was making his speech in Greek before the representatives of the imperial power, and using their language to describe the glorious secret of the gospel. But at the crucial point of his story, where he tells of how God spoke to him, he says that God spoke in Hebrew. Newbigin says that God addresses him, not in the language of public life, but in "the language of the home and heart," in the mother tongue.[60] The nature of God's word to Paul was not affirmative of his "deepest feelings and desires," but of challenge: "Why do you persecute me?" According to Newbigin, these words challenged Paul and the very thrust of his whole life. What Paul took for devotion in God's service was proved to be an attack against God. This divine word called for an abrupt stop and a total turn-around in his life. This is a true missionary communication which has a `double character'. It speaks to the heart and conscience, the language of one's deepest feelings and commitments, and at the same time it profoundly challenges those feelings and commitments.

The implications of this are two-fold. First, the true missionary communication does not come as something in a foreign language, so that one has to emigrate out of one's culture in order to hear it. One hears it as the person that one really is. Second, and on the other hand, a true communication of the message does not merely confirm one's selfhood. It calls the whole direction of one's life in question. For Newbigin, this is true and genuine contextualization. Contextualization can be either true or false, depending on the place it gives to the gospel. It should give the gospel its "rightful primacy," its "power to penetrate every culture" and to speak within each culture, in "its own speech and symbol," the word which is "both No and Yes," both "judgment

---

[60]Ibid., p. 11.

and grace."[61] The true contextualization happens when the word is not a disembodied word, but comes from a community which embodies the true gospel story, in a style of life which communicates both the grace and the judgment. In order to do this, it must be local and truly ecumenical. It is truly local because it speaks the grace and judgment for that people in that context. It is ecumenical because it is open to the witnesses of the churches in all other places. This prevents it from being absorbed into the culture of that place and enables it to represent the universality of God's purpose of grace and judgment for all humanity. The lack of true contextualization might lead to two errors, irrelevance or syncretism. The message can be irrelevant even when it is interesting. The important question is whether it concerns the hearer existentially. Here syncretism would mean that the message is absorbed into the already settled patterns of thought.[62] The gospel is not an empty form into which any content could be poured. Its content is Jesus Christ and the fullness of his work.

The whole question of contextualization, as has been discussed in missiology, has a serious weakness, namely, that it ignored Western culture. Here Newbigin is very successful in drawing our attention to this crucial need of addressing this question in terms of Western culture. He provides a challenge to missiologists to consider ways in which the post-Christian Western culture can be brought into a missionary encounter with the gospel. This issue cannot be ignored, because Western culture is the most widespread, persuasive, and powerful among all contemporary cultures.[63] No missiologist has sufficiently addressed the need for contextualizing the gospel in the West. The church in the West was concerned with the question of contextualization in non-Western

---

[61]*The Gospel in the Pluralist Society*, p. 152.
[62]Ibid.
[63]*Foolishness to the Greeks*, p. 2.

cultures, but it did not have an equally clear vision about the need for contextualization in its own context. Following Newbigin, I believe that this has been a serious deficiency and a lack of missionary concern on the part of the church and its missiologists.

2. NEWBIGIN'S CRITIQUE OF MODERN WESTERN CULTURE

Since 'religion' and 'culture' are inseparable, and, in Newbigin's view, modern Western culture is 'religious' in character, his critique of this (his own) culture can be seen as a form of 'inter-religious dialogue.' His dialogue with modern Western culture includes an analysis of its history, beginning with the 'Enlightenment.'

a. Roots in the Enlightenment

Newbigin outlines in brilliant clarity what he means by 'Western culture.' It is the culture of the West shaped most importantly by the eighteenth century Enlightenment and by all the reactions to it in the nineteenth and twentieth centuries. So it is much more than a body of ideas. It is a "whole way of organizing human life." Culture is "the sum total of ways of living"[64] which includes factors such as language, arts, science and technologies, political and social organizations, and religious beliefs, (including Christianity), etc. When Newbigin speaks of "our culture" to mean modern Western culture, he is referring to both eastern and western streams of European culture which were divided on the basis of ideology for some seventy years. While the eastern stream has been characterized by the ideology of Marxism, the western stream has

---

[64]Ibid., pp. 3, 29.

espoused liberal capitalism.⁶⁵ But both of them have their 'proximate source' in the movement of thought known as 'the Enlightenment'. Both cherish their belief in a 'heavenly city', either by evolution or by revolution.

Although Newbigin traces the genesis of modern Western culture to the eighteenth century Enlightenment, he says that its roots lie further back in history.⁶⁶ Since all movements of thought are continuous, he believes that any decision about where to mark the emergence of something new is arbitrary. Although Newbigin has often been highly critical of the Enlightenment, he acknowledges that post-Enlightenment culture has a 'prehistory' and, according to Newbigin, it had its earlier beginnings in the 'ferment of thought' introduced into western Europe by the translation of Arabic writings into Latin, the impact of Aristotelian philosophy, the rise of the universities, the flood of classical ideas at the time of the Renaissance, the fierce theological and political debate of the Reformation, and the beginnings of modern science in the seventeenth century.⁶⁷ The development of new science was associated with names such as Bacon, Galileo, and Newton. Also, as we have seen, Descartes' philosophical method had a serious impact on the shaping of the European mind.

The word 'Enlightenment' has "profound religious overtones." It is a "very significant pointer to the nature of the experience" that created modern European culture. It expresses the joy and excitement of those who have seen the day of truth dawn over a dark world. What was obscure and confusing is now clearly seen and what was unexplainable has been explained. The word is

---

⁶⁵Lesslie Newbigin, *The Other Side of 1984: Questions for the Churches* (Geneva: WCC, 1983), p. 3.
⁶⁶Ibid., p. 5.
⁶⁷*Foolishness to the Greeks*, p. 23.

a "conversion word" which describes the experience of whole European peoples. Newbigin says that the thinkers and peoples of Europe have passed through a "collective conversion."[68] It is the same word used to describe the experience of the Buddha. It is also a biblical word, as used by St. John, to describe the coming of Jesus into the world. "The Light has come into the world" (Jn 3:14). By the middle of the eighteenth century many thinkers believed that Europe had reached a turning point. The secret of knowledge had been discovered, and as a result, mastery of the world was possible. What happened at the Enlightenment was the replacement of one framework of thought with another. In Newbigin's view, of all the forces that were impressed upon the mind of the eighteenth century, the scientific worldview, was the most significant.

Newbigin presents in broad outlines the scientific methodology of Isaac Newton and the worldview created by his work.[69] He does not sufficiently recognize the positive contributions made to Western culture by Enlightenment philosophy and science. He strongly criticizes the core of the Enlightenment worldview which became available through the new scientific method. Newton's methodology focused on the observation of physical phenomena and on that basis, the formulation of "laws". The most fundamental of all laws are those of mathematics which are applicable to all that really is. `Analysis' is the necessary instrument for the thinking mind, so that the reality behind the appearance of objects can be discerned. This enterprise is cumulative and leads on to greater and greater capacity to exploit nature for human ends. The outcome of this method was the

---

[68]Ibid.
[69]Newbigin's two books, *The Other Side of 1984*, and *Foolishness to the Greeks* are a powerful presentation of the modern Western culture.

picture of the world which was to dominate European thinking for the next two hundred years. The real world is one of moving bodies which have a totally objective existence apart from any human observer. All reality is ultimately intelligible in these terms.

According to this scientific method, though not necessarily in the thought of Newton himself, 'Nature' becomes the totality of all observable phenomena. It replaces the concept of God, which is no longer necessary. Newbigin says that, while the 'Deism' of the eighteenth century retained the concept of God as "a sort of Prime Mover standing behind the processes of nature," the nineteenth century came to the conclusion that there was no place for God.[70] The scientific process which has replaced God with Nature has given rise to a situation where the scientists have become the new 'priests' who can mediate between the human being and the new god. Now science alone can enable the human person to understand nature, and unlock nature's bounty for the benefit of humanity. As a result, no authority other than the authority of the observable facts can be accepted. A disastrous effect of this scientific worldview was the autonomous and reductionistic understanding of knowledge. Due to this autonomous character of the sciences, no alleged revelation can be allowed to interfere. Everything without exception, whether it is a branch of science such as astronomy, or a critical historical study of literature which includes the Bible, has to be studied using scientific principles. Newbigin's criticism of this approach, I believe, is right, because the autonomous sciences have become reductionistic in the sense that they tend to reduce reality to one sphere and not accept authority, truth or wisdom from outside sources. Accordingly, for example, Economics has become an autonomous science separated off from the principles of ethics, and also, of course, from any positive relation to theology. There is an interlocking and

---

[70] The Other Side of 1984, p. 11.

interdependent character of all knowledge, which cannot be reduced to one sphere and absolutized. The world of creation is one, and as John Polkinghorne so ably demonstrates in his book,[71] reality is a multi-layered unity. Newbigin knows well that Western culture was once a coherent whole with the Christian vision at its centre, but it has disintegrated.[72] Therefore, he wants to recapture this integral Christian vision for the whole of human culture, and this vision is an essential aspect of his proposal for a missiology for Western culture.

Further, with 'God' replaced by 'Nature', a new understanding of 'Law' has emerged in Western culture. There is no longer a need for obeying the laws of a personal divine law-giver, because the laws of Nature are the laws of 'God'. Laws are the necessary relationships which spring from the nature of things. The scientific worldview exalts the significance of human reason, which can discover the laws of nature. Reason is a faculty common to all human beings and in principle it is common everywhere unless it has been perverted by unfounded dogmas. Therefore, any authority of dogma, of scripture, or of God, which claims to replace 'Reason' has to be rejected as false and as treason against the dignity[73] of the human being. The idea of the 'autonomous

---

[71] *One World: The Interaction of Science and Theology* (London: SPCK, 1986), p. 97.

[72] *A Word in Season* (Grand Rapids: Wm. B. Eerdmans, 1994), p. 117.

[73] Newbigin says that the word 'dignity' has been used "advisedly." The medieval world used the word 'honour,' which was related to the person's status in society. The word 'dignity' has come to be used after the Enlightenment to imply that every human person has been endowed with dignity, simply from the person's birth and apart from his or her social status. See *The Other Side of 1984*, pp. 12-13.

human person' has become increasingly important. Later on the Romantic Movement developed the idea of the `personality' which produced one of the unquestioned assumptions of western Europe that every human person has the `right' to develop his or her own potential to the maximum limit, limited only by the rights of others. Newbigin points out that, if medieval society emphasized the <u>duties</u> of the human person, from the Enlightenment onwards, the emphasis fell on the `rights of man'. Referring to the new republic in the New World and the preamble of its constitution which promulgates `the inalienable rights' of every individual, he comments that the rights of the human person are the `unquestioned starting point' from which everything else follows.[74] What is included in these rights are life, liberty and the pursuit of happiness.

A mark of the post-Enlightenment culture which Newbigin criticizes is "the pursuit of happiness." He says,

> Happiness (bonheur) was hailed by the eighteenth century philosophers as "a new word in Europe". In place of the joys of heaven to which the medieval person was encouraged to look forward, Enlightenment people looked forward to "happiness" here on earth. This would come within the reach of all through the cumulative work of science, liberating societies from bondage to dogma and superstition, unlocking the secrets of nature and opening them for all.[75]

Referring to Hannah Arendt's *On Revolution*,[76] Newbigin observes

---

[74]Ibid., p. 13.
[75]Ibid., pp. 13-14.
[76](New York: The Viking Press, 1963).

that some American founding fathers had thought of "public happiness," but the course of events led inexorably to an interpretation of happiness as private well-being. The consequence of this was the right of the autonomous individual to pursue happiness in the domestic and privatized sense. The pursuit of happiness in contemporary Western culture has to be seen against any consideration of reality beyond death as "unreliable" and "subversive."[77] No reliable knowledge of what lies beyond death has been provided by scientific methods. It is subversive because it deflects attention from the pursuit of individual `happiness' in this life to an alleged happiness in another life. Politically speaking, this involved the rise of the nation state, who became the guarantor of happiness.

In the post-Enlightenment culture, the `nation state' also has taken the place of God.[78] Once the concept of `human rights' has been established, there ought to be a guarantor of these rights. The "centre-piece" in the political scene in post-Enlightenment Europe which replaces the old concepts of the Holy Church and the Holy Empire is the state. He writes,

> After the trauma of the religious wars of the seventeenth century, Europe settled down to the principle of religious coexistence, and the passions which had formerly been invested in rival interpretations of religion were more and more invested in the nation state. Nationalism became the effective ideology of the European peoples, always at times of crises proving stronger than any other ideological or religious force. If there is any entity to which ultimate loyalty is due, it is the nation

---

[77]*The Other Side of 1984*, p. 14.
[78]Ibid., p. 15.

state.[79]

Accordingly, a case of blasphemy is treated as a "quaint anachronism," while the charge of treason (placing another loyalty above that to the nation state) is treated as an "unforgivable crime." Also Western societies have given to the state responsibilities of education, healing and public welfare which were formerly the sphere in which the Church had control.

Newbigin believes that part of the contemporary cultural crisis is precisely that the explanations of the eighteenth century no longer provide meaning for us and that is why the future is in doubt. In this predicament, a fresh outlook on life is necessary to overcome the emptiness and self-doubt of Western culture. Part of today's problem is that Christians never did respond to the challenge of the Enlightenment. So what is needed now is another model for understanding our world and that model has to have Christian revelation at its centre.

b. The Loss of Teleology in the Modern World

The modern Western scientific worldview is most fundamentally marked by the absence of teleology or purpose. Newbigin argues that Greek physics worked with the idea that change and movement in the world of nature can be explained in terms of purpose.[80] The Bible, of course, constantly testifies to the divine purpose. For Medieval thinkers divine purpose in the world of nature was important to the whole framework of thought. The revelation of that purpose for them had been given in the events confessed in the church's creeds. As a result, all study of nature had its place within the creedal articulation and the condition of entry

---

[79]Ibid.
[80]*Foolishness to the Greeks*, p. 24.

into the world of scholarship was the recognition of that framework. However, the explanatory framework of teleology has been replaced with the Newtonian framework of cause and effect. The new framework influenced the ongoing activities in the field of science. Thus teleology had disappeared from physics and astronomy. As a result,

> All the movements of tangible bodies and the changes in the visible world could be explained without reference to the purpose and in terms of efficient cause. The rotation of the planets manifested not that perfection of the divine will but the uniform operation of the laws of inertia and gravitation. As the methods of science achieved greater and greater triumphs, both theoretical and practical, the old picture of how things are, the picture derived from the Bible and vividly sketched, for example, in the medieval mystery plays, was replaced by a quite different one.[81]

One of the consequences of this scientific method was the belief that all causes are adequate to the effects they produce and everything can be explained on the basis of the law of cause and effect. To discover the cause of something is to have explained it. There is no need to invoke purpose or design as an explanation. This eventually has led to the elimination of categories of explanation such as divine intervention and miracles. `Nature' is the sum total of all that exists and that is "the really real." This has implications for one's understanding of God. In eighteenth century Deism, `God' is the ultimate author of all, but one does not need to know the author in order to read the book. Divine revelation or principles derived from it are not acceptable within this scientific

---

[81]Ibid.

framework, which works by the method of observation and inference. It uses the tools of analysis to dissect, separate, and observe each of the elements that make up the phenomenon. Mathematics has become an aid in quantifying and enabling all reality in a relatively comprehensible structure. Newbigin says that what the eighteenth century celebrated as the 'geometric spirit' is thus applied to all forms of human knowledge.[82]

In Newbigin's vision, there is a link between teleology and eschatology. For the medieval Christian, the biblical vision of the end of history was the second coming of Christ, the judgment of living and dead, and the holy city in which all that is pure and true in the public and private life of the nations is gathered up in eternal perfection. This vision, informed by the Bible, is an integral part of the teleological view of creation and history at the centre of which is the will and purpose of God. The Post-Enlightenment culture transferred the holy city from another world to this. It is no longer a gift of God from heaven, but it would be the final triumph of science and the enlightened peoples of the earth. The predicament was compounded by the "doctrine of progress" in the eighteenth century with its fateful consequences extending into the twentieth century. According to this Worldview,

> The emancipation of the human spirit from the pressure of dogma, tradition, and superstition, and the purposeful exercise of the newly liberated powers of human reason would lead to such a growing understanding and a growing mastery that all the evils that enslave men and women would be conquered.[83]

---

[82]Ibid., p. 25.
[83]Ibid., p. 28.

Another sphere of human life from which teleology has disappeared is the sphere of human labour. This is evident in the work of the traditional craftsman who was involved in the process from the stage of raw material to the finished product. Newbigin notes that "analytical or mathematical reason is not content to deal with physics or astronomy" but has "extended its operation to human behaviour, work, and society."[84] Consequently, the traditional craftsman's work has been analyzed into its smallest parts and then broken up into separate operations, each given over to a different worker. While this "division of labour" as seen in modern culture has increased the output of the finished product, it has created a situation where the individual worker has been deprived of the direct vision of the finished product which governs the whole process. This removal of vision from the individual worker results in the removal of the vision of the end. On the predicament of this situation, Newbigin has this to say:

> His work is assimilated more and more into the repetitive action of a machine rather than to the purposeful work of the craftsman, whose operations are all governed by a vision of the end. Craftsmanship is replaced by labor, and human work is assimilated into the pattern of the Newtonian universe, from which teleology is banished. The individual worker, for example, does not know whether his product is going to make a family car or a fighter plane.[85]

In speaking of the banishment of teleology from the public sphere of work, Newbigin uses Hannah Arendt's observations in

---

[84]Ibid., p. 31.
[85]Ibid.

her book *The Human Condition*.[86] Arendt's study divides human activity into labour, work, and action.[87] Labour is "the activity which corresponds to the biological process of the human body"; it is "man's metabolism with nature".[88] It is the cyclical process that has to be repeated endlessly if life is to continue. Work is the activity that transcends the merely biological character of human existence. It looks to the creation of something that will endure in the world of things after the worker is dead. Action is the activity that goes on in the mutual interaction of human beings. From the observation of these distinctions, Newbigin concludes that the effect of the post-Enlightenment project for human society is that all human activity is absorbed into labour.[89] It results in an "unending cycle of production for the sake of consumption." The production-consumption cycle is kept going and the craftsman's intention to create something enduring is marginal to the economic order. Newbigin observes that the world of action, of politics, is reduced to a conflict of views about how to keep the production-consumption going. Therefore the questions of ultimate purpose are excluded from the public world.

Newbigin states that the consequence of the division of labour is the growth of market economy. When the division of labour gained control, the market moved into the central place as the mechanism that linked all the separate procedures with each other and with the consumers. This gave rise to the modern science of economics of which ethics was no longer a part and finally it was not concerned with the purpose of human life. Thus teleology was banished. The development of economics as a science quite apart from the consideration of ethics brought about a special

---

[86](Chicago: The University of Chicago Press, 1958)
[87]Ibid., p. 7 ff.
[88]Ibid., p. 7.
[89]*Foolishness to the Greeks*, p. 30.

situation. In Newbigin's words,

> It was no longer about the requirements of justice and the dangers of covetousness. It became the science of the working of the market as a self-operating mechanism modeled on the Newtonian universe. The difference was that the fundamental law governing its movements, corresponding to the law of gravitation in Newton, is the law of covetousness assumed as the basic drive of human nature. What does not enter the market is ignored. Gross National Product refers only to what enters the market. It excludes the work of the housewife, of the gardener growing his own food. It includes the operations of the gambling syndicate, the arms salesman, and the drug pusher.[90]

In Newbigin's opinion, this situation, namely, the division of labour, has produced two consequences. First, work has been removed from the home to factory. Second, there has been the creation of huge cities. The removal of work to the factory has produced immense consequences for the nature of society. The home ceased to be the place of work and the family ceased to be the working unit. A divide between the `public world' of work and the `private world' which is withdrawn from it has been created. In the public world of work, workers related to each other "anonymously as units in a mechanical process" which are "replaceable parts."[91] In the home people are known by names and they are irreplaceable persons. It is their mutual understanding as persons that constitutes the home. Newbigin says that at least for the first hundred and fifty years of the Industrial Revolution, it was

---

[90]Ibid., p. 31.
[91]Ibid.

the men who operated the public world of the factory and the market and women were relegated to the private realm. This has divided the sexes.[92]

Furthermore, the growth of huge cities and the mechanization of work and the resultant urbanization in Newbigin's argument "breaks up traditional family-based communities."[93] It "introduces people into a world where there is a multiplicity of human networks, each controlled by different purposes."[94] This new predicament is different from the traditional societies where each individual is "securely fixed in a single human milieu that embraces work, leisure, family relationships, and religion."[95] These are the factors in a traditional society which would give each person a well-defined identity, whereas in huge cities, a person is faced with "multiple possibilities" and a "plurality of worlds among which he chooses." The identity of the person, as a result, becomes a matter of personal choice. Urbanization has made huge cities as a collection of individuals pursuing individual goals. This pursuit of individual goals in a "world without landmarks" can reach the point of despair. The characteristics of modern Western culture, namely, the division and mechanization of labour, the development of a market economy, the dichotomy of private and public worlds, and the growth of big

---

[92] Ibid. Here Newbigin offers an interesting insight into the historical roots of today's feminism which represents in part the revolt of women against "the fissure" in society according to which the man was concerned with the public sector and the woman with the private sector. He was the producer and she was the consumer, even when she has worked in the home as long and as hard as the man in the factory or office.
[93] Ibid., p. 32.
[94] Ibid.
[95] Ibid.

cities, are not found in the premodern cultures of Asia and Africa, except insofar as they have embraced modernization.[96] These characteristics rest upon and in turn reinforce the new view of the human person that marked the birth of post-Enlightenment culture.

To the above two consequences of the division of labour, Newbigin adds what is called 'bureaucratization' which "plays a central role" in modern culture.[97] The pluralization and complexification of society requires the development of techniques for large-scale control. Bureaucracy applies the mechanical model to this task. Newbigin says that

> It provides machinery in which there is a high degree of division of labour, of specialization, of predictability, and of anonymity. It is of the essence of bureaucracy that it sets out to achieve a kind of justice by treating each individual as an anonymous and replaceable unit.[98]

Bureaucracy applies the Enlightenment principles of reason to human life in the public sector, namely, the analysis of every situation into the smallest possible components and the recombination of these elements in terms of logical relationships which can be expressed in mathematical terms and handled by a computer. According to Newbigin, bureaucracy, in its final development, is the rule of nobody and therefore can be experienced as a tyranny.[99] The attempt to interpret human behaviour in terms of models derived from the natural sciences

---

[96]Ibid.
[97]Ibid., pp. 32, 33.
[98]Ibid., p. 33.
[99]Ibid.

will finally destroy personal responsibility. Here Newbigin agrees with Arendt's sense of `action' in which action is absorbed along with work into labour. It becomes part of the cycle of production and consumption. Newbigin concludes that, if the growth of huge cities in the early decades of the modern age was mainly due to the growth of the factories and their power-based mechanization, the contemporary growth in the cities is more largely due to bureaucratization.[100]

Newbigin argues that it is difficult to describe human behaviours without the `category of purpose'.[101] He draws a comparison between Greek science and modern science to show that Greek science did take purpose as a category of explanation in physics. For example, `motion' was seen as inexplicable unless it was purposive. The breakthrough in the sixteenth and seventeenth centuries that gave birth to modern science would have been impossible without the methodological elimination of the notion of purpose from the study of physics and astronomy. The ensuing achievements had the effect of converting in the minds of many this methodological elimination into a disposition which believes that purpose as a category of explanation has no place in what is called `scientific'. This has created the need for another explanation of everything, including both animal and human behaviour, without reference to purpose.[102] This alternative explanation, without the category of purpose, had an enormous impact on the mental world of the post-Enlightenment culture. Newbigin expresses this well:

> The result has been the creation of the mental world
> with which we are so familiar - a world in which

---

[100] Ibid.
[101] Ibid., p. 34.
[102] Ibid., p. 35.

everything will ultimately be explained as the effect of antecedent causes that operate with the precision and the predictability of the Newtonian atoms, and in which no alleged knowledge is regarded secure against doubt unless it conforms to this pattern.[103]

Purpose, as Newbigin views it, is an "inescapable element" in human life.[104] It is a characteristic of human life to entertain purposes and to set out to achieve them. However, the banishment of teleology from the scientific enterprises of modern Western culture does not mean that the activities of the scientists have been purposeless. Rather, the immense achievements of modern science are an evidence of the "purposeful efforts" of scientists who wanted to achieve something valuable. But while criticizing the very nature of this purpose, Newbigin perceives this as a problem of the culture. This problem is the "strange fissure" which has been produced within the "consciousness of modern Western man."[105] It is the dichotomy between the public worlds and the private worlds, and between what are called `facts' and what are called `values'.

Newbigin might be misunderstood as an enemy of modern science and an inadequate interpreter of Western culture, because he tends to ignore major positive elements that are intrinsic to its stability.[106] Newbigin spurs some misunderstanding with the vigor of his argument against the ideology that is so pervasive in his culture. He could have been clearer in his presentation and more attentive to the positive elements in science. However, his attack

---

[103] Ibid.
[104] Ibid.
[105] Ibid.
[106] See David Stowe's criticism "Modernization and Resistance: Theological Implications for Mission," in *International Bulletin of Missionary Research*, Vol. 12 (October 1988), p. 148.

on modern scientific culture is not to be seen as an attack on science itself, but on the tendency to absolutize science without any reference to its origin and purpose. He has indeed admiration for the development and new discoveries in science, and even maintains that the birth and rise of Western science and technology were in part a result of the influence of the Bible on European culture.

c. Dichotomy of Public and Private Life

The root paradigms of Western culture are based in part on dualisms which polarize human experience between public and private, knowledge and belief, facts and values, the objective and the subjective. The dichotomy between the `public' world and the `private' world is based on a dichotomy between `facts' and `values'. Newbigin calls this dichotomy one of the "outstanding marks" of a modern society.[107] He traces it to the thought of the Enlightenment, that colossal turning point in European history.

One of the consequences of this dichotomy may be seen at the intellectual level where there is an intense search for `value-free facts'. In the science of human behaviour, this expresses itself as `objectivity,' which in essence accepts no value judgments concerning its operations. Language, accordingly, has to be purged of any notion of teleology, or purpose. This would ensure a `scientific' theory of how human societies function. In modern Western societies, the value-free facts have become the only valuable thing. Newbigin rejects this ideal which has enormous power in the public life of modern societies.

What separated the `public' from the `private' vision is the framework introduced by the scientific world view. The dichotomy

---

[107] *Foolishness to the Greeks*, p. 35.

between public and private spheres is not congruous with a biblical vision of reality.[108] The biblical vision of the holy city coming down from heaven to earth is the vision of consummation that embraces both the public and private affairs of human beings. The dichotomy, which has become crucial in Western culture, is absent from traditional non-Western cultures. It proposes a private enclave where alone religious certainty can be had, as distinct from the public world, where all experience is to be tested by scientific criteria.[109]

What are called `facts', according to this split-vision, are to be accepted by everyone, as a child in school learns and accepts facts. `Values' belong to a private realm, because they are a matter of personal choice, whether they are expressed in religious terms or otherwise. They are often relegated to the spheres of church and home. For example, the fact that the development of the human person is governed by the programme encoded in the DNA molecule is a public fact, whereas the idea that this person is made to glorify God is not a fact; it is a belief which belongs to the private realm.[110] Here also, as elsewhere, Newbigin criticizes the cultural notion that allows no particular belief about the purpose of human life to be taught as public truth. This does not mean that `purpose' as a category is denied by all scientists. According to the believing scientists, purpose lies in the sphere of revelation, and only God can reveal the `why' of things. However, they also believed that such revelation has to be accepted in faith. It is not public truth, but personal decision. Newbigin says that even a

---

[108] *The Other Side of 1984*, p. 35.

[109] Lesslie Newbigin, "Can the West Be Converted?" in *The Princeton Seminary Bulletin*, Vol. 6, No. 1 (February 1985), p. 28.

[110] Lesslie Newbigin, *Mission and the Crisis of Western Culture: Recent Studies by Lesslie Newbigin*, ed. by Jock Stein (Edinburgh: Handsel Press, 1989), p. 3. Cf. *A Word in Season*, Op. cit., p. 70.

hundred years ago, a child in school in Scotland could study the purpose of human life as being to `glorify God and enjoy him forever.'[111] This was as much a fact as anything in biology or physics, but today it has lost the status of public truth. This shows the fundamental split present in the modern Western culture.[112] The older science had asked questions about cause which opened up enormous vistas of knowledge and power. But if `why' questions, or questions of teleology are eliminated, there is no way to find a factual basis for values; no way of moving from the statement, `This is' to `This is good'.[113] Therefore, it follows from this that if questions of purpose are eliminated, then facts are value-free and they cannot be called good or bad. In Newbigin's opinion, such value-free facts are the currency of contemporary Western culture.

The major consequence that follows from this situation is that one cannot speak publicly of knowledge but only of personal belief, because values are relegated to a private world.[114] Accordingly, `I believe' might mean `I do not know'. Statements about God and his purpose might be prefaced by the words `we believe because we do not know'. Statements in a physics text book require no such preface, as they are impersonal statements of facts. This, according to Newbigin, is misleading, because the

---

[111]Reference is being made to the first question of The Westminster *Shorter Catechism*: "What is the chief end of man?"
[112]Ibid., p. 4
[113]Ibid.
[114]Newbigin cites the example of John Locke whose understanding of `belief' as `that which one falls back on when one does not have the knowledge' has had dominated the thinking of the English-speaking world. An implication of Locke's definition of belief, according to Newbigin, is a belief which is not based on facts.

development of modern physics has shown that all scientific knowledge rests upon `faith commitments', for example, beliefs in the `rationality of things' which cannot be demonstrated by science itself. He affirms, as we have seen in chapter 2, that it is an illusion to think of a kind of knowledge which is totally impersonal. Faith is not a substitute for knowledge, but its starting point.[115]

One of the disastrous effects of this dichotomy is the separation between one's personal life and public life. As a result, Christianity has been completely removed from the public sphere into the private sector.[116] Against this cultural notion, Newbigin argues that the message of Jesus was about the universal sovereignty of God which embraces the whole reality of the world. The biblical message is not about the interior life of the soul considered in abstraction from the public life of the world. Confining Christianity to the private realm means that it cannot address the public life of a nation. The concern of Newbigin is that

> The Church has lived so long as a permitted and even privileged minority, accepting relegation to the private sphere in a culture whose public life is controlled by a totally different vision of reality, that it has almost lost the power to address a radical challenge to that vision and therefore to "modern western civilization" as a whole.[117]

One of the effects of this dichotomy is evident in the area of public educational systems where children are introduced to those areas of knowledge and skills that enable them to function effectively in the public world of facts. While religion is privatized, science in

---

[115]Ibid., p. 4
[116]*The Other Side of 1984*, p. 32.
[117]Ibid., p. 23

educational systems is taught as a true account of how things really are. Newbigin adds that the typical form of Christian faith from the eighteenth century onwards was pietism, a religion of the soul, or of the inner life, of personal morals and of the home. Although the church did struggle to keep the sphere of education within the old framework, it was not successful. First the universities and then the schools became "secular" in their presuppositions. The consequence was that the Bible no longer provided the framework within which world history was understood. Nor is it possible for a public educational system to be neutral. It presupposes and either tacitly or explicitly teaches a certain viewpoint, which is inevitably a secularist, `post-Enlightenment' philosophy. A major burden of Newbigin's writing is to offer an invitation to the church to explore ways in which this rift between the public world of facts and the private world of values can be healed.

As he leads the way in finding a cure for this dichotomy, Newbigin reflects on the medieval worldview which was based on Christian dogma.[118] Its biblically informed vision of reality never maintained a separation between the public sphere and the private sphere. Rather, it embraced the whole life of the society as one single reality in which economics and social order, prayer and the sacraments were equally part of that reality. It assumed that human life is to be understood in its totality, that is to say, as a life in which there is no dichotomy between the believer and the citizen. What Newbigin proposes as a solution is to have another model for understanding which means to recover a proper acknowledgment of the role of Christian dogma. This dogma is based unashamedly on the revelation of God in Christ and attested in Scripture and the tradition of the church.[119] Newbigin views this as a starting point for the exploration of the mystery of human existence and coping

---

[118] Ibid., p. 21
[119] Ibid., p. 27.

with its practical tasks not only in the private and domestic life of the believers but also in the public life of the citizen.

Now an important question has to be posed here: If the Christian revelation is to be taken as the framework for understanding and action in the public sphere -in politics, economics and social organization, how can the church avoid falling again into the "Constantinian trap" of alliance between church and state? The suggestion of a fresh recognition of the role of dogma does not imply going back to the middle ages. Rather, now the church has to face the task of embodying within its own life the claim that Jesus is Lord over all of life, without the Constantinian impasse. This question does not give easy answers. Nevertheless some basic guidelines may be considered.

First, the church has to consider the presence of the 'reign of God' in the midst of history as the reality of which every human being must take account. It is the sovereignty of God's reign over the whole cosmos in all its spheres, visible and invisible.[120] Of this reign of God, Newbigin says,

> The kingship of God, present in Jesus, concerns the whole of human life in its public as well as its private aspects. There is no basis in scripture for the withdrawal of the public aspect of human life from that obedience which the disciple owes to the Lord. The question, therefore, is not: "What grounds can be shown for Christian involvement in public life?" It is: "What grounds can be shown for the proposal to withdraw from the rule of Christ the public aspects of our human living?" The answer

---

[120]Ibid., p. 34.

is:"None."[121]

Second, Newbigin strongly suggests that if Christians do not submit those areas of human life to the rule of Christ, they do not remain free. They fall under another power. Using the Pauline language of Galatians 4:3, they become slaves to the "elemental spirits of the universe." In the same context, Paul insists that the law is a good gift of God but that if it does not yield place to Christ it becomes a power to enslave. The "principalities and powers" have been created in Christ and for Christ (Col 1: 16). But when they fail to acknowledge the absolute sovereignty of Christ, and claim absolute sovereignty themselves, they become instruments of the evil one. The imperial power which has been instituted by God for the maintenance of social justice becomes an embodiment of demonic evil (Rom. 13 and Rev.13). Therefore,

> The decision for Christians is not whether or not to become involved as Christians in public affairs. It is whether our responsibilities in the public sphere are to be discharged under the kingship of Christ or under the dominion of the evil one.[122]

The human person is a unity. It is the same person who lives in the most private prayers and in the most public acts. All human beings have a shared humanity and a shared story. Newbigin's theology has no place for dichotomies, because he has a biblical ground motive which shows the mutual relation and coherence of all the aspects of God's world. The modern worldview is reductionistic. It reduces all of life to its economic, political or scientific dimension. Newbigin teaches that we should not absolutize one aspect and reduce the others, but respect each on

---

[121] Ibid., p. 39.
[122] Ibid., p. 41.

account of its intrinsic worth given by God. As Herman Dooyeweerd points out, each sphere of reality has a God-given sovereignty, given as a 'creational principle,' but they have a "mutual irreducibility, inner connection and an inseparable coherence."[123] Newbigin's biblical worldview does not tolerate a dichotomy of temporal reality into two mutually opposing and mutually separable areas.

d. The Reality of Secularization

The theme of secularization and how this process is to be viewed from a Christian standpoint has been a point of central interest for Newbigin. In one of his earlier writings[124], Newbigin devotes his attention and energy not only to accounting for and evaluating the process of secularization, but also to offering clues to a Christ-centred missionary dialogue with the secular culture. His ideas about secularization are an important part of his dialogue with modern Western culture. Since his critique offers useful insights into the nature of a secularized society and the kind of life that is possible for a Christian in a secularized society, I shall briefly note the salient features of his analysis.

In defining the terms, the author distinguishes the words 'secular' and 'secularization' from 'secularist' and 'the propagation

---

[123] *Roots of Western Culture* (Toronto: Wedge Publishing Foundation, 1979), p. 43.

[124] *Honest Religion for Secular Man* (London: SCM Press, 1966). It is a reproduction of the Firth Lectures, with some changes, given at the University of Nottingham in 1964. In these lectures Newbigin is asking the question, "What must be the religion of a Christian who accepts the process of secularization and lives fully in the kind of world into which God has led us?" See p. 10.

or spread of secularism'. He uses the word `secularism' to refer to "a system of belief, or an attitude, which in principle denies the existence or the significance of realities other than those which can be measured by the methods of natural science."[125] At the Jerusalem meeting of the International Missionary Council (1928), `secularism' was defined as "a way of life and an interpretation of life that include only the natural order of things and that do not find God, or a realm of spiritual reality, necessary for life or thought."[126] Newbigin makes an essential difference, which was not made at the Jerusalem meeting, between `secularism' as a closed system of belief and `secularization' as a historical process.[127]

The process of secularization, according to Newbigin, can be viewed both in its negative and positive aspects. Negatively, it is "the withdrawal of areas of life and activity from the control of organized religious bodies, and the withdrawal of areas of life and activity from the control of what are believed to be revealed religious truths." Positively, it may be seen as "the increasing assertion of the competence of human science and technics to handle human problems of every kind."[128] This, from a biblical standpoint, can be argued as "man's entering into the freedom given to him in Christ, freedom from the control of all other powers, freedom for the mastery of the created world which was promised to man according to the Bible."[129] It provides a personal freedom that is not known in sacral forms of society. It liberates human powers to question, to experiment and make independent

---

[125] Ibid., p. 8.
[126] International Missionary Council Meeting, *Jerusalem Meeting Report*, Vol. 1, (London, 1928) p. 284.
[127] *Honest Religion for Secular Man*, p. 8.
[128] Ibid.
[129] Ibid., pp. 8-9.

decisions. It is indeed a summons to greater personal freedom, and to the responsibility which freedom entails.[130]

The process of secularization is a universal fact, a single movement which unifies peoples of all continents. Important elements such as modern means of communication and travel have rendered all parts of the world inter-related and interdependent. Although there are still parts of the world that are not affected by massive social changes, one could view this world as interdependent and inter-related by innumerable commercial, political and cultural relationships. While this linkage and interdependence may be spoken of as external indications of the movement of unification, it has some internal characteristics which can be expressed both negatively and positively. Negatively, while people are aware of being part of a single world history, they are also aware of standing under the threat of a single world disaster such as a nuclear war. Positively, people share increasingly common expectations about the future, about human rights, technological development, etc.[131] Newbigin notes that this common history, which carries a common danger and common hope is something new; and both are directed towards secular possibilities. He points out that humankind is "not unified on the basis of a common religious faith or even of a common ideology, but on the basis of a shared secular terror and a shared secular hope."[132] It is in this context of secular hope that he discusses the word `Development'.

Development is a new set of goals and values which are different from those of non-Western cultures. These are defined in terms of technical advance, industrialization, economic planning, productivity and the more equal distribution of wealth. To achieve them, there must be a sharing of scientific knowledge and

---

[130]Ibid., pp. 68-69.
[131]Ibid., p. 12.
[132]Ibid., p. 13.

economic planning on a global scale. The pursuit of them draws all races into a common involvement in a single universe of thought as well as a single fabric of economic life. The dynamism of this process changes the shape of human lives, brings unbearable stresses into ancient societies and finally tears them apart. Yet these developments cannot be seen in negative terms only. According to Newbigin,

> Its effect (not recognized at first) is to destroy the cyclical pattern of human thinking which has been characteristic of many ancient societies and to replace it by a linear pattern, a way of thinking about human life which takes change for granted, which encourages the younger generation to think differently from its parents, which looks for satisfaction in an earthly future. It is in the pursuit of secular, this-worldly goals that mankind is being made one. It is in terms of shared secular hopes and a shared secular peril that we can speak today of the human race as a unity.[133]

If the process of secularization has a globally unifying effect upon the entire humanity, especially from a 'this-worldly' point of view, how is this related to the biblical promise of the summing up of all things in Christ? Has this process anything to do with the biblical goal of history? These are the questions with which Newbigin is concerned. Instead of simply deploring the process of secularization, Newbigin is trying to understand it in the light of the Bible. For him, the Bible is also a book of secular events. In his words,

> Whatever else it may be, the Bible is a secular book

---

[133] Ibid., p. 14.

dealing with the sort of events which a news editor accepts for publication in a daily newspaper; it is concerned with secular events, wars, revolutions, enslavements and liberations, migrants and refugees, famines and epidemics and all the rest. It deals with events which happened and tells a story which can be checked- and is being checked- by the work of archaeologists and historians. We miss this because we do not sufficiently treat the Bible as a whole.[134]

Newbigin believes that the Bible is an interpretation of universal human history, beginning with the saga of creation and ending with a vision of the gathering together of all the nations and the consummation of God's purpose for humankind. In other words, the Bible is an "outline of world history."[135] He deals with the central question of the relation of the Bible as universal history to the unifying process of secularization. In exploring this question, he offers three points.

First, the beliefs and the techniques which are drawing peoples of all nations together into a single global civilization have their origin in Western Europe, which is the part of the world most continuously exposed to the influence of the Bible. In order to effectively participate in the process of development, people of any country have to learn a European language and master techniques of study and research which have been developed by European peoples. The leadership of Western Europe, according to Newbigin, has not been due to any superiority of intelligence they

---

[134]Ibid., p. 20.

[135]Ibid., p. 20. Since I shall be addressing Newbigin's view of history elsewhere, my comments on his view of the Bible as history shall be treated here only briefly.

have, but to the biblical belief about the created world and about the place of the human person in the world.[136]

Second, an essential element in the process of secularization is the assumption that the conditions of human life can be bettered. The movement of development has been empowered by the idea that the new order is just beyond the horizon. 'Development', that "innocent-sounding word," has produced a major shift of allegiance for the non-Western peoples. This has radically altered their standards of judgment and contributed to the dissolution of their civilizations.[137] Newbigin identifies the source of this astonishing result as 'the faith' that it is possible to create a new order of human existence in which poverty, disease and illiteracy are banished and all human beings enjoyed the privileges of what are called developed nations. But this faith, Newbigin says, could not have come from the teaching of Asian or African religions. Their dominant teaching has been to show that it is wise to be content with the world, or to be released from attachment to it. The idea of total human welfare, to be pursued as a goal within history, has been part of the Western invasion of Asia. In the last analysis, it is a secularized form of the biblical idea of the Kingdom of God.[138]

The third point which Newbigin offers has to do with the dissolution of the 'ontocratic' pattern of non-Western societies like those of Asia. Newbigin borrows this notion from the work of the

---

[136]Ibid., p. 23.

[137]This has created a situation in which things which had been venerated for centuries are discarded. A specific example the author cites is the neglect of the study of theology, of philosophy, of classical poetry and music and the creation of great new institutions to train men in scientific agriculture, sanitation and metallurgy. See Ibid., p. 26.

[138]Ibid., p. 27.

Dutch scholar, A. T. Van Leeuwen.[139] An `ontocratic' society is one whose pattern rests upon a total identification of the orders of society with the order of the cosmos. Van Leeuwen's interpretation of biblical history is centered in the struggle of the prophetic faith in the living God to overcome the ontocratic pattern of society. All the great human civilizations which have developed from the neolithic period onward, except in so far as they have come under the influence of the prophetic critique, have rested more or less upon this ontocratic pattern. According to Van Leeuwen's survey of ancient world civilizations, the Hebrew kingdom took over the main features of this pattern. He shows that the central theme of the Bible is the prophetic attack upon this pattern in the name of the living God, whose rule can in no way be identified with any earthly rule, and whose will is not completely embodied in any human pattern of society. The triumph of secularization is not the triumph of the Kingdom of God. The driving power of the movement which is drawing all peoples into the single global civilization is a secularized form of biblical eschatology.[140]

However, these three points raise critical questions about the whole process of secularization. First a question may be raised concerning the relation of modern science and technology to the biblical understanding of the human person and nature. Newbigin

---

[139]*Christianity in World History*, trans. *H. H. Hoskins* (London: Edinburgh House Press, 1964). Van Leeuwen's thesis is that the process of secularization is the present form in which the non-western world is meeting biblical history. The great civilizations such as the Middle East, the Mediterranean, India and China have been `ontocratic,' because they were organized upon an apprehension of cosmic totality. Van Leeuwen contends that the Bible is the only place where the `ontocratic' view is rejected in the name of theocracy. See Ibid., pp. 158 f.

[140]*Honest Religion for Secular Man*, p. 30.

says that underneath the exultant sense of mastery of science and technology there is an appalled feeling of anxiety and guilt.[141] The meaninglessness and even terror which go alongside the sense of mastery may be seen in the life of modern societies. There is a reciprocal proportion of suicide rate to technological development. He writes,

> One does not need to be a cynic to notice that the suicide rate varies from nation to nation in something like a direct ratio to what is called development. Suicide is on the one hand an assertion of mastery because it denies that man is finally responsible for his life to another; and on the other hand it is a confession that the burden of this mastery is too heavy to be born, because without responsibility there is no meaning, and if there is no Other, there is no responsibility.[142]

The roots of modern science lie in a society shaped by a biblical understanding of the human place in a created world. Newbigin states that there are two possibilities, namely, slavery to elemental powers, and responsible living as children of God the Father in whose hands lie all created things, all powers and forces, and all history. This responsible living is the essential attitude for human beings to take in order to deal boldly with the created world and all its powers. Newbigin is here proposing a theology of creation which judges the pagan fear of the cosmos as baseless, because "all belongs to God, serves his will," and we are invited to become God's children and heirs and "to have the freedom of the whole estate subject only to his obedience to the Father."[143]

---

[141]Ibid., p. 31.
[142]Ibid., p. 32.
[143]Ibid., p. 32.

An outcome of this biblical understanding of the created world is the freedom with which the human person explores and experiments with the resources of the world. In other words, this desacralizing of nature is the precondition for the development of science and technology. It is this understanding of the creation that has also made missionaries in Africa and Asia the pioneers of technical development.

In biblical terms, this desacralizing has to be seen in the context of the centrality of God's work in Christ. The Bible shows (Gal. 4: 1-7; Col. 2: 13-15) that there was a dethronement of cosmic powers in Christ which has liberated human persons from the control of these powers so that the person can enjoy "through Christ, the freedom and responsibility of sonship."[144]

Newbigin is speaking of a Christ-centered liberation and desacralization, which may not be acceptable to those who use the method of science and technology. The scientific method suggests that the religious ideas and images of the Bible, even the idea of a God who is other than humanity and sovereign over humanity, must be given up. Again, this method suggests that "the Christian too must deal with the world *etsi Deus non daretur*, as if there was no God."[145] So Newbigin argues that there is despair and a sense of meaninglessness which go along with technological development that avoids any reference to the Bible or to God.

Secondly, Newbigin poses the question whether the driving power of the movement that is drawing all the nations into a single history is a secularized form of the biblical eschatology. It is a belief, as seen in some countries of Asia and Africa, in some sort

---

[144]Ibid., p. 33.
[145]Ibid.

of new order towards which history is moving.[146] They are spurred on to make radical and costly changes in their ways of life because of the `faith' in a new order which is on the horizon. In highlighting the vulnerable side of scientific achievements, he is not negating its usefulness. His main concern is to show that if technology is pursued without reference to God's rule over all creation, technology will become a snare. By rejecting the gods and demi-gods, technological development might be bringing in a whole new set of different gods. The pursuit of technology can create an "ideological pull" by going beyond all limits.

Thirdly, in connection with the rapid dissolution of the ontocratic order, the contact of the West with the non-Western world has brought with it not simply a new pattern of society which might replace the traditional one, but rather a new revolutionary principle which questions all settled social structures. It is a question directed against every pattern of society, or a permanent principle of revolution.[147]

With Van Leeuwen, Newbigin sees in the prophetic attack upon the ontocratic pattern of society the element in the Bible which makes biblical faith a secularizing agent. There is "continuity between the prophetic resistance to the claims of a sacral kingship, the Christian refusal to acknowledge the divinity of the Emperor, and the secular spirit which refuses to acknowledge the final authority of any sacred tradition or any official ideology which overrides the right and dignity of the human person." The question here is "whether the truly secular

---

[146]Ibid., p. 34.

[147]In Newbigin's observation, it is this permanent principle of revolution that has come to the aid of Hindu Reformers like Ram Mohan Roy in attacking the evils of Hindu society in the early nineteenth century, and Gandhi, against the British Raj.

spirit can be sustained if it loses contact with that which gave the prophet his authority to speak, namely, a reality transcending every human tradition and every earthly society, a God who is for humanity against all the `powers'."[148]

Newbigin's analysis of the process of secularization, and the scientific and technological development which are its essential products, calls attention to the new possibilities of freedom, but also to the new possibilities of enslavement. The Christian must view the process of secularization neither with fear and hostility nor with uncritical enthusiasm, but with a sober understanding founded upon biblical faith. The question of God's act in Jesus Christ is so important in this understanding that Newbigin says,

> Believing in the God who is the Lord of history we ought to have every confidence in seeking rather to understand, in the light of his revelation of himself in Jesus Christ, what this process of secularization means, and to find the ways by which, in this new situation, we can bear witness to his purpose.[149]

This, however, does not mean that we accept the process of secularization as though it provided in itself the norms by which belief and conduct were to be determined. The ultimate norms for our standpoint are not offered by what is prescribed by Enlightenment thought. The right standing point in understanding the process of secularization is God's revelation of himself in Jesus Christ, as this is testified in the Bible. This understanding has to come from the interpretation of the biblical texts.[150]

---

[148] Ibid., p. 37.
[149] Ibid., pp. 41-42.
[150] Ibid., p. 42.

Newbigin does not believe that increasing secularization would create a society in which there are no conflicting truth-claims of religions. There are limits to the possibilities of a secular society, because humans cannot live in the rarified atmosphere of pure rationality and the needs of the human spirits are to be met.[151] Now what has come into being is a pagan society which worships false gods. Christian affirmation in this context must mean calling people into discipleship of Christ. The model for this discipleship is found in the ministry of Jesus. This discipleship involves challenging the assumptions that govern the worlds of politics, economics, education, etc. Also, evangelism in the context of secularization would mean that the church would equip its members to be agents of the Kingdom of God and to be "the hermeneutic of the gospel." Christian faith, through their evangelistic dialogue, would impinge on their daily work. In this dialogue, they would be able to explain the Christian story and its radically different way of seeing things, including all the things that make up daily life in the secular world.[152] This dialogue is a call to conversion.

e. **The Absence of Hope**

A profound problem of modern Western culture is the widespread absence of hope, despite its 'religious' character and the modern dogma of progress. When Newbigin returned to Britain after many years of life and work in India, he was especially able to sense the differences between the two cultures. He was often asked about the greatest difficulty he faced in moving from India to England. The answer was "the disappearance of hope."[153] He always found even in the slums of Madras that there was always

---

[151] *The Gospel in a Pluralist Society*, p. 213.
[152] Ibid., p. 222; *A Word in Season*, p. 156.
[153] *The Other Side of 1984*, p. 2.

the belief that things could and would be better. In England, notes Newbigin, it is hard to find any such hope. He lists several factors that have compounded the hopelessness of the West.[154]

First, there is what he calls the spiritual poverty of Europe, an evidence of which is

> [T]he sight of young people from affluent homes in England, France or Germany roaming the streets in tattered and unwashed Indian clothes, having turned their backs on Europe in the hope that - even as beggars - they might find in India something to make life worth living.[155]

Second, the disintegration of familiar values. For the elderly and the middle-aged, for the most part, there is only the hope of surviving reasonably comfortably amid this deterioration of human values. Third, for many of the young people, there is only the terrible specter of probable nuclear war, with nothing beyond. Fourth, there is what Newbigin calls the `loss of confidence in the validity' of Western culture. Even after the appalling event of the First World War, there was some confidence in modern science and technology, which were thought to be the keys to unlimited progress. Western civilization was confident even then that it held the key to the coming world civilization, and that free democratic institutions would establish themselves everywhere, that mastery over nature would create a world of well-being. Contrary to this expectation, today science and technology, and even the most benign form of science called medicine, are being viewed with skepticism. They are seen more and more as threats than as ground

---

[154]Ibid., pp. 1-2.
[155]Ibid., p. 1.

for hope. The rise of "green" movements as significant political forces is the most obvious sign of this shift in perspective. A fifth factor is the `collapse of meaning'. The most rapidly growing mental illnesses are related to this factor. Nearly all the fatal diseases have been mastered in principle, and yet the burden on health services in all Western nations is outstripping resources. According to Newbigin, neither scientists nor politicians can bring a solution to these problems. Of course there are those who point out the weaknesses of every age. What surprises Newbigin is the dramatic suddenness with which confidence in the validity of this culture has been lost. His observation leads him to the conclusion that Western culture is approaching death.[156]

If there is no hope in Western culture, what then would give hope to a culture of hopelessness? For Newbigin it is very clear that the primary basis of hope is the resurrection of Jesus Christ, as the pledge of a new creation.[157] The gospel of Christ offers an understanding of the human situation which makes it possible to be filled with a hope which is both eager and patient even in the midst of hopeless situations.[158] It is precisely the loss of this ground of hope that has produced meaninglessness and despair. For Newbigin, `hope' is not a "faint ineffectual desire," a "desire projected into the unknown future," but an "unshakable assurance of that which shall be because God has promised it."[159] The

---

[156] Ibid., p. 3.

[157] Ibid., p. 1. Cf. Lesslie Newbigin, "The Christian Hope." in Norman Goodall, *Missions Under the Cross* (London: Edinburgh House Press, 1953), p. 107.

[158] *The Gospel in a Pluralist Society*, p. 232.

[159] "The Christian Hope," in *Missions Under the Cross*, Op. cit., p. 108. See also Newbigin's "The Kingdom of God and Our Hopes for the Future," in *The Kingdom of God and Human Society*, ed. R. S. Barbour (Edinburgh: T & T Clark, 1993), p. 6.

Christian hope is indissolubly bound up with our membership in Christ who will visibly terminate and consummate the world history in which he is hiddenly at work. It is rooted in a new life in Christ, which has been given to us through the work of the Holy Spirit. In spite of the modern advancement of science and technology, there exists great terror as the human person faces the future. In *Honest Religion for Secular Man*, Newbigin narrates the story of his conversation with a physicist who worked on the team that developed the first atomic bomb during the final years of the last World War.[160] He remembers:

> He described to me what it felt like to work on the job with his colleagues, and the mounting excitement as success came nearer. And then he described the sudden change of feeling which came over the whole team when they realized that they had succeeded, and that the thing they had created was potentially the most monstrous evil that the mind of man had ever conceived and brought forth.[161]

As mentioned above, Newbigin shows a link between technological development and the suicide rate in Western societies. Yet, suicide is an `assertion of mastery' because it denies that the human person is finally responsible for his life to another; and on the other, it is a `confession' that the burden of this mastery is too heavy to be borne, because without responsibility there is no meaning, and if there is no `Other', there is no responsibility.[162]

Newbigin refers to Romans 8: 22: "We know that the whole

---

[160] Op. cit., p. 30.
[161] Ibid., p. 30.
[162] Ibid.

creation has been groaning as in the pains of childbirth right up to the present time. Not only so, but we ourselves, who have the firstfruits of the Spirit, groan inwardly as we wait eagerly for our adoption as sons, the redemption of our bodies. For in this hope we were saved."[163] He sees in Romans 8: 18-25 the relatedness of the Spirit and creation. The liberation of creation and human liberation are the common theme of this passage and they are not to be understood apart from each other. Groaning and suffering here is not meaningless. It is full of hope grounded on the raising of Jesus from the dead. The resurrection is God's signal of the beginning of the new creation. The story of the resurrection of Jesus as the primary basis of hope has to be the starting point for understanding the world.[164] The basis of hope is Christ and there is no dichotomy between the eschatological hope and the hope we realize now in history.[165]

A 'privatized eschatology', which is the mark of modern Western society, is a sign of the loss of faith in a meaningful future.[166] The hope, which Newbigin finds in the New Testament, is the hope for the world, and its horizon is the second coming of Christ and consummation of history. It is the missionary task of the church to act meaningfully in the world until the consummation of history.

---

[163]Lesslie Newbigin, *Come Holy Spirit Renew the Whole Creation*, Occasional Paper No. 6 (Birmingham, U.K.: Selly Oak Colleges, 1990), p. 6.

[164]Ibid., p. 7.

[165]Lesslie Newbigin, "The Nature of the Christian Hope," in *The Ecumenical Review*, Vol. 4 (1952), pp. 282, 284.

[166]Lesslie Newbigin, "The Kingdom of God and Our Hopes for the Future," in *The Kingdom of God and Human Society*, Op. cit., p. 9.

Concluding Critical Comment

Newbigin offers a brilliant critique of modern Western culture as an alternative `religious' outlook which has its roots in part in the Christian tradition itself. Many of the stances he has articulated here are of a piece with what he will say about inter-religious dialogue generally, and so his discussion of Western culture is inseparable from his theological position regarding the nature of religion, and the relationship between Christian faith and the world religions.

Newbigin's criticism of the privatization of faith and appeal for `public truth' is lucid and compelling. However, we might ask whether his vision of society governed under the Lordship of Christ is convincing. Can he really envisage an educational system which acknowledges Christ as public truth, while yet denying that he seeks a return to `Christendom'? Newbigin is not sufficiently critical of the negative and imperialistic character of `Christendom'. He seems to assume that pre-modern Western culture was authentically `Christian'. His uncompromising insistence on the Lordship of Christ for all of culture is to be appreciated for its honesty and forthrightness. But he has not helped us to see what it might mean to live as Christians - socially, politically, culturally, during an extended period of minority status.

Newbigin is one of the fiercest critics of the Enlightenment, who details the negative influence it has had upon European culture. But seldom does he speak of the profoundly positive elements, such as the movement of critical thought, and the aspects of human emancipation and freedom of thought and tolerance, which came with the Enlightenment. It is not right to put the whole blame for our current malaise on the Enlightenment. As David J. Bosch notes, the modern Western worldview was in a sense the "logical consummation of a way of thinking the roots of which lay far back in Greek antiquity, whence it penetrated Christian thinking."[167] Newbigin does not altogether ignore this truth. However, he does not stress the fact that the progenitors of the Enlightenment, for instance, Bacon, Descartes, Newton, Leibniz, were all Christians, who believed that they were serving God through their works. Descartes, whom Newbigin chastises heavily, was rooted in scholastic theology, and the ideas of Bacon, an English puritan, grew in part out of John Calvin's attitude to scientific investigation. Newton was a biblical scholar and a mathematician, who sought to formulate a natural philosophy that would preserve the role of God in the cosmos and vindicate the faith. Descartes himself was not an enemy of the faith. His purpose, in the words of Stuhlmacher, was "to observe certain `first principles' or causes of everything that is or might be in the world, and without paying that world any mind apart from the God who created it."[168] So the Enlightenment, including its preceding events, cannot be considered simply as a disaster, nor can it be pitted against the Christian faith, as if they were implacable enemies.

Newbigin calls for a dialogue with Western culture, with its science and politics. A dialogue with science is necessary to deal with the questions of `What can we know?' and `How can we know?' Likewise, a dialogue with politics should entail the question of `What is to be done?' Answers to these questions can become the contours of a missiology for the West. This area needs to be fully developed; Newbigin does not spell out sufficiently what the new approach to politics should be, though he surely encourages the recovery of a more confident approach to all of life.

---

[167]*Believing in the Future: Toward A Missiology of Western Culture* (Pennsylvania: Trinity Press International, 1995), p. 6.

[168]Peter Stuhlmacher, *Historical Criticism and Theological Interpretation of Scripture*, trans. Roy A. Harrisville (Philadelphia: Fortress Press, 1977), p. 8.

He articulates very powerfully the apostasy and the resultant despair of Western culture, which needs to regain its confidence in the gospel of Christ. He shatters the persistence of a unidirectional understanding of mission from the West, often still controlled by the spirit of the old Christendom.

CHAPTER 5

THE QUESTION OF THE UNITY OF ALL RELIGION
A RESPONSE TO THE PLURALIST CHALLENGE

In a religiously plural world, Newbigin seeks to present Jesus as the unsurpassable revelation of God. In presenting Christ in this way, he is not alone, but stands with other theologians such as Hendrik Kraemer, Karl Barth and Karl Rahner. He also fervently debates the issue of religious pluralism with its proponents, like Wilfred Cantwell Smith, Diana L. Eck, Paul Knitter, John Hick, and Gordon D. Kaufman.

What I propose to do in this chapter is to clearly outline and discuss Newbigin's understanding of Jesus and the non-Christian religions with a particular focus on the question of `Continuity/Discontinuity' debate. A topic which ensues from this question is the `Salvation of non-Christians.' In order to grasp the distinctiveness of Newbigin's thought on these matters, I shall compare his ideas to those of certain conversation partners. But to begin with let us explore how Newbigin understands the relation of Christ to the religions.

1. CHRIST AND THE RELIGIONS

As one who spent his life in the task of primary evangelism, Newbigin is profoundly interested in defining the Christian faith in relation to non-Christian religions. In an essay written on the Vancouver Assembly theme `Jesus Christ, the Life of the World,' he explores the meaning of the theme for an understanding of inter-faith relationships.¹ How we are to relate this claim to the spiritual experience of millions of non-Christians is the heart of Newbigin's concern. This is a legitimate question in a world which has millions of non-Christians devoted to other religious traditions. Is Christ *the life* of the millions of Hindus, Buddhists and Muslims? This question cannot be set aside. For Newbigin, the question of Jesus Christ being the life of the world cannot be answered apart from an explication of the New Testament witness on the matter.

The New Testament bears testimony to the life-giving reality of Jesus. The resurrection of Jesus from the dead is the pivotal point in the whole reality of the Christian. Jesus has been variously described as `the author of life' (Acts 3: 14), whose flesh is that which gives life to the world (Jn 6:51). Jesus is the giver of eternal life and he is contrasted with Adam, who brought death into the world (Jn 6:51; 1 Cor 15:22). Newbigin makes a distinction between Jesus as life *for* the world and Jesus as life *of* the world.² Jesus is life for the world, because he has brought life into the world through his reconciling death on the cross. The gift of life is almost always made against the background of death, as in the fourth Gospel, for example, which in its prologue contrasts life and death. On the other hand, John proclaims that the coming of Jesus into the world was not the coming of a stranger, but the coming of the one to whom the world owes its life and being. This life is identified as the light of all people. He is the light of the world. The presence of life in Jesus is confronted by the total hostility of the powers of darkness and death which rule this world and "which have their primary focus in the world of religion." The existence of the Christian church derives from this source of life and empowerment.

---

¹Lesslie Newbigin, "Christ and the World of Religions," in *The Churchman*, 97 (1983):16-30.
²Ibid., p. 16.

How does this Christological affirmation square with the goodness and the nobility, indeed the evident 'life' of those people who follow other faiths? This is a crucial question. Newbigin says,

> How much good there is, even in this dying world! Does not God appreciate it as much as we do? How much nobility there is in men and women who live and die without faith in Jesus! Does God condemn them all to eternal perdition? And can it really be that all the millions of men and women and little children who have lived and died before Jesus came, or before the gospel reached them, are consigned to the bonfire? Can a God who does - or even allows - such things, be the object of our love and reverence? Questions such as these cannot be silenced.[3]

The questions that Newbigin raises about Christ in relation to other religions are pertinent to the matter of inter-religious dialogue and the ongoing theological discussion about the salvation of 'good' non-Christians. If 'life' comes through Christ only, what are the Christians to think of the nobility, goodness and 'life' of non-Christians? Is the death of Jesus really the crucial event in which God's grace and power met and mastered the powers of evil? Or, has the event of Jesus been simply one of many manifestations of God? And if it is indeed the decisive event for the deliverance of the world from death, does it follow that all who have not explicitly accepted that gift of life in the name of Jesus are condemned to eternal death?

Here, as elsewhere, we shall see that the 'centrality of Christ'

---

[3] Ibid., p. 17.

is basic for Newbigin's thought. These and similar questions lead us to consider the concept of `religion' and the question of `continuity/ discontinuity' of non-Christian religions with Christianity.

a. Newbigin's Concept of `Religion.'

For Newbigin, the word `religion' is very difficult to define, as we have already noted in the last chapter. However, it is important to clarify this concept once again so as to understand its use in inter-religious dialogue. `Religion' may be defined as "all those commitments which, in the intention of their adherents, have an overriding authority over all other commitments and provide the framework within which all experience is grasped and judged."[4] When the word is understood in this very broad sense, it will include an ideology such as Marxism, which carries ultimate commitments for its adherents. The word `religion' is often used to describe any system of belief and practice which implies some kind of transcendence of the experience of the senses. But this is too vague to be useful. If the term `religion' is used to imply certain beliefs and practices about God and the immortal soul, it becomes too narrow, for it excludes many Buddhists. Because of this difficulty Newbigin prefers to use the word to refer to that which has final authority for a believer or a society, both in the sense that it determines a scale of values, and in the sense that it provides the models, the basic patterns through which the believer grasps and organizes experience. This definition would be more comprehensive and it would include both `religions' and ideologies.[5]

There is another distinction one has to make here between

---

[4] Lesslie Newbigin, *The Open Secret*, p. 181.
[5] Ibid., p. 182.

'implicit religion' and 'explicit religion'. Newbigin thinks that what one calls one's religion may in fact be other than the ultimately authoritative factor in one's thinking and acting. For example, one may call oneself Christian and yet limit the operation of the Christian commitment to a restricted area of life, while one's ultimate commitment may be to some other way of understanding and judging experience, such as the modern scientific world view. Consequently, one's commitment to Christ will be conditioned by the commitment to the "overriding myth," and the latter will be one's real religion.[6]

In one of Newbigin's earlier writings,[7] written in connection with the debate about Birmingham's syllabus on religion in the U.K., he says that the meaning of the word 'religion' changes in a religiously plural society. The syllabus used phrases such as 'religious and moral dimensions of human experience' and 'stances for living'. In Newbigin's opinion, a religion which is simply one of a class, as used in the plural setting, cannot be an ultimate commitment and a stance for living.[8] He insists on the need for commitment in religion. For example, a faithful Muslim cannot consider Islam as one of a class called religions, because he or she holds to the finality of the Qur'an and Muhammad as the Messenger of God. Another example is the Hindu recognition of many ways to salvation such as Saivism, Vaishnavism, Buddhism and even Christianity. But the Hindu, Newbigin says, has a standpoint from which to view these religions as ways to salvation

---

[6]Ibid.

[7]"Teaching Religion in a Secular Plural Society," in *Learning for Living*, vol. 17, No. 2 (Winter 1977). This essay later appeared in John Hull, ed., *New Directions in Religious Education* (Sussex, England: The Falmer Press, 1982), pp. 97 - 107.

[8]Lesslie Newbigin, "Teaching Religion in a Secular Plural Society," in *New Directions in Religious Education*, Op. cit., p. 98.

and that standpoint is *Sanatanadharma*, the eternal order to which the ultimate key is found in the Upanishads. Therefore, Newbigin argues that to say that *Sanatanadharma* is itself just one of the possible ways to look at things would be to cease to be a Hindu.[9] Likewise, Marxism has a highly developed interpretation of religion and to regard its stance as one of the many is not possible for a Marxist.

Now the question is, what meaning can the word 'religion' have in a plural society? Newbigin distinguishes three types of answers. First, one can look at religion from a standpoint outside of any one of them. This, he says, has been the characteristic approach to the 'comparative study of religions' done in Europe since the age of the Enlightenment. This method calls for an impartial view of religions from outside, "being uncommitted to the beliefs of any of them."[10] This, according to Newbigin, is a commitment to a method rather than to any religion. This allegedly impartial, non-committal approach to the study of religion is often found in writers who, in Newbigin's opinion, do not reveal the standpoints from which they judge these religions.

Second, religions can be studied from the vantage point of their social function. They can be seen as forces of 'conservation and cohesion' among the groups which professed them. A third possible approach is to see religions as varied manifestations of one common experience. This experience has been defined in many ways. It could be mysticism, or belief in God or of the soul,

---

[9]Ibid.

[10]The representative thinkers who provided models for this approach to religion, according to Newbigin, were Descartes, Newton, Leibnitz and Kant. This approach has religion 'within the limits of pure reason.' See Ibid., p. 98. Cf. Lesslie Newbigin, *The Finality of Christ*, p. 16.

or life after death. But Newbigin contends that

> 'God' in this case is conceived in unitarian rather than trinitarian terms. In any case the formulation of the 'essence of religion' by which all the varieties of 'religion' are brought into a single class is that of the individual thinker, and will always contain elements which are vehemently denied by other people claiming to be religious.[11]

All three points mentioned above have one thing in common: they represent one particular stance among the many which are available. In each case, whether consciously or unconsciously, the way 'religion' is understood is governed by a prior commitment of the person who is trying to understand the religion. There is no standpoint above all standpoints. Newbigin demands that the person who regards all religions as members of a class should expose for examination his or her understanding of religion, and the claim that this is in fact the truth about all religions.

The inevitable presence of a standpoint in studying religion has been overlooked by the Birmingham syllabus. It insists on studying religions objectively and for their own sake. But the call for this objectivity is an illusion, because the syllabus itself rests upon one particular view according to which religions should be regarded. Newbigin asks whether an objective study of religion is possible at all. He examines the problem further by saying,

> If 'objectively' in this context means without any presuppositions about what counts as evidence and what makes 'sense', then it is impossible. If it does not mean this, then it means that all 'stances' are

---

[11]"Teaching Religion in a Secular Plural Society," p. 99.

> open for examination except the `stance' of the Syllabus itself.[12]

This affirms the truth that in the teaching of religion, one cannot avoid operating out of some particular standpoint. Thus Newbigin says: "I do not understand anything except when I have related it somehow to the rest of my experience, and therefore to the models in which I have (provisionally) grasped my experience up to now."[13] He detects an ideology wherever the particular standpoint is not being made explicit. It is the ideology of a "secular, liberal inhabitant of the Western capitalist post-Christian world."[14] For Newbigin, religion is concerned with realities, and therefore it must be taught with a real passion for the truth.

Since the word `religion' covers an extremely wide and varied range of entities, it is difficult to achieve a fine division of various religions. What one calls religion is integrally inter-related to so many other aspects of human culture. Religions can be classified in numerous ways, using different features. To show this, Newbigin calls attention to various methods of classification which have already been employed by others.[15] One of them is the classification of Nicol MacNicol who, in his book, *Is Christianity Unique?*[16] classifies world religions into two main categories. First, there are those religions such as Christianity, Judaism and Islam, which regard God's self-revelation in historical terms. The

---

[12]Ibid., p. 100.

[13]Ibid. This is equally true in the matter of inter-religious dialogue where, Newbigin says, the real decisions are made at the beginning of the argument, not at the end. See *The Finality of Christ*, p. 15.

[14]"Teaching Religion in a Secular Plural Society," p. 100.

[15]*The Gospel in a Pluralist Society*, pp. 171-72.

[16](London: SCM Press, 1936).

second group of religions, such as Hinduism, Buddhism and Sikhism sees the essential religious experience as a-historical. But even this cannot serve as a homogenous category. For example, in the first group, one has to distinguish between Christianity, for which the Messiah has already come, and Judaism, which still looks for the Messiah to come. Islam affirms rather a succession of messengers culminating in the Prophet Muhammad.

A second method examined is that of Harold Turner[17], according to whom there are only three possible ways of understanding the world: the atomic, the oceanic, and the relational. This classification is based on worldviews rather than religions, but it must be recognized that every religion embodies some kind of worldview. The atomic view sees `atom' as the ultimate constituent of matter. Thus by analogy, the individual is the ultimate constituent of the society, a notion which characterizes the description of contemporary Western society. The oceanic view sees all things ultimately merged into one entity, which includes both the soul and all that exists. The third view sees everything as constituted by relationships, whether the material world or human society. Newbigin sees this view, which is characteristic of what is known as "primitive societies," as the one that comes closer to the biblical worldview. This is why the Gospel is more readily accepted by people of "primitive societies" than those who inhabit atomic and oceanic worldviews.

The difficulty in precisely defining the word `religion' leads Newbigin to the conclusion that in using the word `religion' one is

---

[17] Harold Turner has written extensively on religious movements in primal societies. See his *New Religious Movements in Primal Societies [Microform]: A Collection of Primary Source Documents*, edited by Stan Nussbaum (Birmingham, England: Selly Oak Colleges, 1993).

making many unacknowledged assumptions which need to be closely scrutinized. One of the unacknowledged assumptions is the integral relationship between religion and culture. He does not see religion as a separate activity set apart from the rest of life.[18] The cultural life of a society is permeated by religious belief. Here Newbigin's thought is similar to that of J. H. Bavinck,[19] who says that, although there is a strictly personal element in religion, the great religions of the world have been and still are great social powers. Religion appears to be a social phenomenon, because human beings act collectively, especially when they respond to what is called the deepest realities of life.[20] A fundamental clarification that Newbigin brings to this discussion is that religious activity is part of human culture.[21] The sharp line that has been drawn in Western culture between 'religious affairs' and 'secular affairs' should be seen as a forced separation, according to

---

[18] *The Gospel in a Pluralist Society*, p. 172. The integral relationship between religion and culture increases the complexity of the word 'religion' and the task of its precise interpretation. Clifford Geertz expresses the same opinion when he speaks of the sociological nature of religion. He points out that 'religion' describes social order to a great extent, and it has a direct bearing on a people's secular life. See his essay, "Religion As a Cultural System," in *The Interpretation of Cultures* (New York: Basic Books, Inc., 1973), pp. 119, 124.

[19] *The Church Between Temple and Mosque* (Grand Rapids, Michigan: Wm. B. Eerdmans Publishing Co., 1967), p. 19.

[20] Ibid.

[21] See George R. Hunsberger, *The Missionary Significance of the Biblical Doctrine of Election as a Foundation for a Theology of Cultural Plurality in the Theology of J.E. Lesslie Newbigin*, (Ph.D. Thesis, Princeton Theological Seminary, 1987), p. 356, who describes religious plurality as a subset of a larger category called cultural plurality.

Newbigin's thought. This is a "false dichotomy" and he addresses this issue in his writing elsewhere.[22] He says that the contemporary debate about Christianity and the religions of the world is often carried out with the unspoken assumption that `religion' is the primary medium of human contact with the divine.[23] This assumption has to be questioned.

Schleiermacher

Newbigin refers briefly to Friedrich Schleiermacher[24] and Rudolf Otto in his discussion about the classification of religion. For Schleiermacher, religion is based on the feeling of absolute dependence. Here `feeling' is not a subjective emotion; it denotes a kind of intuition by which an individual has an immediate awareness of the divine. It is a feeling of being absolutely dependent and it is one and the same thing with consciousness of being in relation with God.

Newbigin sees Schleiermacher as a "paradigmatic figure" who takes the universal human religious experience as the presupposition of all theologies and as the clue to the human situation.[25] Schleiermacher's was one of the massive attempts, says Newbigin, "to affirm the gospel in the context of post-Enlightenment culture."[26] Newbigin sees that all subsequent theological work in the Protestant West has been done under his shadow. He especially refers to

---

[22] *Truth to Tell: The Gospel as Public Truth*, chapter 3.
[23] *The Gospel in a Pluralist Society*, p. 172.
[24] See *The Finality of Christ*, p. 16, for a passing reference to John Oman's classification of religions based on Hegelian, Schleiermacher, and Kantian types.
[25] Lesslie Newbigin, *Foolishness to the Greeks*, p. 12.
[26] Ibid., p. 44.

Schleiermacher's *The Christian Faith*[27] and points out the flaw of doing theology in this way. In this work, Schleiermacher, in Kantian fashion, defined the nature of theology in terms that place it firmly on one side of the divide between the world of public facts and the world of private values. Christian doctrines, for Schleiermacher, are "accounts of the Christian religious affections set forth in speech."[28] They are transcripts of religious consciousness. Insofar as Christian theology incorporates statements about the attributes and acts of God or about the constitution of the world, it must be understood that these are not properly part of dogmatics, that they belong respectively to metaphysics and natural science; they belong to the objective consciousness and its conditions, and are independent of the inner experience and the facts of the higher self-consciousness. Schleiermacher believes that "we must declare the description of human states of mind to be the fundamental dogmatic form; while propositions about the second and third forms [i.e., about the attributes and acts of God, or the constitution of the world] are permissible only insofar as they can be developed out of propositions of the first form; for only on this condition can they really be authenticated as expressions of religious emotions."[29] That matter becomes very clear to Newbigin in Schleiermacher's treatment of the resurrection of Jesus. He constantly speaks of the resurrection as a fact but absolutely denies that it has any bearing on faith in Jesus as Redeemer[30], which is the heart of the self-

---

[27]English translation of the second German edition (Philadelphia: Fortress Press, 1928)

[28]Ibid., para. 15, pp. 76, 77.

[29]Ibid., para. 30, p. 126.

[30]The "right impression of Christ can be, and has been, present in its fullness without a knowledge of these facts.", Ibid., Para 99, p. 418.

consciousness of the Christian believer. Newbigin says that it is clear from these statements that Schleiermacher was 'fencing off an area of inward religious experience that would be protected from the otherwise total dominance of an "objectifying consciousness" (to use his phrase), from a world of hard fact ultimately explicable on the terms provided by Newtonian science.'[31] Furthermore,

> It is also clear why subsequent Protestant theology has always seemed to tremble on the edge of falling into pure anthropology, so that theological statements were thought to have no referent except the religious consciousness itself. And it is clear that Feuerbach was only drawing the obvious conclusion when he said that the very idea of God is a *brockenspecter*, the projection of an image of the human ego onto the cosmos. Such an understanding of theology could perhaps, at least until the arrival of modern psychology, provide a hiding place for religion from the searching light of science, a space within the modern world for the continued cultivation of an archaic form of self-consciousness. But it could not challenge the ideology that ruled the public world.[32]

Newbigin is criticizing what he calls the "grand theological underpinning" of Schleiermacher who redefined the task of theology as the study of religious experience, and denied that theology had anything to say directly about God (because it applies to metaphysics) or about the world (because it applies to natural

---

[31]*Foolishness to the Greeks*, p. 44.
[32]Ibid., p. 45.

sciences.)³³ The impact of this kind of approach to theology has been enormous, as Newbigin outlines. For example, the Church struggled to retain a place in education, but even then, it was to hold only the private sector, without challenging the public faith. As a result, in a modern university there may be 'religious studies' offered because it is a fact that there are people with religious experiences and that they have resulting religious beliefs. Newbigin comments:

> These are facts and can be scientifically studied. But though the beliefs are facts, the things believed in are not facts as our culture uses the term. So you can have 'religious studies', but not 'dogmatics'- not the exploration of another way of understanding the world which would pose radical questions to the whole of the rest of the curriculum. There is no place for 'dogma' in the school.³⁴

So what we find is a critical view of Schleiermacher's understanding of religion and its impact upon doing theology in the post-Enlightenment culture.

Rudolf Otto

Rudolf Otto was strongly attracted by theologians like Schleiermacher. A scholar of the history and phenomenology of religions, Otto interpreted the religious phenomenon, especially in

---

[33] Lesslie Newbigin, *England As a Foreign Mission Field: An Address Given to the Assembly of the Birmingham Council of Christian Churches* (U.K.: Birmingham Council of Churches, 1986), p. 5.
[34] Ibid.

his book *The Idea of the Holy*,[35] as a synthesis of a transcendental *a priori* and as a reality beyond any merely sociological or psychological interpretation. Religion begins in itself and remains related to the Wholly Other. The sacred or holy is an *a priori* category not reducible to other categories such as the good or the valuable.

Except for a passing observation of Otto's view of Indian religions, Newbigin does not engage his work extensively.[36] Newbigin is clearly at variance with any view which includes Christian faith as one instance of a universal anthropological dimension. But our point here is that there has been a tendency to see Hinduism and Christianity as preparation and fulfillment, a theory which Newbigin does not accept. The Papal Encyclical *Ecclesiam Suam*, which represents religions in concentric circles with the Roman Catholic Church at the centre, is not a sufficient model. Around the centre are Christians and beyond this are other theists and non-Christian religions. According to Newbigin, the non-Christian religions are not to be understood and measured by their proximity to or remoteness from Christianity. They are not beginnings which are completed in the gospel. These religions "face in different directions, ask fundamentally different questions and look for other kinds of fulfillment" than that which is given in the gospel.[37]

In this context, Newbigin agrees with Otto's comment that the "the religion of India turns upon an altogether different axis from the religion of the Bible, so that the two cannot be regarded as

---

[35] Translated by John W. Harvey (London: Oxford University Press, 1924)
[36] *The Finality of Christ*, p. 28.
[37] Ibid., p. 44.

preparation and fulfillment."³⁸ To fit them into the *Ecclesiam Suam* model is to lose any possibility of truly understanding them.

Is Christianity a religion according to Newbigin? Of course, it shares many of the characteristics of other religions. He points out that

> If the word `religion' covers such things as the practice of individual and corporate worship, prayer, the reading and treasuring of sacred scriptures, then it requires no argument to prove that Christianity is a religion.
>
> But it is also clear that Christianity has much in common with movements which are not normally included under the word `religion'. It could be convincingly argued, for example, that Christianity has much more in common with Marxism than with Buddhism. There is much evidence to show that modern secularism has its roots in the Bible.³⁹

However, while Christianity is one of the religions, it cannot be fully understood <u>merely</u> as one of the religions - even if it is the "supreme and culminating" one.⁴⁰

Newbigin distinguishes Christianity from religion in general by speaking of the Gospel as a "secular announcement". It is the announcement of an "event which is decisive for all men and for the whole of their life."⁴¹ This event, which is described in

---

[38] Quoted by Newbigin, ibid., p. 28.
[39] *The Finality of Christ*, p. 46.
[40] Ibid., p. 47.
[41] Ibid., p. 48.

"universal cosmic terms," is dealing with an announcement of God which concerns the end of the world. He adds,

> This announcement, then, is something unique. It is neither simply the announcement of a new religious doctrine, nor the launching of a new secular programme. It is not an answer offered to the `questionableness of human existence', if by that is meant the existence of the individual human person.
>
> It is rather addressed to the questionableness of all things considered in their totality. It is the announcement of the decisive encounter of God with men - not just with man as individual `souls' detachable from their place in human history, but with mankind as a whole, with human history as a whole, indeed with the whole creation. It concerns the consummation of all things. Its character as `final' lies in this fact.[42]

b. The Question of Continuity/Discontinuity

The discussion of Christianity and other religions takes Newbigin to the question of whether there is continuity between non-Christian religions and Christianity. To address this question in its proper context, one has to begin by addressing Newbigin's assessment of the related questions which were dealt with in the two world missionary conferences. The reports and discussion at the missionary conferences dealt with the relationship between Christianity and other religions.

---

[42] Ibid., p. 49.

First, we shall look at Newbigin's interaction with the substance of the World Missionary Conference of Edinburgh in 1910. The Edinburgh Conference can be described as the first notable gathering in the interest of the world-wide Christianity ever held, not only in missionary history, but in all Christian history.[43] In many respects, it was a unique gathering and it was also unique in the impetus it gave to Christian activity in many directions. It opened a new era in the missionary enterprise and was "a fountainhead of international and inter-Church co-operation on a depth and scale never before known."[44] What interests us here are the Commission reports about the "nobler elements" in other religions.

Newbigin calls attention to the report of the Commission on the Christian Message.[45] The report, which is the result of a survey of evidence from various missionary fields, speaks of the true attitude of the Christian missionary to the non-Christian religions as one of understanding and sympathy.[46] However,

That there are elements in all these religions which

---

[43] The reports of the Commissions of the Conference, together with the abstracts of the debates upon these reports are accounted in nine volumes by W. H. T. Gairdner, *Echoes From Edinburgh, 1910: An Account and Interpretation of the World Missionary Conference* (London and Toronto: Fleming H. Revell Company, 1910).

[44] Hugh Martin, *Beginning at Edinburgh: A Jubilee Assessment of the World Missionary Conference, 1910* (London: Edinburgh House Press, 1960), p. 3.

[45] *The Finality of Christ*, pp. 24, 25.

[46] World Missionary Conference, 1910, *The Missionary Message in relation to Non-Christian Religions*, Vol., IV (New York, Chicago, and Toronto: Fleming H. Revell Company, 1910), p. 267.

lie outside the possibility of sympathy is, of course, recognised, and that in some forms of religion the evil is appalling is also clear. But nothing is more remarkable than the agreement that the true method is that of knowledge and charity, that the missionary should seek for the <u>nobler elements</u> in the non-Christian religions and use them as steps to higher things, that in fact all these religions without exception disclose elemental needs of the human soul which Christianity alone can satisfy, and that in <u>their higher forms they plainly manifest the working of the Spirit of God</u>. On all hands the merely iconoclastic attitude is condemned as radically unwise and unjust.[47]

The report points out that there are nobler elements in non-Christian religions, but asserts that Jesus Christ "fulfills and supersedes" all other religions. Moreover, there is the idea that the "higher forms of non-Christian religions manifest the working of the Holy Spirit."[48] Newbigin interacts also with the speech of Robert E. Speer, who concluded the discussion of the Commission report.[49] Newbigin observes that when the Commission spoke of `Christianity' it did not mean the entire body of belief and practice which has been characteristic of Christians in history. But it meant the essential revelation which none of us has fully grasped and obeyed. Newbigin summarizes the position of the Edinburgh

---

[47]Ibid., p. 267. Emphasis added.

[48]Ibid., pp. 25- 26. Newbigin is critical of these Edinburgh observations.

[49]*The Finality of Christ*, pp. 25-26. Speer's speech can be found in *The Missionary Message in Relation to Non-Christian Religions*, Op. cit., pp. 324-326.

Conference in the following sentences.[50] First, Christianity is absolute. 'Jesus fulfills and supersedes all other religions.' Second, Christians should seek out the nobler elements in non-Christian religions and use them as stepping stones by which members of those religions may be brought to higher things. Third, all religions disclose the needs of the soul which only Jesus can satisfy. Fourth, the Holy Spirit is at work in higher forms of non-Christian religions. Fifth, Christianity, understood here as empirical and historic is enriched by treasures from the other religions through sympathetic contact between Christians and non-Christians.

Newbigin raises several critical questions in response to the positions of the Edinburgh Conference: "In what sense does Jesus fulfill the other religions?", "Is it only that he satisfies needs which other religions manifest but cannot satisfy?", "Or does he in some sense complete that which they have only in part?"[51] He rejects the idea of the nobler elements in other religions as stepping stones to Christian faith. His rejection is based on the reality (and his personal experience) that it is precisely those who represent the nobler elements in the non-Christian religions who are often most bitterly hostile to the preaching of the Gospel. The classic example of this is the case of the Pharisees who represented the "ethically highest elements" in Judaism, yet who took the lead in destroying Jesus. He raises the question as to the specific ways in which it can

---

[50] See *The Finality of Christ*, pp. 25, 26.

[51] Ibid., p. 26. Newbigin here refers to the Indian philosopher Aurobindo, who apparently claimed that it was one of the glories of Hinduism that it has the courage (which Christianity lacks) to worship the evil principle of the universe, represented by *Durgha*, as well as the good. He expresses his concern in two questions: "Can the gospel be said to fulfill in any sense something which is incomplete in this faith? Is there not a choice between two mutually incompatible beliefs?"

be said that the Holy Spirit is active in non-Christian religions, and whether one would be able to gather any substantial measure of agreement about a list of such evidences.[52]

The second World Missionary Conference of Jerusalem[53] in 1928 is more important for our discussion, because of the entry of Hendrik Kraemer onto the scene. Kraemer wanted to know what the "value of the religious values" of the non-Christian religions was.[54] Although I shall deal in more detail with Kraemer in relation to Newbigin later in this chapter, mention should be made of

---

[52] Ibid., p. 27.

[53] For an account of the discussion and the material on which the discussion was based, see [Robert E. Speer], ed., *The Christian Life and Message in relation to Non-Christian Systems: Report of the Jerusalem Meeting of the International Missionary Council, March 24th-April 8th*, Vol. 1, (London: Oxford University Press, 1928). Kraemer's statement may be found on pp. 347-349. As Newbigin notes, the dominating fact at the 1928 meeting was the rise of secularism. Yet the central question was the quest for the spiritual values of non-Christian religions. There was a tendency to consider the non-Christian religions as allies in the battle against secularism. Newbigin is doubtful about this. Cf. *The Finality of Christ*, p. 29.

[54] In the final position of the Conference, there are some examples of the value of non-Christian religions. In Islam, there is "the sense of the Majesty of God and the consequent reverence in worship," "the deep sympathy for the world's sorrow and unselfish search for the way of escape" in Buddhism, and in Confucianism, there is the "belief in a moral order of the universe and consequent insistence of moral conduct." See Robert E. Speer, ed., *The Christian Life and Message in Relation to Non-Christian Systems: Jerusalem Meeting Report*, Vol. 1 (London: Oxford University Press, 1928), p. 491.

Kraemer's provocative question. Referring to Kraemer's point, Newbigin thinks that the Jerusalem Conference "did not really get to grips with the question" of Kraemer.[55] In fact it was never answered. Looking at the discussion of the Jerusalem conference at a later stage, Newbigin doubts if the use of the term "values" was a useful language. In Newbigin's words, Hendrik Kraemer was a person who took the world of religions "with immense seriousness and studied with profound and scholarly understanding." Kraemer's key distinction between Christianity and the revelation of God in Jesus Christ is an "important clarification" of what was less precisely indicated in the Edinburgh Conference. According to Kraemer's distinction, Christianity as such can claim no absoluteness or finality and it belongs to the world of religions. Speaking of this distinction, Newbigin says that it is an important one, but it leaves us with some difficult questions about the relation of Christianity to the Gospel. Newbigin thinks they can be distinguished, but cannot be separated. Similarly difficult is the distinction Kraemer made between God's act of revelation in Christ and religious experience outside the Christian revelation. It is questionable how far this dichotomy between revelation and religious experience can be pushed, according to Newbigin.[56]

Newbigin makes some critical remarks about this distinction. First, if God's revelatory act has not been in some measure understood and accepted, says Newbigin, there has been no revelation. But if it has been understood and accepted, then there has been a religious experience. Second, if there has been a religious experience, for example of a non-Christian, (and we recognize, as Kraemer certainly does, sublime elements in this experience) can we say that there has been no self-disclosure from the side of God? Third, if we admit that there has been a self-

---

[55]*The Finality of Christ*, p. 30.
[56]Ibid., p. 34.

disclosure from the side of God, what becomes of the *sui generis* character of the revelation in Christ?[57] Newbigin sheds some light on this question within his discussion of continuity and discontinuity.

While Newbigin shares Kraemer's vision of God's unique revelation in Jesus Christ, he takes a slightly different stand on the `continuity/ discontinuity' debate. In order to understand Newbigin's position better, we should examine Kraemer's view on the Christian revelation and the non-Christian religions.

Kraemer, (who was commissioned to write on the relation between Christianity and non-Christian religions as a preparation for the Tambaram conference of 1938) took his standpoint within the sphere of Christian revelation, a stance which he maintained in subsequent years with a high degree of consistency. There are two fundamental theses which are to be identified in his theology of religion.

The first thesis of Kraemer is that the Christian revelation as the record of God's self-disclosing revelation in Jesus Christ is absolutely *sui generis*.[58] The Christian revelation is the story of God's redeeming acts which have become "decisively and finally manifest" in Jesus Christ. Kraemer terms this as "Biblical realism" which expresses the idea that

> [T]he Bible, the human and in many ways historically conditioned document of God's acts of revelation, consistently testifies to divine acts and

---

[57] Ibid., pp. 34-35.
[58] Hendrik Kraemer, "Continuity and Discontinuity" in *The Authority of the Faith*, Vol. 1, p. 1 where Kraemer reiterates his main theses as a response to his critics at Tambaram.

plans in regard to the salvation of mankind and the world, and not to religious experience, or ideas.[59]

This does not mean that the Bible does not contain religious experience or ideas, but rather that they are not "central and fundamental" in the Bible. What are central and fundamental is God's creative and redemptive dealings with the world.

Kraemer's second thesis is that the reality of the various non-Christian religions forbids one to construe a relation of 'preparation and fulfillment' between the non-Christian religion and the Christian revelation. In other words, it is erroneous to view them as continuous with each other. On the basis of these two theses, based on his concept of 'biblical realism', Kraemer proposes a radical discontinuity between Christianity and other religions. He does not think 'reason', 'nature', or 'history' can afford preambles, avenues or lines of development towards the realm of grace and truth as revealed in Jesus Christ.[60] Concerning the point of 'longing and fulfillment' Kraemer says that "there are longings and apperceptions" in the religions outside the special sphere of the Christian revelation, of which Christ, what he is and what he has done may be termed "in a certain sense" the fulfillment. But it is "mistaken and misleading" to describe the religious pilgrimage of humankind as a preparation or a leading up to a so-called consummation or fulfillment in Christ.[61]

Kraemer teaches that, even when we recognize that Christ may *in a certain sense* be called the fulfillment of some deep and persistent longings and apprehensions that everywhere in history manifest themselves in the race, this fulfillment never represents

---

[59]Ibid., p. 2.
[60]Ibid., pp. 2-3.
[61]Ibid., p. 3.

the perfecting of what has been before. It is "blind and misdirected."[62] Of course, these longings and apprehensions are "humanly" speaking heart-stirring and noble, but this should not obscure the fact that in Christ "all things become new". He is the "crisis" of all religions. He further argues that God in Jesus Christ is "contrary to the sublimest pictures" we made of him before we knew him in Jesus. Kraemer uses the biblical teaching of reconciliation (2 Cor. 5: 17) which emphasizes how God reconciled an alienated world to Himself in Jesus Christ. Humanity in its totality is in a state of hostility towards God as God really is.[63]

A major consequence of Kraemer's thesis of discontinuity is that it excludes the possibility and legitimacy of a *theologia naturalis*. He rejects the notion of the Christian revelation as a "superstructure." Therefore, representing the non-Christian religions of the world as somehow a "schoolmaster" to Christ is a "distorted presentation of these religions" and a "misunderstanding of the Christian revelation."[64] Christ `the power of God' and `the wisdom of God' stands in opposition to the power and wisdom of humankind. Concerning the matter of `fulfillment', the best allowance Kraemer makes is to speak of it as "contradictive or subversive" fulfillment. Kraemer believes that his position is based upon revelation in Christ, and if this is a prejudiced position, he believes there can be no position which is not `prejudiced'. The standard of evaluation and judgment for Kraemer comes from the decisive and unique revelation of Christ. He is convinced that this revelation and nothing else must be his authoritative guide.

Newbigin agrees with Kraemer concerning revelation in

---

[62]Ibid.
[63]Ibid., p. 4.
[64]Ibid., p. 5.

Christ. The standpoint one takes is decisive in criticizing the religions or understanding the world. The `world' is not a "tenable" standpoint. Newbigin can think of no standpoint other than "Jesus Christ incarnate, crucified and risen Lord," and it is "in Christ" that Christians learn to deny and affirm the world.[65]

In Newbigin's understanding, however, there is a radical discontinuity and yet, not total discontinuity.[66] The total fact of the cross which is the focus of the Gospel makes it impossible for him to describe the relationship between faith in Christ and other forms of religious commitment in terms simply of continuity and discontinuity. He illustrates this in different ways. First, the story of the conversion of Paul, in which he looks back to his pre-conversion days and to the story of his own race. Paul sees that it is the same living God who had been dealing with him as a Pharisee, even though he was fighting against God.[67] Similarly, about the "Unknown God" of the Athenians in the book of Acts, Paul tells them that it was the living and true God they were seeking. This element of continuity, says Newbigin, has been confirmed in the experience of new converts to Christianity. Even though their conversion involves a radical discontinuity, yet there is a strong conviction afterwards that it was the living and true God who was dealing with them in the days of their pre-Christian wrestling. So, Newbigin believes that

> [T]he Gospel has a double relationship to man's experience and to the wisdom founded upon it, apart from the knowledge of God in Jesus Christ. It is a relationship both of continuity and of discontinuity. The Gospel demands and effects a radical break

---

[65] Lesslie Newbigin, *Honest Religion for Secular Man*, p. 147.
[66] *The Finality of Christ*, p. 59.
[67] Ibid.

with, and conversion from, the wisdom that is based upon other experience; yet mature reflection by those who have experienced this break suggests that it is the same God who has been dealing with them all along. He has never been without witness even when they did not know him as he has revealed himself in Jesus.[68]

Newbigin thinks that we have to take account of the fact that it is precisely those who are most religious and nearest to God who have rejected God's revelation of himself in Jesus Christ. This is so, not only in the case of the Jews, but also in the case of those who belong to the so-called higher religions.[69] The question whether there is a real communion between God and the believer in non-Christian religious experience should be answered, in Newbigin's opinion, with a plain affirmative.[70] Nevertheless, this raises questions as to the relation of the non-Christian `faith' to faith in God through Jesus Christ.

Furthermore, one could also look at the experience of translating the Bible or communicating the gospel in a foreign culture. No one can communicate the gospel without using the word `God' and missionaries take this word from the non-Christian culture. This has been possible only because of the continuity that exists between the non-Christian experience and the Christian experience. If there were no continuity, the translators of the Bible who borrowed this word would have had to invent a word or transliterate a Hebrew or Greek word.[71]

---

[68] Ibid., pp. 59-60.
[69] Ibid., p. 39.
[70] Ibid., p. 38.
[71] Ibid., p. 36. Cf. "The Christian Faith and the World Religions," in Geoffrey Wainwright, ed., *Keeping the Faith* (Philadelphia: Fortress Press, 1988), p. 326.

c. Salvation of Non-Christians

Neither Kraemer nor Newbigin deny the graciousness and work of God outside the range of the Christian revelation. For Kraemer, the problem whether, and if so, where, and how far, God the Father of the Lord Jesus Christ, has been working in the religious history of the world is a "baffling and awful" problem.[72] His rejection of a *theologia naturalis* does not, however, include the denial of the work of God in the lives of people outside the sphere of the Christian revelation. He says that "there may be acceptable men of faith" who live under the sway of the non-Christian religions, "products, however, not of these non-Christian religions, but of the mysterious working of the Holy Spirit."[73] Kraemer argues that one should not be so irreverent as to dispose of how and where the Sovereign God has to act. Kraemer, as Newbigin comments, was of the strong opinion that the work of God outside the direct range of the gospel is to be evaluated in the light of the unique revelation in Christ, and not the other way around.[74] Concerning the salvation of non-Christians, Kraemer has nowhere said that those who have not accepted the gospel are lost. It is often assumed to follow from his affirmation of the uniqueness of the gospel event.[75] It should be emphasized that Kraemer refused to recognize any of the non-Christian religions as ways of salvation alternative to Christ. Kraemer did not, however, derive from this the conclusion that all non-Christians are lost. Newbigin defends this posture of Kraemer; it is not a "failure of logical

---

[72]"Continuity and Discontinuity," in *The Authority of the Faith*, p. 14.
[73]Ibid., pp. 4-5.
[74]Lesslie Newbigin, "The Christian Faith and the World Religions" in *Keeping the Faith*, p. 330.
[75]Ibid.

rigour."[76] The assumption that this is the only possible conclusion stems from the fact that the whole discussion is dominated by the question about the salvation of the individual soul.

For Kraemer, the question of how God works in other religions cannot be passed by in silence. He says that "Biblical realism requires us to wrestle with it, for the world is still the creation of God" who does not abandon his works."[77]

Newbigin thinks that the debate about the salvation of non-Christians has been "fatally flawed", because it has been conducted around the question, "Who can be saved?"[78] It has been taken for granted that the only question was, "Can the good non-Christian be saved?", and by that question what was meant was not, "Can the non-Christian live a good and useful life and play a good and useful role in the life of society?" Or, to put it plainly, the question was, "Where will one go when one dies?" In the debate about Christianity and the religions of the world, according to Newbigin, there has been an almost unquestioned assumption that the only question is "What happens to the non-Christian after death?" In his opinion, it is a wrong question and a wrong question will bring only confusion and silence. This way of putting the question is wrong for several reasons.

First, it is a question to which God alone has the right answer. Newbigin is astounded at the "arrogance of theologians" who think that it is their duty to inform the world as to who is to be vindicated and who is to be condemned at the last judgment.[79] He

---

[76]Ibid.
[77]*The Christian Message in a Non-Christian World* (London: Edinburgh House Press, 1938), pp. 120-21.
[78]*The Gospel in a Pluralist Society*, p. 176.
[79]Ibid., p. 177.

criticizes Hans Küng who, in Newbigin's opinion, is "scathing in contempt" for Protestant theologians who say that this question has to be left in the hands of God.[80] Hans Küng says that Protestant theologians are dismissing the problem as a whole with a supercilious "we do not know," as if it were no concern of theirs. In Küng's words,

> If Christian theologians have no answer to the question of the salvation of the greater part of mankind, they cannot be surprised when people react again as they have done in the past: Voltaire pouring out his scorn for the Church's presumption in claiming to be the sole way of salvation; Lessing content with an enlightened indifferentism, with his fable of the three rings, all supposed to be genuine and yet perhaps none of them really belonging to the father. It is all too easy to reverse the assertion of "dialectical theology," that the world religions are merely human projections, and declare that Christianity itself is a pure projection, the expression of absolutist-exclusive wishful thinking.[81]

On this point, Newbigin's position is different from that of Küng, and also of some Protestants, like Wesley Ariarajah, who rebukes Visser't Hooft for saying, "I do not know if a Hindu is saved; I

---

[80] Reference has been made to Hans Küng's discussion of the "Challenge of the World Religions" in his *On Being a Christian*, Edward Quinn, trans., (London: Collins, 1977), p. 99. Here Küng accuses a number of theologians like Barth, Bonhoeffer, Emil Brunner and Hendrik Kraemer who are "without a closer knowledge and analysis of the real world of the religions."

[81] *On Being a Christian*, p. 99.

only know that salvation comes in Jesus Christ."[82] In Newbigin's opinion, we are not in a position to know in advance who is going to be saved and who is going to be lost. The judge on the last day is God and no one else. The Day of Judgment is a day of "surprises, reversals and astonishment." In the parable of the sheep and goats, a parable of the Day of Judgment, both the saved and the lost are equally surprised. The story of the rich young ruler who had kept all God's commandments turned away from the call to surrender his wealth, which prompted Jesus to say that it is harder for a rich man to enter the Kingdom of heaven than for a camel to go through the eye of a needle. Newbigin declares that theologians must first of all learn the "impossible possibility of salvation." He draws our attention to the tension in the apostle Paul, who says that nothing can separate him from the love of God in Christ Jesus (Romans 8), but has to exercise severe self-discipline "lest having preached to others I myself should be disqualified" (1 Cor. 9:27). This is because the Christian life is lived in a "magnetic field between the amazing grace of God and the appalling sin of the world." The Christian lives in "godly confidence" and "godly fear."[83]

Newbigin's second objection to putting the question in this way is its abstractness. It is not the right view because it "abstracts the soul from the full reality of the human person as an actor and sufferer in the on-going history of the world." It is a reductionistic view, because the human person is not, essentially, a soul which can be understood in abstraction from the whole story of the person's life. This reductionism is also typical of the materialists and behaviourists who see the human person as a bundle of physical activity.[84] The question of salvation, therefore, is wrongly put if it is posed in respect of the human soul abstracted from God's

---

[82] *International Review of Mission* 77 (July, 1988), pp. 419-20.
[83] *The Gospel in a Pluralist Society*, p. 178.
[84] Ibid., p. 178.

history of salvation, and abstracted from the questions, "How do we understand the human story?", and "What is the end which gives meaning to this person's story as part of God's whole story?"[85]

The third objection is that it first of all deals with the individual's need for ultimate happiness, and not with God's glory. Newbigin is not suggesting that the individual has no such longing for ultimate happiness; rather he is stressing the chief end of the human person as glorifying God. He is against "privatizing the mighty work of God's grace" and giving it a selfish bent which culminates in the words "For me; for me." The most important question is not, "How can I be saved?", but, "How shall God be glorified?" He thinks that

> The whole discussion of the role of the world religions and secular ideologies from the point of view of the Christian faith is skewed if it begins with the question, who is going to be saved at the end? That is a question which God alone will answer, and it is arrogant presumption on the part of theologians to suppose that it is their business to answer it.[86]

To the question of the salvation of the non-Christians, Newbigin would answer, 'I do not know'. To use the words of Gabriel Fackre, Newbigin shows an "intentional silence," maintaining "an eschatological agnosticism about the non-knowers of Jesus

---

[85]Ibid., pp. 178-79.
[86]Ibid., p. 180.

Christ."[87] To those who argue that a "good" Hindu will be saved, Newbigin asks about the criterion by which this goodness is measured. He wants to know how this goodness is related to the Biblical emphasis upon the fact that Jesus came not for the righteous but for the sinners.[88] He does not believe that there are alternative ways in which God works and saves. He argues,

> The Bible gives us no ground for believing that God has other plans for the unity of mankind than that which he has set forth in Jesus Christ and of which he has made the Church to be first fruit, sign and instrument.... This is not popular doctrine at the moment, but it is scriptural.[89]

2. NEWBIGIN'S CONVERSATION PARTNERS

Newbigin's writings are replete with the names of theologians who represent diverse Christian traditions. However, it is to be pointed out here that, although he is not comprehensive in his treatment of any of them, he uses their theological views to strengthen or clarify his arguments. Some of the theologians he engages, whose views resemble his own, can be called his conversation partners, and others his opponents.

I shall include in this section some theologians who, I think,

---

[87]"The Scandals of Particularity and Universality", *Mid-Stream*, Vol. XXII, No.1 (1983), p. 42. Also see George Hunsberger, Op. cit., p. 407.
[88]*The Finality of Christ*, p. 42.
[89]"Which Way for 'Faith and Order'?" in *What Unity Implies: Six Essays After Uppsala*, World Council Studies No. 7, ed. by Reinhard Groscurth, pp. 131, Geneva: WCC, 1969.

are helpful for clarifying Newbigin's theology of religion and interfaith dialogue. They are Karl Barth, Hendrik Kraemer, Walter Freytag and Karl Rahner. Of these names, that of Walter Freytag has to be reserved for a later chapter which deals with the goal and manner of dialogue. All of them can be named as Newbigin's conversation partners, but his theological interactions with Barth and Kraemer are more extensive than with Freytag and Rahner. I have placed Rahner as a link between his conversation partners and theological opponents, because Newbigin is both very critical and appreciative of Rahner's view of non-Christian religions. I cannot adequately expound the voluminous thought of these major thinkers here. My purpose is to see how Newbigin relates to their key ideas about Christian faith and the world religions.

a. Karl Barth

Newbigin was introduced to Karl Barth during his work with the World Council of Churches. In 1953 Newbigin served as chairman of the committee of the 'Twenty-five' on which Karl Barth was a member, and Newbigin recollects that he assigned Barth the job of writing the final section of the committee's work. In his autobiography, Newbigin has taken time to reminisce about his friendship with Barth and reflect on his theology. He remembers in one place the "tremendous oration" of Barth at the assembly which constituted the World Council of Christian Churches, on the theme of 'Man's Disorder and God's Design.'[90] Newbigin describes this oration as "real prophecy" and adds that "Barth demolishes all one's plans with his terrific prophetic words, and one is left wondering what to do next; and his answer always is, just get on with the next plain duty."[91]

---

[90] *Unfinished Agenda: An Autobiography*, p. 115.
[91] Ibid., p. 117.

From the perspective of this chapter, the most important point of similarity in Barth and Newbigin is their understanding of `religion'. Newbigin, reflecting on his time in Kanchipuram (1939-46) and the long discussions which he had on religious subjects with Hindu friends, says that the `point of contact' for the gospel is rather in the ordinary secular experiences of human life than in the sphere of religion.[92] Newbigin sees both positive and negative aspects of religion. He thinks that Karl Barth's attack upon `religion' has a "large element of truth."[93] He adds,

> I happen to have spent most of my working life in two cities dominated by famous temples and dedicated to the propagation of religion on a massive scale. I have seen enough to know how powerful a source of evil religion can be. Nor is it necessary to go outside Europe to have that demonstration. In one sense the Gospel is indeed the end of religion.[94]

Newbigin at that time had not read Karl Barth and "did not know that `religion is unbelief,'" but he says that "I was certainly beginning to see that religion can be a way of protecting oneself from reality."[95]

Religion is much too great and permanent an element in human experience to be ignored. Positively, it can be `reliving the moment of revelation' or the visible forms in which the knowledge of God is expressed and renewed. Negatively, There is plenty of religion in the world which is indeed an escape from reality, and

---

[92] Ibid., p. 58.
[93] *Honest Religion for Secular Man*, p. 9.
[94] Ibid.
[95] *Unfinished Agenda*, p. 58.

the pagan heart of man, in all ages and places, has always a tendency to hanker after it. The fact that an activity is religious, is pious in the sense of the great traditions of human religion, by no means guarantees that it is concerned with reality. Religious practice can be the place where our escape from reality, our hypocrisy and sheer selfishness are at their maximum.[96]
Religion can become a "cave where one escapes from the presence of the living God."[97] After living in two major Hindu cities in India, Newbigin is convinced that "the forms of religion can become an occasion for idolatry" and `religion can become the "enemy of faith." '[98] Like Barth, he does not exclude Christianity from this characterization.

Karl Barth's discussion of the `Revelation of God as the abolition (*Aufhebung*) of religion' presents some interesting similarities with Newbigin's own discussion of the topic.[99] Barth states that "religion is unbelief."[100] However, as Newbigin points out in a later essay, Barth, when he made this statement, was not thinking primarily of the world religions.[101] Rather, he was speaking of the religion that he knew all around him, the religion of Protestant Europe. Newbigin believes that Barth was rejecting Schleiermacher's understanding of religion, including Christianity, as essentially an aspect of human experience.[102] As he rightly

---

[96]Ibid., pp. 146-147.
[97]Ibid., p. 146.
[98]Ibid., pp. 95, 146.
[99]Karl Barth, *Church Dogmatics*, Vol. 1/2, edited by G. W. Bromiley and T. F. Torrance (Edinburgh: T & T Clark, 1956), pp. 280-325.
[100]Ibid., 299.
[101]Lesslie Newbigin, "The Christian Faith and the World Religions," in *Keeping the Faith*, p. 329.
[102]Ibid.

understands, Barth is not attempting a comparison of Christianity with other religions. He is concerned with a fundamental question which had been prevailing in European theology. Theology has to be faithful to the gospel and the nature and method of theology are to be judged by God's self-revelation in Christ, not by human capacity for religion. As David Lochhead clarifies,

> Barth's conclusion that religion is unbelief is primarily directed against the position that Christianity is the fulfillment of religion, and that human religion in general should be viewed as a preparation for the Gospel. His objection is that to take human religion as the "given," as the starting point of theological reflection, is to be unfaithful to that which is truly "given" as the basis of theology, namely God's self-revelation in Jesus Christ.[103]

To understand Barth's statement of religion as unbelief, one has to look at religion from the standpoint of revelation attested in Holy Scripture. According to Barth, revelation is God's "self-offering and self-manifestation" and it encounters the human person and confirms the fact that to know God from the human standpoint is futile. In revelation God tells the human person that he is God. In Barth's words, the activity which corresponds to revelation would have to be faith.[104] Genuine believers will not say that they came to faith in Christ from faith, but from unbelief. So, From the standpoint of revelation religion is clearly seen to be a human attempt to anticipate what God in His revelation wills to do and does do. It is the attempted replacement of the divine work by a

---

[103] *The Dialogical Imperative: A Christian Reflection on Interfaith Encounter* (Maryknoll, New York: Orbis Books, 1988), p. 34.
[104] Karl Barth, *Church Dogmatics*, Vol. ½, p. 301.

human manufacture. The divine reality offered and manifested to us in revelation is replaced by a concept of God arbitrarily and willfully evolved by man.[105]

Religion, as the human activity, contradicts revelation, which is the divine activity. In religion, the human person ventures to grasp at God. Because it is a grasping, religion is the "concentrated expression of human unbelief, an attitude and activity which is directly opposed to faith."[106] Likewise, revelation does not link up with a human religion which is already present and practiced. Rather, it contradicts it, just as religion previously contradicted revelation.

Karl Barth, in his discussion of 'religion as unbelief,' did not consider a distinction between Christian and non-Christian religion. This is because Christianity is not an exception. Newbigin has a similar understanding of Christianity as a religion. However, Barth does speak of true religion, and revelation singles out the Church as the *locus* of true religion. But,

> It does not mean that the Christian religion is the true religion, fundamentally superior to all other religions. We can never stress too much the connexion between the truth of the Christian religion and the grace of revelation. We have to give particular emphasis to the fact that through grace the Church lives by grace, and to that extent it is the *locus* of true religion.[107]

The Christian religion has no autonomous role detached from the

---

[105]Ibid., p. 302.
[106]Ibid., pp. 302, 303.
[107]Ibid., p. 298.

name of Jesus Christ which alone justifies it. For Barth, the Christian religion is the "sacramental area created by the Holy Spirit" in which God continues to speak through the sign of His revelation.[108] This is not to imply that Christian religion is the content of revelation nor is it a revealed religion. Barth is, rather, attempting to maintain that there is a genuine response to God through the gospel of Jesus Christ within the religious tradition that is known as Christianity.[109]

Newbigin and Barth share the same concern about the question of religion. Newbigin is of the opinion that religion, including the Christian religion, can be the "sphere in which evil exhibits a power against which human reason and conscience are powerless."[110] What should be the standpoint from which one could examine the question of religion? For both Barth and Newbigin, it is the standpoint of God's revelation in Jesus Christ. Newbigin says that

> `The world' is not a tenable standpoint. The only possible standpoint is that of faith in Christ, in whom alone both God and the world are made known as they are.[111]

The only standpoint from which one could understand both God and the world, the only basis for a true criticism of religion, is "Jesus Christ the incarnate, crucified and risen Lord."[112]

---

[108] Ibid., p. 359.
[109] David Lochhead's explication of Barth is useful here. See Op. cit., p. 35.
[110] *The Open Secret*, p. 193.
[111] *Honest Religion for Secular Man*, p. 147.
[112] Ibid.

Newbigin warns that, when the New Testament says that God has nowhere left himself without witness, there is no suggestion that this witness is to be found in the realm of what is called `religion'. The light of the Logos who came to the world in Jesus that shines in every human being, as affirmed by the Fourth

Gospel, does not identify this light with human religion.[113] On the contrary, says Newbigin, the ensuing story of the Gospel suggests that it is "religion which is the primary area of darkness," and it is the "unlearned in religious matters" who respond to the gospel. Therefore, religion may well be an area of damnation. This understanding of other religions has implications for the way in which Newbigin engages those who argue for the unity of all religions.

b. Hendrik Kraemer

Hendrik Kraemer[114] essentially followed Karl Barth in his theology. He was appointed professor of the History of Religions at the University of Leiden, Holland, in 1937, and later became Director of the Ecumenical Institute of the World Council of Christian Churches, *Chateau de Bossey*, Switzerland. A member of the Netherlands Reformed Church, Kraemer went to the Netherlands East Indies in 1921 as missionary to serve as translator

---

[113] Lesslie Newbigin, *The Gospel in a Pluralist Society,* p. 172. In Barth's thinking, the sovereign activity of God cannot be confined to Christian religion. God is free to reveal, redeem, and reconcile outside the sphere of Christianity. These words outside the Bible and Church are called "secular parables of the Kingdom." See Barth's *Church Dogmatics* Vol. IV/3, 1 (Edinburgh: T & T Clark, 1961), pp. 116-117 for the discussion.

[114] I have already discussed certain views of Kraemer in an earlier section of this chapter, and will not repeat what was said there.

and to act as advisor on matters involving the relation of Christianity and missionary work to non-Christian religions and cultures in that part of the world. He was a scholar of great reputation, who authored various publications on Islam, missions, religious life in the Dutch East Indies, colonial politics, etc. Kraemer's contribution to the discussion of the relationship between the Christian faith and non-Christian religions has been both significant and controversial. His understanding of the non-Christian religions can be found pre-eminently in his book, *The Christian Message in a Non-Christian World*,[115] published for the World Missionary Conference at Tambaram,[116] India, 1938.

Kraemer developed this book also as a major response to the pre-Tambaram report directed by William. E. Hocking entitled, "Re-thinking Missions," which, as Newbigin notes, "looked towards the convergence of all the religions in a common way of life which could be described as the "kingdom of God," and which

---

[115] (London: Edinburgh House Press, 1938, Reprinted, 1947). In preparation for the Tambaram conference, the Committee of the International Missionary Council (IMC) asked Kraemer to write a book upon the "evangelistic approach" to the non-Christian religions. The result was this book which has provoked serious thinking on the very bases of the missionary enterprise.

[116] The International Missionary Council (IMC) which was held at Tambaram, India, on 12th -29th December, 1938, was attended by four hundred and seventy delegates, including Newbigin and Kraemer, from seventy nations, to consider how the church may "better make known to the world the love of the eternal God as He has revealed Himself in Jesus Christ." The record of the findings of this conference is contained in *The World Mission of the Church, Tambaram 1938* (London and New York: International Missionary Council, 1938)., See especially pp. 10, 184.

Christians found exemplified in Jesus Christ."[117] Kraemer's work was a rebuttal to the theology found in the report directed by Hocking. He was deeply influenced by Karl Barth's theology, but was not uncritical of it. While Kraemer followed Barth in affirming the gospel as news about a unique action of the sovereign God, he declined to follow Barth's refusal to discuss the ways in which God works outside the unique revelation in Jesus Christ. For Kraemer, the latter point "cannot be passed by in silence or left untouched."[118]

By way of observation, we shall look at a few characteristics of Kraemer's approach to religion, including Christianity. First, his approach was theological. He understood and interpreted religion in the light of his faith in Jesus Christ. The Christian thinker, he says, cannot take a standpoint detached from the basic views implied in the Christian faith. Kraemer says that under all conditions, he or she remains "primarily a disciple, a captive of Jesus Christ, in whom God disclosed Himself, full of grace and truth."[119] Second, for Kraemer, Jesus Christ is "the criterion of truth, the standard of judgment and evaluation."[120] What does this mean? It means that he sets the religions, including Christianity, "in the light of the Person of Jesus Christ, who is the Revelation of God." And Christ alone has the authority to criticize, that is, "to judge discriminately and with complete understanding, every

---

[117] Lesslie Newbigin, "The Christian Faith and the World Religions" in *Keeping the Faith*, p. 314.

[118] Hendrik Kraemer, *The Christian Message in a Non-Christian World*, p. 120.

[119] *Religion and the Christian Faith* (London: Lutterworth Press, 1956), p. 144.

[120] *Why Christianity of All Religions?* (London: Lutterworth Press, 1962), p. 16.

religion and everything that is in man or proceeds from him."[121] By Jesus Christ he means that " Jesus whom we know from the total witness of apostles and evangelists in the New Testament; the Jesus who says, not: This or that is the truth, but "I am the Truth."[122] He recognizes that this is not an easy task. "It requires a persistent effort of the mind at every step to learn what it means to see light in His light alone, in and over all things and all men."[123] So for Kraemer, the measure of what is true and what is real is Jesus Christ, the Truth Himself. Third, for Kraemer, Christianity is not absolute. He says,

> It is not even in all respects the "best" religion, if by that we mean the religion which has found, comparatively speaking, the "best" and noblest way of expressing religious truth and experience. During those parts of my life spent amidst other religions it has struck me many a time that certain religious attitudes and emotions are more finely expressed in those religions than in Christianity.[124]

Christianity is attached to Christ by indissoluble ties. What is absolute is not Christianity, but the revelation of God in Jesus Christ. Newbigin, like Kraemer, was profoundly interested in understanding the Christian faith in relation to non-Christian religions. It is important to consider here how Newbigin interacts with the ideas of Kraemer.

---

[121] Ibid., p. 15.
[122] Ibid., pp. 15-16.
[123] Ibid., p. 16.
[124] Ibid., p. 115. One example of finely expressed emotion is the idea in Islam of `Allah's sovereign majesty' ("*Allahu Akbar*") for which, Kraemer says, one looks in vain for any parallel in Christianity.

Both Newbigin and Kraemer write about `comparative religion' as an academic area of study. Kraemer, as Mulder says, has wrestled during his whole life with the relation of theology and the science of religion.[125] While he admired the achievements of the science of religion, he believed that the religious history of the human race can only be rightly understood in Christ. In other words, Christ is the measure of true religion. With Barth and Newbigin, Kraemer affirms that Jesus Christ is the crisis of all religion. Just as Newbigin uses the `fact of Christ' as the criterion of judgment, Kraemer uses `Jesus Christ' as the criterion by which to judge religion.[126]

For Newbigin also, religion cannot be studied and taught without a prior commitment. Whether it is in teaching religion or in inter-religious dialogue, this prior commitment has to be recognized. And it is the question of this commitment which makes Newbigin critical of the scientific study of religions. The "enterprise" of what is known as `Comparative religion' or `History of Religions', (*Religionswissenschaft*) as defined by one of its pioneers, Max Müller, can hardly serve as a suitable method for Newbigin. For Max Müller, the ultimate commitment was to the `scientific method' as the clue to the apprehension of truth. He was calling upon the scientific community to take possession of this new territory in the name of true science.[127] This enterprise, in

---

[125]D. C. Mulder, "The Dialogue Between Cultures and Religions: Kraemer's Contribution in the Light of Later Developments," in *The Ecumenical Review*, Vol. 41, No. 1 (January 1989), p. 14.

[126]Ibid., p. 13.

[127]Lesslie Newbigin, *The Open Secret*, p. 183. Here reference has been made by Newbigin to Eric Sharpe, *Comparative Religion* (London: Duckworth, 1975), p. xi.

Newbigin's thinking, does not envisage the possibility of the meeting of different ultimate commitments. He is concerned with the issues which arise from the meeting of different discordant commitments, which, for the participants, are their ultimate commitments. There is a major flaw in this approach to religions. It does not foresee that the very foundations of "true science" can be called into question by one of the religions to be studied.[128]

Kraemer distinguished between the `scientific' and `missionary' study of non-Christian religions. The area of "Comparative Religion" is helpful in opening up to "wider horizons of historical contacts." The "Science of Religion" is in itself "quite legitimate," provided it is done in a "spirit of self-criticism and readiness for self-revision."[129] Kraemer speaks of the "approach of love" to other religions. He favoured this view because a missionary study done through this approach would offer a more congenial understanding of the subject. This is a missionary approach by which a missionary, who, moved by "love to those he had to serve" tries to enter into their religious conditions and to understand these from within.[130] The "results of the so-called comparative study of religion" have helped us to better understand the varieties of religious life than ever before. The "painstaking and

---

[128] *The Open Secret.*, p. 183.

[129] Hendrik Kraemer, *World Cultures and World Religions: The Coming Dialogue* (London: Lutterworth Press, 1960), p. 240.

[130] Carl F. Hellencreutz, *Kraemer Towards Tambaram: A Study in Hendrik Kraemer's Missionary Approach* (Uppsala: Almqvist & Wiksells, 1966), pp. 102-3. Also see Kraemer's introduction of W. Brede Kristensen's book, *The Meaning of Religion* (The Hague: Martinus Nijhoff, 1960), where Kraemer points out that his approach to other religions was theological and that he has always defended the "ultimate rightness of a theological approach" (p. xxiv).

brilliant research" in this area have enabled us to understand the characteristic features of the various religions, their historical development and their spiritual habits. Kraemer speaks on a positive note in describing the results of the comparative study of the religions. Their similarities and differences, phenomena and institutions, history, psychology and philosophy are better known to us today than ever before. However, in his opinion, the important function of this "fruitful labour" in this field is to serve as an "eye-opener, paving the way for a more adequate - adequate *in bonam et in malam partem* - and intelligent judgement and evaluation about the meaning and function of religion in its many forms to the life of man."[131] Kraemer's advice is to develop the attitude of an "attentive and teachable hearer" to the results presented by this branch of study. His warning is that

> Comparative religion, however, can and must never become our authoritative guide. Its proper function is to be our intelligent and much appreciated informant. So used, and combined with the guidance we derive from biblical realism, it can help us enormously to combine, in our attitude towards the non-Christian religions as systems of life and experience, that downright intrepidity and radical humility about which I spoke in my book [*The Christian Message in a Non-Christian World*].[132]

Kraemer too had his thought on dialogue with people of other faiths and cultures. Although, like Newbigin, he believes that

---

[131] Hendrik Kraemer, "Continuity and Discontinuity," in *The Authority of the Faith* (London: Oxford University Press, 1939), p. 11.

[132] Ibid., p. 12.

there is a dark side to religion, he is in favour of dialogue with people of non-Christian religions. Kraemer was well aware of the Eastern religions and cultures and their influences in Western countries. The mutual appreciation of cultural values is a "precious and necessary gift" in a multi-cultural world.[133] The great religions of the world can no longer afford to ignore one another. In dialogue with people of other religions there should not be any need for arrogance on the part of Christians. On the other hand, Kraemer notes that amongst many Christians there is a `dominant an attitude (although somehow keeping to the conviction that the Christian Faith stands secure and supreme) of being deeply concerned about appearing humble and inclusive and avoiding any semblance of what is *called* religious arrogance or looks like "exclusiveness." '[134] Kraemer repudiates this compromising attitude, calling it a "spiritual disease."[135] The Christian Church must take more care to interpret the exclusive claim of Christianity, but this has to be done without arrogance, intolerance or dogmatic absolutism. This has to be seen as a real openness to truth wherever it may be found. Nevertheless, dialogue should not only be the concern of a few so-called experts. Rather,

> The time has now arrived when all theological thinkers have to include these new worlds of thought and apprehension in their sphere of interest. Not only for the *theoretical* reason of joining issue in philosophical and religious respect with thought- and life-systems, whose key concepts were for a long time mainly marginal in the cultural and religious world debate, but for *pastoral* reasons.

---

[133] Hendrik Kraemer, *World Cultures and World Religions*, p. 355.
[134] Ibid., p. 364.
[135] Ibid.

This pastoral aspect deserves special mention, because the "ordinary" people turn in their perplexity in the first place not to the leading Christian thinkers, but to their ministers and pastors.[136]

In Kraemer's view, there are two aims in dialogue, namely, a pragmatic aim and a fundamental aim. The pragmatic aim is to remove mutual misunderstandings and to serve common human tasks. The fundamental aim is the open exchange of witness, experience, cross-questioning and listening.[137] To become a partner of the dialogue, the Christian should have the conviction of the exclusive claim of the biblical message. The Christian position is founded on historical revelation. Asian religions, on the contrary, are ultimately "religious intuitionist-rationalist philosophies".[138] They teach the sublimity of unqualified Being with the mystic or sage triumphant through his or her victory in self-awakening. Over against this stands the image of the humility of God, incarnate in the humble suffering servant, Jesus Christ.

Being deeply influenced by the theology of Karl Barth, Kraemer refused to regard the Christian faith as merely one example of the larger phenomenon called 'religion.' He believed that Christian revelation must be distinguished from Christianity as a religion. Newbigin, commenting on Kraemer's method called 'biblical realism,' says that Kraemer was clear that God's work of grace outside the direct range of the gospel must be evaluated in the light of the unique event of the revelation in Christ, not the

---

[136]Ibid., p. 365.

[137]Hendrik Kraemer, *World Cultures and World Religions*, p. 356.

[138]Ibid., p. 370.

other way around.[139] Kraemer says that the "Man on the Cross" is the decisive revelatory act of God, whereas the Eastern religious philosophies posit "Self-Awakening over against Revelation as the true Way."[140] In Kraemer's view, inter-religious dialogue is not an end in itself, it is subordinated to the goal of mission. The exclusivist claim of the Bible cannot be compromised in the dialogue. Without being arrogant, the Christian participants should "show openness of mind and eagerness to learn" from the partners.[141] There is much to learn from others, and teachableness is as necessary as firmness.

While Kraemer is an exclusivist, Newbigin assumes a position which is a combination of inclusivism, exclusivism and pluralism. In the debate about continuity between non-Christian religions and Christianity, Kraemer proposes a radical discontinuity, while Newbigin believes that there is a radical discontinuity but not a total discontinuity. Newbigin and Kraemer agree on a wide range of issues on religion and inter-religious dialogue. But there are other conversation partners with whom Newbigin has less agreement. One such theological partner is Karl Rahner, who represents a major stream within the Roman Catholic tradition.

c. Karl Rahner

Karl Rahner's writing about the relation between Christianity and non-Christian religions has been a point of criticism in

---

[139]Newbigin, "The Christian Faith and the World Religions," Op. cit., p. 330.
[140]*World Cultures and World Religions*, p. 369.
[141]Ibid.

Newbigin's writings. While Newbigin does not treat Rahner's work in a comprehensive way, he is certainly interested in probing his idea of `Anonymous Christianity.'[142] Newbigin describes Rahner as a theologian who rejects both exclusivism on the one hand, and a total pluralism, on the other, taking an inclusivist position which acknowledges Christ as the only Saviour, while affirming that his saving work extends beyond the bounds of the visible church. What Newbigin is highlighting here is not the salvation of non-Christians, but Rahner's view of the salvific nature of non-Christian religions.[143] Four arguments by Rahner which Newbigin examines are to be noted here.[144]

First, Christianity understands itself as the absolute religion, which cannot recognize any other religion beside itself as of equal right.[145] Christianity rests on the incarnation, death and resurrection of Jesus Christ. This event of Christ did not always exist, but occurred at a certain point in history. Rahner points out,

> As a historical quantity Christianity has, therefore, a temporal and spatial starting point in Jesus of Nazareth and in the saving event of the unique Cross and the empty tomb in Jerusalem. It follows from this, however, that this absolute religion-even when it begins to be this for practically all men-must come in a historical way to men, facing them

---

[142]*The Open Secret*, pp. 195-197. Cf. *The Gospel in the Pluralist Society*, p. 174 f.
[143]*The Gospel in a Pluralist Society*, p. 174.
[144]Ibid.
[145]Karl Rahner, *Theological Investigations*, Vol. 5, translated by Karl-H. Kruger (London: Dartman, Longman & Todd, 1966), p. 118.

as the only legitimate demanding religion for them.[146]

Therefore, one has to ask about the relation of this founding event of Christianity to those who lived before it and to their religion. In Rahner's words, "Man who is commanded to have a religion is also commanded to seek and accept a social form of religion."[147] Second, non-Christian religions, even if they contain error, are salvific up to the time at which the gospel enters into the historical situation of the non-Christian individual.[148] But after the gospel has been preached and heard, the non-Christian religion is no longer lawful. Third, the faithful non-Christian believer must be regarded as an `anonymous Christian'. And he or she can be saved through his/her faithful practice of religion. But the one who accepts Christ has a still greater chance of salvation than someone who is merely an anonymous Christian.[149] Fourth, the other religions will not be displaced by Christianity and religious pluralism will continue and conflict will become sharper.

Newbigin believes that the notion of `anonymous Christianity' is "vulnerable at many points."[150] First of all, he is of the opinion that to call a devout non-Christian an anonymous Christian is to fail to take his or her faith seriously. To argue from the universal saving purpose of God to the salvific efficiency of non-Christian religions is to assume, without proving, that it is `religion' among all the activities of the human spirit which is the sphere of God's saving action. Newbigin rejects this view. Secondly, Newbigin wants to take a serious look at the world,

---

[146]Ibid., p. 119.
[147]Ibid., p. 120.
[148]Ibid., p. 121.
[149]Ibid., p. 132.
[150]*The Open Secret*, p. 195.

which includes the world of religions, as in a state of "alienation, rejection, and rebellion" against God.[151] The agony and the death of Christ compels him to say that

> Calvary is the central unveiling of the infinite love of God and at the same time the unmasking of the dark horror of sin. Here not the dregs of humanity, not the scoundrels whom all good people condemn, but the revered leaders in church, state, and culture, combine in one murderous intent to destroy the holy one by whose mercy they exist and were created.[152]

Newbigin wants to hold the doctrine of sin and the resultant alienation together with the doctrine of the divine grace of God. On this matter, his thoughts are closer to those of Hendrik Kraemer, who holds that the world is in a state of alienation and that it is in need of being reconciled to God.

Further, Newbigin's understanding of the wholeness of salvation calls in question aspects of Rahner's position. This may be expressed in line with the words of Harry McSorley, who considers Rahner's grounding of the mission of the Church to be inadequate.[153] McSorley offers two reasons for this inadequacy. First, the view that life in the Christian community makes the chance of salvation greater is not clear. Second, the term `Salvation' has been used by Rahner to denote only the final or ultimate dimension of salvation.[154] One way to overcome this

---

[151] *The Gospel in a Pluralist Society*, p. 175.

[152] Ibid.

[153] Harry McSorley, "God's Saving Activity and the Mission of the Church," unpublished paper, (Toronto: St. Michael's College, June 23, 1992), p. 3.

[154] Ibid.

problem is to think of salvation as a multidimensional reality as the Bible depicts it. What McSorley points out in this connection is consistent with the New Testament usage of the word. Accordingly, believers in Christ are said to have been saved; yet they are now being saved, and they will be saved. This is a past, present and future experience of salvation. There is a "Word" or "Noetic" dimension of salvation that can only be found in "obedience" to Jesus who speaks words of everlasting life. The saving knowledge involves both mind and heart. According to Paul's teaching, confessing with the mouth and believing with the heart are essential to salvation. Salvation comes by hearing the word of God.[155] Therefore, "anonymous Christianity is not enough; it is not commensurate with the "fullness of life" which Christ offers those who hear and heed his voice (Jn 10: 1-16)."[156] McSorley is right when he says,

> The very faithful Jew is told by Jesus that he is still lacking something that will be found only in the explicit following of Jesus (Mk 10:21; Lk 18:22). Similarly, the most enlightened Buddhist will be lacking something until he is enlightened by the One who is the Light of the world (Jn 8:12; II Cor 4:6).[157]

But McSorley's critique stems from the Roman Catholic position of grace perfecting nature, which differs from Newbigin's understanding. The one thing "lacking" is not supplied by an addition, but a radical turn-about. Thus Newbigin would argue that what is needed is a radical conversion which results in the following of Jesus. In this way McSorley and Newbigin differ in

---

[155]Romans 10: 9-10, 17.
[156]McSorley, Op. cit., p. 6.
[157]Ibid.

their criticisms of Rahner.

However, Newbigin is in support of Karl Rahner's basic understanding of the inclusiveness of the divine grace in other religions, a theme which I shall expound later in this chapter. It suffices us to say at this point that Newbigin recognizes the grace of God in other religions. God, who is the creator and sustainer of the world, is an "ocean of infinite love overflowing to all his works in all creation and to all human beings."[158] Jesus welcomed the signs of faith among persons outside the house of Israel and he welcomed those whom others cast out. His prayer of forgiveness on the cross for those who crucified him is a sure sign of a grace, mercy and lovingkindness which reaches out to every creature.[159] Newbigin is close to Rahner's inclusiveness when he affirms:

> I believe that no person, of whatever kind or creed, is without some witness of God's grace in heart and conscience and reason, and none in whom that grace does not evoke some response - however feeble, fitful, and flawed.[160]

3. NEWBIGIN AND THE PLURALIST THEOLOGIANS

Although there are several major 'pluralist' theologians with varying degrees of commitment to the idea of pluralism, they have a common emphasis on 'truth-in-all-religions'. Newbigin engages several of them in his writings, some of them in more detail than others. I shall cite here the arguments of Wilfred Cantwell Smith, Diana L. Eck, Paul Knitter, John Hick and Gordon D. Kaufman.

---

[158] *The Gospel in a Pluralist Society*, p. 175.
[159] Ibid.
[160] Ibid.

Some of them, with Lesslie Newbigin, participated in the celebration of the fiftieth anniversary of the World Missionary Conference at Tambaram in 1988. The discussions and essays occasioned by the celebration are a clear example of the contemporary pluralistic approach to the Christian faith, and they are published in the *International Review of Mission* for July, 1988. These essays are an important source for this study, because all of these writers interact with Newbigin and Hendrik Kraemer. Therefore, it is appropriate for me to refer to the writings of these theologians to show how Newbigin differs from them.

a. Wilfred Cantwell Smith

Wilfred Cantwell Smith is author of many books and countless articles. It is not my purpose here to expound his ideas thoroughly. He showed a tremendous interest in developing a "meaning" for Christian mission from a pluralist point of view.[161] How does he come to explore this new meaning?

Smith's starting point is his realization that the present age in which we are called upon to think and to act is drastically different from any other. There are reasons for his understanding of the novelty of this age. First of all, in this new age all humankind is living "intertwined" in the realms of thought, knowledge, of understanding, including inter-religious, interfaith, awareness.[162] Secondly, when the Christian mission began to expand at the beginning of the nineteenth century, Western Christendom was enormously ignorant of the rest of the world and especially of the

---

[161] "Mission, Dialogue, and God's Will for Us" in the *International Review of Mission*, Vol. LXXVIII, No. 307 (July, 1988), pp. 360-374.

[162] Ibid., p. 360.

"majority of the great religious complexes." Even in New Testament times, he claims, Paul suffered from ignorance of other religions. For example, he had never heard of Buddhism. If he had, he might have thought and written differently than he did.[163] Paul and other biblical writers were aware of only two spiritual movements besides their own Judaism, namely, Greek Philosophy (in the realm of thought) and the Roman Empire (in the realm of social order). Religious plurality, as it is known today, was neither well-recognized nor exclusivistically dealt with by the Church in New Testament times, argues Smith.

The non-Christian religions - Hinduism, Buddhism, Islam, Sikhism and the rest - are great movements of the human spirit, each with historical legacies of cultural moment, and of scientific, theological, sociological, political, and artistic heritage, and also of "great spiritual depth," and as some people now add, "salvific force."[164] The Christian missionary enterprise was not aware of this richness, but it eventually ran into it. It is the lack of adequate response to this richness of other religions until now that requires us to move forward in our understanding of the meaning of mission. Smith proposes the idea that the mission of the Church, God's active purpose in world history being carried out by the Christian movement, need not be, and is not, God's only mission in the world. It cannot be confined within the limits of one geographical segment or one ecclesiastical organization or one historical religious movement.[165] Therefore, the Church has to understand the activity of God in all other religious movements. God's mission in the Church is only part of His whole mission to humankind, not His whole mission to one part of humankind, which Smith calls the "fallacy of indifference," nor His sole

---

[163]Ibid., pp. 360, 361.
[164]Ibid., p. 361.
[165]Ibid., p. 366.

mission to the whole of humankind, which is the "fallacy of arrogance."[166] The exclusivism of "narrow mission people" is "blasphemous," and they are disloyal to Christ. In favour of pluralism, which demands equal standing for all religions, Smith argues that

> It is an impoverishment of life, but an impoverishment also of theology, not to take seriously God's mission to us all through all traditions, all his servants everywhere. In a way, this constitutes my central presentation here: that it is not only intellectually, and morally, wrong, to fail to recognize God's mission to other people through their traditions; and nowadays, through those traditions and those other people, to us. More than simply wrong, theologically one may say that it is blasphemous.[167]

This argument is based on what Smith calls "affinity" between religions. For example, he sees that there is often more affinity between certain Christians and certain Muslims, or certain Hindus, than there is among Christians themselves. If the Church is called a "divine - human complex in action," it is imperative that we recognize that the Islamic movement, the Hindu, the Buddhist and the others have been that also.

The Christian church needs a combination of "sensitivity and historical awareness" in order to discern both the "divine and the human dimensions" in their ever-changing relation to each other from day to day, millennium to millennium, both in our own

---

[166]Ibid.
[167]Ibid. p. 367.

case and in that of other religious traditions around the world.[168] This discernment would be "enriching, rewarding, liberating," and "theologically constructive", because it enables humankind to discern "God's ways of entering human life" and humankind's various ways of living up to that presence only approximately.[169] For Smith, theology is a "human construct" like a work of art, as it has been always, and as we do the same thing today, we should take into account all the new perceptions of our own age. Smith vehemently opposes the views of Hendrik Kraemer, whose ideas about the non-Christian religions stirred up controversy at the Tambaram Conference of 1938. Smith's contention is that Kraemer, although a "great-hearted man," has failed in doing justice either to himself or to "modern awareness" in his theories. Smith believes that doing theology means correlating the Christian heritage with this modern awareness of our time in the best possible way, consonant with the thought of our time.[170]

Smith supports the view that people of non-Christian religions "richly participate in the grace of God and in his bounty", and like Christians, they have inherited formulations from an earlier age articulating this fact in theoretical patterns."[171] The destinies of the people of all religions are "intertwined both here on earth and spiritually ("in heaven"). What follows from this theory is that Christians should join Christianly with people of all other religions in collaborative exploration of their various visions of truth and good. Each religious tradition is severally participating in the one mission of God. They should aim at a better world which is different from the modern gloomy and unpromising world. According to Smith's scheme, participation in this venture in this

---

[168] Ibid., p. 371.
[169] Ibid.
[170] "Mission, Dialogue, and God's Will for Us," p. 372.
[171] Ibid.

interrelated world is the mission of the Christian church.

Newbigin intensely criticizes Smith's idea of the Transcendent. In his review of Smith's book *The Meaning and End of Religion*,[172] Newbigin states that his use of this term is "purely formal." It could be personal or impersonal, benevolent or malevolent. But in Smith's writing, because he is a Christian, his use of the term is filled with Christian content. If this were absent, the argument would lose much of its persuasiveness. All religions, in Smith's view, have as their core some experience of the Transcendent. In his essay on "Idolatry," Smith expands this concept by saying that the Transcendent makes himself or herself or itself present to humans by means of images made of wood and stone or images made in the mind or even of such an image as the man Jesus.[173] To claim uniqueness for one form of response to the Transcendent is preposterous and blasphemous. In Newbigin's view, Smith's category of the Transcendent (whether he, she, or it) may be conceived in any way the worshipper may choose.[174] This would lead to the conclusion that there is no false or misdirected worship since the reality to which it is directed is unknowable. Further, the uniqueness of the Christian concept of the Transcendent present fully in Jesus Christ becomes wholly unacceptable. There are therefore no criteria by which the Transcendent may be tested. As a result, one is "shut up to a total

---

[172](London: SPCK, 1978) reviewed by Newbigin in *Theology*, Vol., LXXXII, No. 688 (July 1979), pp. 294-296.

[173] John Hick and Paul Knitter, eds., *The Myth of Christian Uniqueness: Toward a Pluralistic Theology of Religions* (Maryknoll, New York: Orbis Books, 1987), p. 65. Newbigin's review of this book may be found in *The Ecumenical Review*, Vol. 41, No. 3 (July 1989), pp. 468-69.

[174] *The Gospel in a Pluralist Society*, p. 161.

subjectivity: the Transcendent is unknowable."[175] Newbigin argues, it is one thing to say that 'God has not fully revealed himself to me in Jesus Christ' and it is another thing to say that 'God has fully revealed himself in Christ, but my grasp of this revelation is not comprehensive.' But Smith is claiming that God reveals himself everywhere to every human person however varied may be the forms in which they express that revelation. Smith himself may not accept them as equally valid, because, for example, Hitler believed that he had a divine mission.[176] On what grounds would one reject his claim? By making this distinction and asking this question, Newbigin has shown Smith's argument to be self-defeating.

Smith has hesitations about the term 'dialogue'. He believes that it might convey the idea of a "confrontation: an encounter between two parties; a 'we-they' or at best a 'we-you' orientation."[177] For him, it suggests two groups, who come together to converse yet remain two and distinct. Two is inadequate, and even three is preliminary. He says that the Jewish-Christian dialogue is inevitably skewed, because it has not included also Muslims. Smith's concern is that dialogue should not be seen as an opportunity for a "bilateral encounter" between two opposing parties. He believes that people of differing religions and culture and language have one thing in common, namely, they are all human and they are all potentially or actually genuine in their devotion to truth.[178] Smith believes that both mission and dialogue

---

[175]Ibid.

[176]Ibid., p. 165.

[177]"Mission, Dialogue, and God's Will for Us," pp. 368-69. Even better, Smith prefers colloquy to dialogue, because the former has multilateral connotations. The latter has a face-to-face confronting of each other. See his *Towards a World Theology* (Philadelphia: Westminster Press, 1981), p. 193.

[178]Ibid., p. 371.

should converge, or they are to be moved forwards to the point where they coalesce. The Christian mission today is to co-operate with all humankind.[179]

b. Diana L. Eck

Another pluralist theologian who battles Newbigin's exclusivism is Diana Eck of Harvard University. She is moderator of the sub-unit on Dialogue with People of Living Faiths of the World Council of Churches. In her book *Encountering God*,[180] she criticizes the stance taken by Newbigin, Barth, and Visser t'Hooft as "unpersuasive."[181] She contends that Jesus is unique only as all human beings are unique, with particular parents, place and time of birth, etc. But uniqueness, for her, does not mean the story of Jesus "is the only story of God's dealings with humanity, nor the only true and complete story." And she goes on to say that the language of <u>only</u> is the language of faith, not of statistics.[182]

Eck affirms with Newbigin that "God's incarnation in Jesus Christ is unique," and "there is nothing to put beside that revelation."[183] However, she also maintains that

> People of other faiths also witness to the truth, the transcendence, the universality, the uniqueness of what they have seen. It is not weak-hearted relativism to recognize this as a fact, nor is it a

---

[179] Ibid., p. 374.
[180] (Boston: Beacon Press, 1993).
[181] Ibid., p. 87.
[182] Ibid., p. 89.
[183] "The Religions and Tambaram: 1938 and 1988" in the *International Review of Mission*, vol. LXXVIII, No. 307 (July, 1988), p. 375.

> betrayal of our faith in Christ. The question posed by this fact is an urgent one. How does our knowledge of and life with people of other faiths - be they neighbors, colleagues, friends, or even members of our own families - recast our understanding of ourselves as Christians and our understanding of the task and mission of the church?[184]

This is a call for reformulating the Christian message in relation to the people of other faiths. Like some other participants of the Tambaram conference, she criticizes the "very specific" and "narrow way" in which Hendrik Kraemer treats Christian revelation. For Kraemer, God's revelation found its full, unique and decisive fulfillment in Jesus Christ. This is a view that she opposes strongly, because in her words:

> As a Christian, I can bear witness to what God has done for me, for the people in my family of faith, for those of us who call ourselves Christians, and indeed for all people. But I cannot make claims as to what God has *not* done for the Hindu or for the Muslim. For the affirmation of the Hindu or Muslim as to God's revealing, I must listen to the witness of the Hindu or Muslim and seek to understand what he or she has to say.[185]

Eck affirms with Wilfred Cantwell Smith that the good news is not only that God did something in first century Palestine, but also that God goes on doing something, so that the "locus of revelation is

---

[184]Ibid., p. 376.
[185]Ibid., p. 382.

always the present, and always the person."[186] Eck finds no difficulty in accepting the central emphasis of Lesslie Newbigin's sermon,[187] namely, the revelation in Jesus Christ is a real historical event, with a date and place, but she insists with Cantwell Smith that the date and place of God's revelation is not only in first century Palestine, but in "each century, in each decade, on each continent."[188] Therefore, she sees in the worship of Krishna, something of the "humility and vulnerability of God's incarnation in the person of Jesus."[189] She claims that this kind of understanding and discovery about the revelation of God will not lead to the relativization or domestication of Jesus. Rather, it "unleashes the incarnate One from domestication in first century Palestine into a world of life and death, diversity and struggle, today."[190]

For Newbigin, Eck's statement about God's revelation being "always in the present and always to the person"[191] has the tone of a "purely individualistic spirituality, the understanding of the human person as a being existing apart from the history of which every human life is a part."[192] Newbigin does not ignore the deeply personal spiritual experiences which may share common elements, even though occurring in different cultural contexts. But these cannot be taken in isolation from the shared life of the human race

---

[186] Ibid., p. 385.
[187] Lesslie Newbigin, "A Sermon preached at the Thanksgiving Service for the Fiftieth Anniversary of the Tambaram Conference of the International Missionary Council" in the *International Review of Mission*, Op. cit., pp. 325-331.
[188] "The Religions and Tambaram: 1938 and 1988," p. 385.
[189] Ibid., p. 386.
[190] Ibid.
[191] Ibid., p. 385.
[192] *The Gospel in a Pluralistic Society*, p. 164.

as the clue to the ultimate meaning of life. Human life is both personal and corporate. Each life-story is a part of the whole human story. In Newbigin's words,

> The trinitarian faith brings together these two aspects of human existence, assuring us that the one who is the source and sustainer and goal of all reality, and the one who is made known in the deepest experiences of the human spirit, is one with the man, this particular man, who went his humble way from Bethlehem to Calvary. There is thus no dichotomy between the inward experiences of the heart and the outward history of which each of us is a part.[193]

God's revelation in Christ is not simply an event which recedes farther and farther into the past; rather, through the work of the Holy Spirit we are led into an ever fuller understanding as the Spirit takes of the things of Jesus and shows them to us through the experiences of our place and time.[194] Therefore, Newbigin rejects Eck's and other pluralists' "individual subjectivity." The individual experience has to be sustained, nourished, and tested by continual reference back to the original witnesses of the revelation and by reference to the continuing experience of those who share with us the allegiance to Jesus.[195]

While Newbigin and Eck are in profound disagreement with each other on the nature of Christian revelation, their views come closer to each other on the purpose of inter-religious dialogue. Dialogue, for Eck, is for mutual understanding and questioning.[196]

---

[193]Ibid.
[194]Ibid.
[195]Ibid.
[196]"The Religions and Tambaram: 1938 and 1988," p. 378.

In dialogue, partners do not talk about other partners; they talk with them. We do not settle for "one-way proclamation, announcement and witness," but also invite the testimony and witness of the partners.[197] To turn away from such mutuality is to settle for a "totalitarian regime of faith."[198]

c. Paul Knitter

Paul Knitter is co-editor with John Hick of the popular book *The Myth of Christian Uniqueness*, which Newbigin has reviewed. The kind of pluralistic theology set forth in this volume has aroused much controversy in theological circles and was directly responded to by Newbigin and other writers. Before considering the Newbigin-Knitter interaction, we have to see the thrust of the theology proposed by Knitter in this book. Knitter explains in the preface why the authors are calling the Christian uniqueness a "myth." He says that it is not because they think that talk of the uniqueness of Christianity is purely and simply false, and so to be discarded. Rather, like all mythic language, such talk must be understood very carefully.[199] "Christianity is unique," says Knitter, "in the precise and literal sense in which every religious tradition is unique - namely that there is only one of it and that there is therefore nothing else exactly like it."[200] Knitter charges that the uniqueness of Christianity has taken on a mythological meaning, because it has come to signify the "unique definitiveness, absoluteness, normativeness, superiority of Christianity in comparison with other religions of the world."[201] It is this mythological sense that the authors of the book are criticizing. The

---

[197]Ibid.
[198]Ibid.
[199]*The Myth of Christian Uniqueness*, p. vii.
[200]Ibid.
[201]Ibid.

pluralistic model they are suggesting is to be understood as a new paradigm shift in theology.

This method of approaching religions is quite different from and opposed to the position Newbigin takes, because the pluralistic shift is a "move away from insistence on the superiority or finality of Christ and Christianity toward a recognition of the independent validity of other ways."[202] Such a move has been described by Knitter as "the crossing of a theological Rubicon."[203]

Knitter, along with others, writes with a motivation to confront the "sufferings of humanity and the need to put an end to such outrages."[204] To accomplish this, people of all religions must promote justice. According to Knitter,

> Economic, political, and especially nuclear liberation is too big a job for any one nation, or culture, *or* religion. Therefore a crosscultural interreligious cooperation in liberative praxis and a sharing of liberative theory is called for.[205]

The religions of the world have to accept a shared concern for justice as the starting point and guiding norm for their efforts at dialogue.

---

[202]Ibid., p. viii.

[203]Ibid. The essays are in three groups, each group representing a theological bridge, namely, `The Historico-Cultural Bridge: Relativity,' `The Theologico-Mystical Bridge: Mystery,' and `The Ethico-Practical Bridge: Justice." Knitter's essay "Toward a Liberation Theology of Religions" appears in the third group which deals with the criterion of justice.

[204]Ibid., p. xi.

[205]The Myth of Christian Uniqueness, p. 179.

Newbigin sees two main problems with the ethico-practical bridge which uses `justice' as the criterion. First, the concept of justice could be one's own understanding of justice. Newbigin says that it is notorious that the demand for justice is precisely what fuels war. In the absence of a Judge, each one is judge in one's own cause.[206] He adds, it is part of the corruption of human nature that we overestimate what is due to ourselves. Newbigin's reference point for justice is the gospel, which affirms a justice which is the gift of God through God's own acceptance of the cost of human injustice. The justice of God has been revealed in the real history of the crucifixion of Christ and it relativizes our rival claims for justice.[207] Second, if there is no firm statement about the ultimate Mystery, there is no ontological ground for the "preferential option for the poor."[208] There is a reason for law courts, argues Newbigin. None of us can be trusted to be judge in our own cause. Newbigin, in his essay "Religion for the Marketplace," warns against absolutizing words like `justice' and `liberation', because by absolutizing them one remains locked into one's own definitions of what these words mean.[209] The concept of justice and its realization, in Newbigin's words, cannot be viewed separately from the centrality of the cross of Christ who is the Lord and Judge. This centrality is essential for the realization of a justice and a freedom which are truly God's gift, and for deliverance from one's own

---

[206]Lesslie Newbigin, Review of *The Myth of Christian Uniqueness* in *The Ecumenical Review*, Vol. 41, No. 3 (July 1989), p. 469.
[207]Ibid.
[208]Ibid.
[209]Gavin D'Costa, ed., *Christian Uniqueness Reconsidered: The Myth of a Pluralistic Theology of Religions* (Maryknoll, New York: Orbis Books, 1990), p. 146.

imperial pretensions.[210]

Knitter's understanding of religion from a soteriocentric view, as he suggests in his essay, is grounded on concepts such as *moksha* and liberation. It is the common search for salvation that offers the basis for human unity.[211] A soteriocentric approach is "less prone to (though never fully immune from) ideological abuse," because it does not impose its own views of God or the Ultimate on other religions. He claims that this approach would be more faithful to the data of comparative religions. All of these religions, says Knitter, have a thrust that is soteriological in nature.

Against Knitter's contention, Newbigin affirms his Christocentric view, the view of Christ whose historic records are available for examination.[212] Knitter is fully aware of Newbigin's `salvation is only in Christ' position, which he discusses in his major book *No Other Name?*, alongside that of other mainline Protestant theologians.[213] Knitter charges that Protestant theologians, including Newbigin, "exclude an authentic understanding of salvation in other religions."[214] This Protestant model of understanding other religions is inadequate, according to Knitter, because it ties salvation specifically to the Christ-event. Although he thinks this model offers insights, especially in the area of general revelation, Knitter proposes that it should be modified and radically revised.[215]

---

[210] Ibid., p. 147.

[211] *The Myth of Christian Uniqueness*, p. 187.

[212] *Christian Uniqueness Reconsidered*, Op. cit., p. 142.

[213] Paul F. Knitter, *No Other Name?: A Critical Survey of Christian Attitudes Toward the World Religions* (Maryknoll, New York: Orbis Books, 1985), pp. 97, 108.

[214] Ibid., p. 118.

[215] Ibid., p. 119.

d. John Hick

John Hick is a prominent and influential theologian who vehemently argues for a pluralistic approach to religions. He has published many essays and books to explain and defend his view of religion, some relevant points of which shall be considered here. Newbigin is a strong critic of Hick and their views on central issues of Christianity are radically contradictory to each other. He views Hick as "one of the most influential of those who disclaim any uniqueness or centrality for Christianity" among the world's religions.[216] In this section I shall introduce briefly some of Hick's religious presuppositions, and in a later section, shall comment further on his work on 'Inter-religious Dialogue.'

As co-editor and one of the authors of *The Myth of Christian Uniqueness*, Hick advances his ideas from a historico-cultural perspective. Standing with Gordon Kaufman, Hick uses "Historical consciousness" as his starting point for doing theology. Hick, speaking from this perspective, directs his criticism against the exclusivist understanding of Christianity. In his essay, "The Non-Absoluteness of Christianity," he attacks the absolutist claim of Christianity for many reasons.[217] First, there is a new explosion of knowledge among the western Christians about the "immense

---

[216] Lesslie Newbigin, "The Christian Faith and the World Religions," in *Keeping the Faith*, p. 316.

[217] *The Myth of Christian Uniqueness*, pp. 16-36. See also his *The Myth of God Incarnate* (Philadelphia: Westminster Press, 1977) and *The Metaphor of God Incarnate* (Louisville, Kentucky: Westminster/ John Knox Press, 1993) where he argues that the idea of divine incarnation is better understood as metaphorical than as literal (p. 12).

spiritual riches" of other religions. He claims that after the two world wars, "ill-informed and hostile Western stereotypes" of the other religious faiths have been increasingly replaced by "more accurate knowledge and more sympathetic understanding."[218] This modern knowledge has tended to erode the plausibility of the old Christian exclusivism. Second, the realization that Christian absolutism, in collaboration with "acquisitive and violent human nature," has damaged the relationships between the Christian minority and the non-Christian majority of the world.[219] By referring here to "aggressive imperialism," Hick charges western Christianity with "sanctifying exploitation and oppression on a gigantic scale."[220] He adds that the link between Christian absolutism and the historical evils of the colonial West is "not one of a priori logical necessity" but is a factual link via "fallen human nature that Christianity has been largely powerless to redeem."[221] However, it should be emphasized that Hick is not accusing Christianity alone of the harmful effects of religious absolutism; almost every religion is guilty of it.

Hick's approach does not allow an "ultimate religious superiority" of any one religion. According to this vision, Christianity is seen as one of the world religions having no claims to superiority and "one of the streams of religious life" through which human beings can be "savingly related to that Ultimate Reality" which for Christians is the heavenly Father. Since salvation takes place in every religious tradition, for Hick, it seems "arbitrary and unrealistic" to keep on highlighting that the "Christ-event is the sole and exclusive source of human salvation."[222] The

---

[218] *The Myth of Christian Uniqueness*, p. 17.
[219] Ibid.
[220] Ibid.
[221] Ibid.
[222] Ibid., p. 22.

Christian tradition is "one of a plurality of contexts of salvation - contexts, that is to say, within which the transformation of human existence from self-centredness to God- or Reality-centeredness is occurring."[223] Hick asks:

> When it is acknowledged that Jews are being saved within and through the Jewish stream of religious life, Muslims within and through the Islamic stream, Hindus within and through the Hindu stream, and so on, can it be more than a hangover from the old religious imperialism of the past to insist upon attaching a Christian label to salvation within these other households of faiths. This would be like the anomaly of accepting the Copernican revolution in astronomy, in which the earth ceased to be regarded as the centre of the universe and was seen instead as one of the planets circling the sun, but still insisting that the sun's life-giving rays can reach the other planets only by first being reflected from the earth![224]

The "transformation from self-centeredness to Reality-centeredness" is a much used expression in Hick's writing. Although this is not a sufficiently clear concept, he uses this to refer to a kind of a salvation experience. This transformation is being promoted by each religion more or less to the same extent. Because of this, Hick sees "no good grounds for maintaining that

---

[223] Ibid., p. 23.

[224] Ibid., pp. 22-23.

Christianity has produced or is producing more saints, in proportion to population, or a higher quality of saintliness, than any other of the great streams of religious life." However, he recognizes that this point cannot be proved or disproved.[225]

Since each religion, according to Hick, has its own "unique mixture of good and evil," and each is a "long-lived social reality", some of its aspects promote human good and others damage the human family. Therefore, it is wrong to judge that any particular religion has contributed more good or less evil, or "a more favorable balance of good and evil than the others."[226]

Hick has no difficulty in rejecting the assumption that it is God's will that all of humankind should be converted to the Christian faith. What supports his rejection is the argument from numbers, that is, the Christian faith is held only by a minority of the human race.[227] The small number of Christians compared to the large majority of non-Christians existing outside the church has been a vexing problem for Hick. These non-Christians have up to the present moment lived and died before Christ or outside the periphery of Christendom. This vision of the non-Christians has brought about in him a change of view, a change from an

---

[225]Ibid., p. 24.
[226]Ibid., p. 30.
[227]John Hick, " Whatever Path Men Choose is Mine" in *Christianity and Other Religions*, John Hick and Brian Hebblethwaite, eds. (Philadelphia: Fortress Press, 1980), p.172. The inspiration of Hick's essay appears to have come from a verse from the *Bhagavad Gita*, IV. II, which says, "Howsoever man may approach me, even so do I accept them; for, on all sides, whatever path they may choose is mine."

exclusivist to a pluralist understanding of religions.[228] He criticizes and rejects the old slogan, *extra ecclesiam nulla salus*. It is a "moral contradiction" to conclude that the God of love who seeks to save all humankind would nevertheless ordain salvation in such a way that only a small minority in the church would be eligible to receive this.[229]

Hick finds a "phenomenological similarity of worship" in all religions. Non-Christian places of worship have the "same kind of thing" as the Christian church. This observation contributes to his conclusion that there is but one God and the people in the various great religions are worshipping that one God, but "through different, overlapping concepts or mental images of him."[230] There are many forms but the same worship.

In Hick's understanding, the great world religions arose within the different "streams of human life" and have flowed down the centuries within different cultural channels. Each of them has undergone immense historical "developments, revolutions and transformations."[231] He predicts that the future of Christianity will be formed partly by influences from Hinduism, Buddhism and Islam. Consequently, differences between world religions will be less important in an age of "growing world ecumenism."[232] However, this prediction of Hick should not be construed as a forecast of a single world religion, but a situation in which the

---

[228] John Hick, *God and the Universe of Faith: Essays in the Philosophy of Religion* (London: The Macmillan Press Ltd., 1973), p. 122.

[229] Ibid., pp. 122-123.

[230] "Whatever Path Men Choose is Mine," in *Christianity and Other Religions*, pp. 174, 178.

[231] Ibid., p. 187.

[232] Ibid.

different traditions no longer see themselves and each other as "rival ideological" communities. A "single world religion is never likely, and not a consummation to be desired."[233]

In Newbigin's opinion, writers like John Hick, identifying Christianity with western imperial power, miss the present reality of western culture where Christianity has long ceased to be its public doctrine.[234] Hick's idea of salvation, that is, the salvific "transformation of human existence from self-centredness to Reality- centredness" draws severe criticism from Newbigin.

Newbigin's major contention is that Hick has no "accepted account of Reality." There is no "compelling evidence" about the nature of what Hick calls "Reality." Therefore, there is no criterion available to pass judgments on the different conceptions of 'Reality' embodied in the different religions and the secular traditions.[235] Hick's position is "logically self-defeating," because there is no way of knowing that there is a Reality which is unknown. He says,

> There are, after all, confident affirmations by Muslims and Marxists and Christians and Buddhists about what reality is. On the basis of what prior knowledge is it possible to deny that any of these claims is true? If something is truly unknown, then there is nothing to be said.[236]

Accepting Hicks' understanding of "Reality" would lead one to

---

[233] Ibid., p. 189.
[234] Newbigin, Review of *The Myth of Christian Uniqueness*, p. 469.
[235] Newbigin, *Christian Uniqueness Reconsidered*, p. 141.
[236] Ibid., pp. 141-142.

invent one's own conception of it. And by doing this, one becomes oneself the centre by implication. Hick's move from a Christocentric worldview to a Reality-centric view[237] is a move from a view "centered in the objective reality of the man Jesus Christ" to a view centered in a subjective conception of ultimate Reality.[238] Newbigin believes that Hick is trying to avoid the claims of truth. To separate the quest for salvation from the business of understanding the truth about the cosmos is a "recipe for disaster."[239] Religions offer ways to salvation because they make truth claims. These claims are in many cases "mutually irreconcilable."[240] No one can evade the question of distinguishing truth from error. A pluralism that evades this question is a "sign of the approaching death of a culture."[241]

We shall have reason to return to Hick's thought again in the next chapter.

e. Gordon D. Kaufman

Gordon Kaufman expresses his concern for the unity of humankind and the need for world peace in the face of the threat of a nuclear holocaust. It is with the aim of unity in mind that he proposes the new task for Christian theology. Writing from the perspective of what is called, `modern historical consciousness,' Kaufman argues that there is a limitation of all knowledge and religious beliefs and therefore it is difficult, if not impossible, to judge the truth claims of another culture or religion on the basis of

---

[237] *The Myth of Christian Uniqueness*, p. 23.
[238] *Christian Uniqueness Reconsidered*, p. 143.
[239] Ibid.
[240] Ibid.
[241] Ibid.

one's own.[242]

In his essay on "Religious Diversity, Historical Consciousness, and Christian Theology," Kaufman draws the picture of a world which faces the threat of nuclear war. This should drive all religions to dialogue and cooperation. A necessary condition for such dialogue should be the understanding of the historical relativity of all religious forms, which disallows the uniqueness of any one religion. Kaufman says,

> The tendencies toward absoluteness and exclusivity in traditional Christian faith easily lead to a kind of idolatry that makes it difficult to take other faiths seriously in their own terms, searching out their insights into human existence and deepest human problems, attending carefully to their proposals regarding how those problems should be approached.[243]

To address this problem, Kaufman proposes that Christians follow certain implications of our modern historical consciousness, and the kind of reflection it engenders, as they work out the theological understanding of their faith. The way to break through the tendencies toward absoluteness and self-idolatry that often obstruct interaction between Christians and others can be provided by historical and comparative studies of human religiousness.[244] Kaufman says that neither Christians nor non-Christians possess absolute or final truth, truth adequate to orient humankind in face of the enormous problems of the world. The understanding and

---

[242] *The Myth of Christian Uniqueness*, p. ix.
[243] Ibid., p. 5.
[244] Ibid.

insights of our forebears are "finite, limited and relative."[245] He vigorously argues that Christians must "break the grips of absolutistic commitments" that have characterized much traditional Christian faith and theology. This would clear the way to an encounter with other religious and secular traditions "in their own terms" instead of Christian terms.[246] Here Kaufman seems to give a one-sided call to Christians to meet others in their own terms. Does he want the non-Christian believers to meet Christians in Christian terms?

Inter-religious dialogue is important in Kaufman's scheme. Because the threat of nuclear war has pushed people of all religions into a common fate, and in order to escape from this danger, all religions must bring together all the wisdom, devotion, and insight that humanity has accumulated through its long history.[247] Inter-religious dialogue is an opportunity to learn from each other and to bring together all resources for the promotion of peace in today's world. The purpose of the dialogue is not "to get information about points of view different from our own." Rather, it is to help humanity "to find adequate orientation in today's world" and "to construct religious frameworks that can provide genuine guidance with respect to the unprecedented problems" of the world.[248] Dialogue can help each one to understand each other, to evaluate each one's strengths and weaknesses, and to appreciate the insights and understanding of positions quite different from one's own. How does Newbigin react to Kaufman's propositions?

Newbigin understands Kaufman's need for human unity, but he thinks that Kaufman's 'historical consciousness' requires

---

[245] Ibid., p. 13.
[246] Ibid., p. 14.
[247] Ibid., p. 13.
[248] Ibid.

Christians to abandon Christ's uniqueness. He points out,

> It is true that modern historical studies enable us to see that people in other times and places were looking at the world through culturally conditioned lenses and that their claim to "see things as they really are" is relativized by our studies in the history of cultures. But to suppose that modern historical consciousness gives us a privileged standpoint where we really do see things as they really are, is of course unsupported dogma. Modern historical consciousness is also the product of a particular culture and can claim no epistemological privilege.[249]

Newbigin believes that Kaufman's theology also rests on his own truth claims and ultimate commitments, but his "modern historical consciousness" also makes culturally conditioned truth claims and it is a culture-product.

Newbigin disagrees with Kaufman's scheme for human unity which ignores the viable centre for such a unity in the gospel. There has to be some centre, some vision of what it is to be human which can hold together the diversity of human desires. Newbigin uses the centrality of the gospel as a rallying point for humankind. He believes that a centre has been provided in the gospel around which it is possible for human beings to become one, because "their sins against one another are forgiven and their conflicting wills and desires are cleansed of their egotism and directed toward their true goal."[250]

---

[249] *The Gospel in a Pluralist Society*, p. 160.
[250] *Christian Uniqueness Reconsidered*, p. 139.

Every religious tradition, not just Christianity, makes truth-claims, says Newbigin. In this respect, religions are in the same category as the scientific tradition. Newbigin opposes the theological task outlined by Kaufman, for it is suggesting that Christians should give up their tradition and accept a different tradition.

Concluding Critical Comments

In conclusion, one could say that in the works of all the pluralist theologians cited above, we find a persistent argument for the unity of religions based on the interrelated, intertwined and interdependent nature of human existence. Most often the motivating factor for promoting this unity is the need for contributing solutions to the many sociological, ecological and political crises of the world. The belief that Christianity alone can address these issues in an intertwined and interrelated world appears preposterous to them. The capacity of the gospel to transcend the cultural and linguistic barriers, its universal salvific appeal and the central point of unity are neglected.

Pluralism poses a great challenge to some of the basic doctrines of the Christian church concerning Christ as the only Saviour of the world, and the need to proclaim Christ to all people. Smith opposes the biblical notion of the church's mission by developing an alternative meaning of mission. He does not want the Christian mission to be understood as God's only mission in the world.

Generally speaking, we may observe that the arguments of religious pluralists make little distinction between 'religion' and 'culture'. Especially in many non-western cultures, because of their integrated worldview, religion and culture cannot easily be separated, and Newbigin recognizes this. However, to eliminate the distinction is to reduce the significance of particular truth claims. Among the proponents of religious pluralism, there is a consolidated effort to reduce all religions to the same phenomenon, which is to deny the unique question that each religion asks and answers. Hick's argument that the different religions are different responses to the same God can be very problematic for two reasons. First, truth in religion becomes a matter of where a person was born. To use the expression of Alister McGrath, this is a "shockingly naive view of truth" which ends up "destroying the notion of truth itself."[251] Second, this understanding of pluralism destroys the very notion of mission, which is a biblical command to the Church.

Newbigin rightly condemns pluralism as an ideology, while allowing the plurality of religions, in the sense of tolerating and respecting the existence of other religions. Pluralism, which denies the uniqueness of Jesus Christ, poses serious problems to the life and witness of the church. Newbigin's responses to the pluralists' challenge are powerful and convincing.

However, one should criticize Newbigin's lack of stress on the salvation of the individual soul. This does not mean that the individual's salvation is not important for his thought. But any question which deals with the salvation of the individual is cast aside as "abstracting" the soul from a corporate understanding of salvation. He is right to assert the corporate dimension of salvation and the glory of God, but his posture is vulnerable when he keeps on stressing this at the expense of genuine concerns about the salvation of individual souls. Concerns about life after death and personal salvation are extremely important for individuals, and

---

[251]"The Challenge of Pluralism for the Contemporary Christian Church," *Journal of the Evangelical Theological Society*, Vol. 35, No. 3 (September 1992), Op. cit., p. 370.

should not be neglected.

CHAPTER 6

THE NATURE OF INTER-RELIGIOUS DIALOGUE

The relationship of Christianity to non-Christian religions has become a crucial theological question of our time. The attempts to define and formulate this relationship have been many and varied. There are at least three major lines of thought which have been identified in current theological discussion, namely, `exclusivism', `inclusivism', and `pluralism'. These three dominant paradigms are well documented by Paul F. Knitter[1] and Gavin D'Costa[2]. Our concern in this chapter is to see the unique contribution of Newbigin to this area of theological discussion. Following this, I shall proceed to discuss Newbigin's theology of inter-religious dialogue, the question of the unity of religions, and finally, the unity of humanity in Jesus Christ.

1. EXCLUSIVISM, INCLUSIVISM, AND PLURALISM

a. Exclusivism

Christian exclusivists believe that God's revelation in Jesus Christ is definitive and final, and salvation is to be found nowhere else. One of the best representatives of this position has been Hendrik Kraemer. Although this exclusivist position is adopted by many within the evangelical tradition, there is significant diversity among those who share this paradigm. Newbigin's position is

---

[1]*No Other Name?: A Critical Survey of Christian Attitudes toward the World Religions* (London: SCM Press, 1985).
[2]*Theology and Religious Pluralism* (Oxford: Basil Blackwell, 1986).

exclusive in the sense that it affirms the unique truth of the revelation in Jesus Christ.[3] However, he is not exclusivist in the sense of denying the possibility of the salvation of the non-Christian.

There are some theologians, like Raymond Panikkar, who think that God provides for the salvation of every person.[4] But for Newbigin, salvation is not a logical deduction from the revealed nature of God. Nor is Hinduism the starting point of a religion that culminates in Christianity. What Newbigin introduces here is the terrible necessity of the Cross of Christ upon which the gospel story is centered. The Cross was necessary because of human estrangement from God. If salvation had been a logical deduction from the character of God, Christ would not have died for estranged humanity.

Newbigin claims finality for Jesus. This claim is neither to assert that the majority of human beings will someday be Christians, nor that all others will be damned. It is to claim that commitment to him is the way in which human beings can become truly aligned to the ultimate end for which all things were made.[5] Therefore, conversion is a necessity, and for this purpose, repentance and forgiveness of sin should be preached in Christ's name to all nations. The universality of Christ's lordship over all nations and over all creation is not a ground for leaving all the nations as they are. Paul's words in Romans 10:12 f. is a complete statement on the universality of Christ's lordship. Three things can be noticed here: the universality of God's love and grace, a radical

---

[3] *The Gospel in a Pluralist Society*, p. 182.
[4] Raymond Panikkar, *The Unknown Christ of Hinduism* (London: Darton, Longman and Todd, 1964) referred to by Newbigin in The Finality of Christ, p. 41.
[5] *The Finality of Christ*, p. 115.

insistence upon the freedom of God over against his own people, and the need for repentance.[6] God's grace is not limited by any ecclesiastical barriers. It does not discriminate between Jew and Greek. God bestows his riches upon all who call upon him. God is not the property, says Newbigin, of the ecclesiastical establishment and is free to manifest himself to the pagans ("I have been found by those who did not seek me." Isa 65:1a). However, "conscious belief and explicit verbal confession of Jesus as Lord" are the conditions for salvation (Rom. 10: 9-10).[7]

How important is membership in the Church? Is membership in the visible community integral to conversion? These questions arise in relation to Cornelius and his family (Acts 10), and Newbigin answers by noting that they were recipients of the Holy Spirit while being both uncircumcised and unbaptized. But Peter baptized them, and they were incorporated into a visible and definite community. Thus Newbigin argues that conversion does involve incorporation into a community.[8] The relationship with Christ is not purely mental and spiritual, unembodied in any of the structures of human relationship. Therefore, a Christian is, "one who is baptized, who regularly shares in the Lord's Supper, who abides in the teaching of the apostles through faithful study of the Scriptures, and in their fellowship through his participation in the common life of prayer and service."[9] The Christian community is constituted by the words, deeds and the sacraments of Christ. It exists in him and for him; he is the centre of its life.[10] It is the context in which its members find that the gospel gives them the framework of understanding and coping with the world. Because of

---

[6]Ibid., p. 101.
[7]Ibid., pp. 101-102.
[8]*The Finality of Christ*, pp. 104-105.
[9]Ibid., pp. 109-110.
[10]*The Gospel in a Pluralist Society*, p. 227.

the given character of the community, Newbigin will not ask a Hindu, who has been born again in Christ by the work of the Holy Spirit, to remain a Hindu and worship Jesus in the context of Hindu faith and practice. The person has to be a participant in the Christian community, which is characterized by its worship, love for truth, and mutual responsibility in the common priesthood of believers in the world.[11] Conversion to Christ brings a person into fellowship and visible solidarity with those similarly committed and it enables the person to act in history in a way that bears witness to and carries forward God's real purpose for creation.

Does faithfulness to the revelation in Christ as attested in Scripture require us to believe that all those who have not made an explicit commitment of faith in Christ are eternally lost? If this is the real situation of those who are outside the Church, the need for inter-religious dialogue does not arise. If all non-Christians are destined for eternal fire, any method should be used to convert them. Newbigin does not favour the view that it would be unjust on the part of God to condemn millions who, through no fault of their own, have never heard the gospel. Here argument from justice cannot stand, because if sin has been committed against a holy and loving God, punishment is not unjust.[12] However, from the point of inter-religious dialogue, it is to be noted that every proposal to deny all knowledge of God outside explicit Christian confession breaks down in actual missionary practice. This is because it is impossible to assert a total discontinuity between the gospel and the non-Christian religions.[13]

Here certain affirmations about the human situation are

---

[11] Ibid., pp. 227-231.
[12] "The Christian Faith and the World Religions," in Geoffrey Wainwright, ed., Op. cit., p. 316.
[13] Ibid.

necessary, and they describe, in Newbigin's words, the "drama of salvation."[14] It starts with the creation of the cosmos and the care of it by a gracious God. His tender mercies are over all his works. And yet there runs through all being "a dark mystery, a perversion, an apostasy," which has resulted in the alienation of human life from its divine source.[15] That humankind is in enmity with the Creator is clearly seen in the enmity of human beings with Christ in his crucifixion. God's dealing with the human situation has been focused on a particular time and place. He has chosen a people among all peoples, and one human being, namely Jesus Christ among all the people, who was called for the sake of the many.[16] The redemption planned by God has an exclusive focus on the work of Christ, so that through this one man, all can be saved. After the resurrection of Christ, there is a choosing of the Twelve for the proclamation of the redemptive message. Newbigin notes that

> The victory over sin and death which they are to proclaim and embody is one that lies on the other side of death and the grave. It is a consummation that will gather into one glorious event both the story of every human soul and the story of all the nations.[17]

Those who have embraced the redemption in Christ become a learning community, not pretending to possess all the truth. It is a community which has the promise of the Holy Spirit that they would be led into all the truth as they continue to bear witness among all the nations.

---

[14]Ibid., p. 331.
[15]Ibid.
[16]Ibid., p. 332.
[17]Ibid.

b. Inclusivism

This approach, which is often called Karl Rahner's approach, affirms the salvific presence of God in non-Christian religions while still maintaining that Christ is the definitive and authoritative revelation of God. As Paul Knitter explains this view, Rahner's positive view of religions stems from the biblical teaching that God desires to save all humankind.[18] Here there is a clear understanding of the universality of God's grace and God's universal salvific will. John Hick, who is a pluralist, criticizes Rahner's concept of `anonymous Christianity' in this context. He argues that it creates a paternalism and chauvinism which erects barriers against open inter-religious dialogue.[19]

Newbigin is also inclusivist in the sense that he refuses to limit the saving grace of God to members of the Christian Church, but rejects the kind of inclusivism (e.g. that of Karl Rahner) which regards the non-Christian religions as vehicles of salvation.[20]

All human beings are created in the image of God and they are embraced in the love of God. Every human person is illuminated by the light who is Jesus Christ. Newbigin affirms that there is no human being in whom there is no evidence of the grace of God, of the mercy of God, of the kindness of God. However, he says that this does not mean that there is no final judgment. There is a possibility to miss the way and to be lost.[21] The final judgment

---

[18] *No Other Name?*, Op. cit., p. 125.
[19] John Hick, *God Has Many Names* (US), p. 68.
[20] *The Gospel in a Pluralist Society*, p. 182.
[21] "The Christian Faith and the World Religions," in Geoffrey Wainwright, ed., Op. cit., p. 333.

is a reality. The New Testament teaches that the final judgment is in accordance with what each person has done. The main thrust of the warnings about judgment is directed against those who think that they are safe. One has to strive to enter by the narrow gate.[22] Jesus came into the world, to his own people, but they did not receive him. The light of Christ which enlightens every human person is also the light of judgment at the same time. The coming of the light is also the "showing up of all that is not the light."[23] This is an element of judgment which the New Testament teaches and which cannot be evaded.

Newbigin sees the goodness and grace of God in the people of other faiths, but he refuses to label this as *gratia communis*, common grace. In Reformed theology, the idea of grace can be distinguished into *gratia particularis* and *gratia communis*. The concept of common grace has been used to explain the evidence of integrity and goodness of the non-Christian people. Newbigin, however, is not comfortable with the distinction between common grace and saving grace, because it "smacks of the old Catholic idea of grace as a kind of commodity which God may dispense in various strengths."[24] He believes that it is a "very unbiblical idea." He writes:

> It seems to me that the witness of the Bible is that God's tender mercies are over all his works and that the grace of God is not, as it were, a commodity. It is the graciousness of God. It is that tender, gracious, loving care of God which surrounds every

---

[22]Ibid.

[23]Lesslie Newbigin, "Confessing Christ in a Multi-Religion Society," *Scottish Bulletin of Evangelical Theology*, Vol. 12, No. 3 (Autumn 1994), p. 129.

[24]Ibid., pp. 128-129.

human being.[25]

Newbigin's inclusivist position, therefore, allows him to see the grace of God in every person. God works in every person and it is God who imparts salvation. In the meantime, he believes that Christians should welcome and appreciate the evidence of the grace of God in people outside the periphery of the Church. His position does not see non-Christian religions as vehicles of salvation, because of the particularity of the work of God in Christ. The fact of Christ, which he uses as criterion, is important here also. If God has done this in Christ, then this should be the factor that controls everything else. It cannot be seen as one of a series of facts, but should be seen as the central fact which shapes, determines, and evaluates everything.[26]

Although Newbigin's inclusivism is limited, he wants Christians to acknowledge and welcome the goodness in people of other religions. He maintains that factual claims are made by other religions, which contradict the central tenets of Christianity. For example, Islam "flatly contradicts the central affirmation of the gospel."[27] For a Muslim, it is a blasphemy to state that God in Christ has died for human sin. Similarly, Hinduism might find the facts about Christ interesting, but these facts belong to a world which does not touch ultimate reality. It might belong only to a

---

[25]Ibid., p. 129. But in an earlier article co-authored by Newbigin, a distinction has been made between 'common grace' and 'general grace', which contradicts his present opposition to such a distinction. See Dan Beeby and Lesslie Newbigin, "The Bible and Inter-faith Relations," in *Using the Bible Today*, ed. Dan Cohn-Sherbok (London: Bellew Publishing, 1991), p. 186.

[26]"Confessing Christ in a Multi-Religion Society," Op. cit., p. 127.

[27]Ibid., p. 128.

shifting world of *maya*, where ultimate truth is not found.[28] Neither is the fact of Christ 'the ultimate fact' to the post-Enlightenment society, where this is only one of the facts. Newbigin's inclusivism, then, does not override his insistence upon particular Christian truth claims.

c. Pluralism

According to this paradigm, other religions are equally salvific paths to the one God, and Christianity's claim that it is the only path, or the fulfillment of other paths, should be rejected. As we have seen there are a number of exponents of this view, with their differences, and Newbigin is overwhelmingly negative about this stance.

However, 'Pluralism' is not a single notion in Newbigin's work. There is a pluralism of cultures (cultural pluralism) and a pluralism of religions (religious pluralism). Newbigin appreciates cultural pluralism which is the presence of people of various cultures and ethnicity living together and sharing in the public life of a society. This fact of 'plurality' must be distinguished from an ideology of religious pluralism, which Newbigin criticizes strenuously. He defines religious pluralism as the "belief that the differences between the religions are not a matter of truth and falsehood, but different perceptions of the same truth."[29] According to this view, to speak of religious beliefs as true or false is unacceptable. This is total pluralism, which should be distinguished from a 'provisional pluralism'.[30]

A key example of this is the Hindu *Vedanta*, the end of the

---

[28] Ibid.
[29] *The Gospel in a Pluralist Society*, p. 14.
[30] "The Christian Faith and the World Religions," p. 320.

Vedas. It points to that in which all religion reaches its true goal. That goal is the point at which all duality between subject and object disappears and one is enabled to realize the identity of the individual soul with the world soul. A long and hard road of spiritual discipline is needed to realize this end, and few will reach it. This road defines the religious quest for many. Three paths[31] are available to reach the end- the *karma marga* (the path of good works), the *bhakti marga* (the path of devotion) and the *gnana marga* (the path of knowledge). Evangelical Christianity will be seen as a *bhakti marga*. Newbigin points out that

> Here the names and forms and events that belong to the various world religions disappear in the white light of truth, for indeed they were only shadows. Here any claim for final validity on behalf of one of these names or forms is ruled out. An assertion by the Christian that Jesus is the truth by which all else is to be tested must necessarily be uncompromisingly rejected.[32]

This Provisional pluralism, in the case of the *Vedanta*, does not encourage conversion from one religious allegiance to another. Newbigin, while refuting the ideology of pluralism, looks appreciatively at a positive feature of it, namely, the operation of the divine grace in all peoples.

Newbigin's 'pluralist' position acknowledges the gracious work of God in all human lives, but it rejects a pluralism which denies the decisiveness and uniqueness of the work of God in Jesus

---

[31] Newbigin uses the word 'stages' which I believe is a wrong translation of the Sanskrit *marga*. See Ibid., p. 321.

[32] Ibid., p. 321.

Christ.[33] He notes the argument for pluralism which stems from the need for human unity and global peace in the face of nuclear and other threats to society. Nevertheless, the recognition of this need does not give any clue as to how it is to be met. It does not justify the assertion that `religion' is the means by which human unity is achieved. The question of truth cannot be evaded.

2. THE MANNER AND THE GOAL OF INTER-RELIGIOUS DIALOGUE

Newbigin has identified different types of dialogue, which I shall discuss in the following few pages. He believes that, like all intellectual activity, inter-religious dialogue always implies presuppositions, and it is important that these be identified and made explicit. Presuppositions belong to the very "grammar and syntax" of the participants' thought.

a. Types of Dialogue

Newbigin distinguishes three types of dialogue, two of which he approves and one he rejects.[34] His views on this stem in part from his years of life and experience among people of various

---

[33] *The Gospel in a Pluralist Society*, p. 183.

[34] "Confessing Christ in a Multi-Religion Society," in *Scottish Bulletin of Evangelical Theology*, Op. cit., p. 132. In a sense he is "allergic" to the word `dialogue,' because it seems to give the impression that this word is used when partners cannot have an ordinary conversation. The very use of the word often indicates to him that ordinary conversation has broken down or not even started. However, there exists a "dialectical" relation between the New Testament Church and the non-Christians around, which makes inter-faith dialogue a necessity. See "The Bible and Inter-faith Relations," in *Using the Bible Today*, Op. cit., p. 187.

religions in India, and his extensive study and rather formal conversation with Hindu monks at the Ramakrishna Mission in Madras. This is the first type of inter-religious dialogue. He and his Hindu friends studied the Gospels and the *Upanishads*, each out of his own religious convictions and commitments. This type of dialogue helped them to understand each other's deepest convictions, but it could go only so far as a dialogue, because both parties were speaking from "prepared positions." Nevertheless, formal interfaith dialogue is a "very valuable exercise." It is not part of evangelism. The inter-faith discussions at the Ramakrishna Mission were not aimed at converting each other; rather the goal was mutual understanding of where each one stood, and this mutual understanding was a "necessary basis for a true evangelism."[35] To participate in such a dialogue is significant, although it has only limited possibilities. Such an activity differs from the classical Socratic idea of dialogue, which involves the mutual criticism of each other's positions so as to lead on to a fuller truth, on the assumption that there are fundamental agreements already on the basis of which both parties argue. This is not the case in the matter of inter-faith dialogue, because if the gospel is true, if Jesus is the *Logos*, the Word made flesh, then there is no other basis from which we can work except the recognition of Jesus as Lord. This is why Newbigin believes that there are strict limits to the possibilities of dialogue.[36]

A second type of dialogue has to do with the involvement in civic responsibilities and participation in the common tasks of society.[37] Concerns for `nation-building' and `national unity' in some countries like India have triggered a political need for inter-religious dialogue. The basis of dialogue for this task, according to

---

[35]"Confessing Christ in a Multi-Religion Society," p. 133.
[36]Ibid., p. 134.
[37]Ibid., p. 132.

some Indian Christian theologians, was in their Christian faith.[38] Newbigin is of the opinion that Christians are indeed to become meaningful participants with people of other religions in the common tasks of society. Sharing in common tasks is an important way of opening up relationships. Newbigin speaks of his experience in Madras, where, as bishop, he had to cooperate with people of different faiths, including Marxists, Gandhians and others. There should be an eagerness on the part of Christians to cooperate with people of all faiths and ideologies in all projects "which are in line with the Christians' understanding of God's purpose in history."[39] No matter what a person's religious or ideological background is, each person has his or her own understanding of the meaning and end of history. But this should not turn Christians away from participating with others in the common societal tasks, because along the way there will be many issues in which Christians and others can "agree about what should be done."[40] Christians can join hands with others "to achieve specific goals," even though the ultimate goal, for Christians, is Christ and his coming in glory and not what their collaborators imagine. Newbigin repeatedly states that the heart of the faith of a Christian is the belief that the true meaning of the story is that which is revealed in Christ. In other words, it is the centrality of Christ that occupies the core of his argument. Being part of the story, Christians are to play their part intentionally in the story.

This second form of dialogue, i.e., "shared commitment to the business of the world" provides the context for true dialogue.[41]

---

[38] Examples of two theologians in this category are Paul Devanandan and M. M. Thomas. See Newbigin, "The Basis, Purpose, and Manner of Inter-Faith Dialogue," Op. cit., p. 255.
[39] *The Gospel in a Pluralist Society*, p. 181.
[40] Ibid.
[41] Ibid.

Newbigin's understanding of this dialogue becomes clearer when he adds,

> As we work together with people of other commitments, we shall discover the places where our ways must separate. Here is where real dialogue may begin. It is a real dialogue about real issues. It is not just a sharing of religious experience, though it may include this. At heart it will be a dialogue about the meaning and goal of the human story. If we are doing what we ought to be doing as Christians, the dialogue will be initiated by our partners, not by ourselves.[42]

The non-Christian partners will be aware of the fact that Christian actions in the common task are set in a different context from their own. The Christian motivation and goal are different from that of any secular ideology. Christians do not invest their ultimate confidence in the "intrahistorical goal" of their labours.[43] For Christians, the horizon is both nearer and farther away than that is for non-Christians. Newbigin states very clearly that

> They will discover that we are guided by something both more ultimate and more immediate than the success of the project in hand. And they will discover that we have resources for coping with failure, defeat, and humiliation, because we understand human history from this side of the resurrection of the crucified Lord. It is or it ought to be - the presence of these realities which prompts

---

[42] Ibid.
[43] Ibid., pp. 181-82.

the questions and begins the dialogue.[44]

Every programme for teaching, healing, feeding the hungry, or for freedom and justice, must point beyond itself to a greater reality, namely, Jesus Christ. In his address on *Mission in Christ's Way*,[45] Newbigin expands this theme in relation to the Kingdom of God. Here he warns against separating the meaning of the Kingdom of God from the name of Jesus Christ, lest the activity of the church be reduced to a mere "ideological crusade."[46]

A third type of dialogue, which Newbigin rejects, takes as its presupposition a common core of reality within all the varieties of religious experience. The classic statement which supports this position comes from *Rig Veda*, which states that "Real is one, though sages name it variously." Newbigin points out that, according to this view, it is axiomatic that there is one reality behind or within all forms of religion.[47] As we have seen in the previous chapter, the question of unity among religions is an ensuing concern within this model, and not only Hindus, but many Christians adopt this approach. Various models and schemes have been proposed by theologians in this category with a view to achieving human unity through religion. There have been many attempts to find a basis of unity which all could accept, but the difficulty has been in finding a common framework. One such attempt comes from Newbigin's British contemporary, John Hick, who has proposed a so-called 'Copernican revolution' in theology.

---

[44] Ibid., p. 182.

[45] Lesslie Newbigin, *Mission in Christ's Way* (Geneva: WCC Publications, 1987).

[46] Ibid., p. 9.

[47] Lesslie Newbigin, "The Basis, Purpose and Manner of Inter-Faith Dialogue," in *The Scottish Journal of Theology*, Vol. 30 (1977), p. 254.

John Hick

We have already explored something of Hick's views in chapter four, and we shall not review all of that here. However, Hick's position is a prime example of what Newbigin opposes in inter-religious dialogue, and warrants further consideration.

Hick's proposal has been to solve the problem of inter-religious understanding by means of a shift from the dogma that "Christianity is at the centre to the realisation that it is *God* who is at the centre."[48] Thus Hick calls for a change from a 'Ptolemaic' to a 'Copernican' theology, from a view that places one's own religion at the centre, to a view that places God at the centre. Previous Christian theological analyses, according to Hick, are like Ptolemaic "epicycles," or supplementary theories ("Implicit faith," "Baptism by desire," "Anonymous Christianity," etc.,) added on to the original to accommodate new information about religions. The fixed point of the Ptolemaic theology is the principle that outside Christianity there is no salvation.[49] The Copernican revolution in astronomy was a transformation in the way in which people understood the details of the universe. Hick writes:

> It involved a shift from the dogma that the earth is the

---

[48] John Hick, *God and the Universe of Faiths: Essays in the Philosophy of Religion* (London: The Macmillan Press, 1973), p. 131. Much of this volume is taken up with the question of the relation of Christianity to other religions.

[49] Ibid., p. 125. Hick points out that the epicycles of Ptolemaic Christianity can also be used in a Ptolemaic Hinduism, or Buddhism or Islam and so on, in which case the adherents of that particular religion can assume that their own religion is fully true and that all the others are more or less true according as they approximate to or diverge from it (p. 132).

centre of the revolving universe to the realisation that it is the sun that is at the centre, with all the planets, including our own earth, moving around it. And the needed Copernican revolution in theology involves an equally radical transformation in our conception of the universe of faiths and the place of our own religion within it. It involves a shift from the dogma that Christianity is at the centre to the realisation that it is *God* who is at the centre, and that all the religions of mankind, including our own, serve and revolve around him.[50]

The Copernican paradigm, in Newbigin's view, is defective. Hick is interested in a shift from a Christocentric to a theocentric model, but this shift, in Newbigin's opinion, is unnecessary, because of what he considers the historically credible "fact of Jesus Christ". It is his belief that there are "historical records that can be read, probed and analyzed," which impart, in Jesus Christ, the truth about God. In the light of this fact, Hick's approach could offer us only a vague and unclear notion of `God.' The word `God' has almost as many meanings as there are human beings. So `God' as the centre means not God as revealed in Jesus Christ, or in any other specific religion, but `God' as an undifferentiated notion conceived of in a subjective way.[51] It is a move from an objective to a subjective view of God. At the root of this move is an individual search for wholeness, "a search that is surely in some sense different for every human being."[52]

---

[50] Ibid., pp. 130-131.

[51] Lesslie Newbigin, "Religious Pluralism and the Uniqueness of Jesus Christ," in the *International Bulletin of Missionary Research*, Vol. 13, No. 2 (April, 1989), p. 51.

[52] Ibid.

Newbigin thinks that Hick's Copernican paradigm is fallacious. First of all, astronomers of Copernicus' day were genuinely searching for the truth about the cosmos. Ptolemy's view was found to be inadequate. The suggestion that different ideas should be pooled together would have been rejected, as it is still rejected today in the sciences, which have no interest in synthesizing truth and error. Further, according to Newbigin,

> The sun, the planets, and the earth are all objects capable of investigation by the same methods of observation; they are equally objects of sense-perception. God and the religions are not objects in the same class. If the analogy of the Copernican revolution is to be applied to the relation of Christianity and the other religions without logical fallacy, then like must be compared with like. God is not accessible to observation in the same sense in which the world religions are, and we have no frame of reference within which we can compare God as he really is with God as conceived in the world religions.[53]

The realities which are accessible and comparable are 'God' as the Christian conceives him, and 'God' as the world religions conceive him. Hick's scheme for the unity of religions turns out to be the claim that one theologian's conception of God (his own) is the central essence of all religions.[54]

The fact that each religion involves an ultimate commitment can never be ignored in inter-religious dialogue. Because commitments can clash with each other, it is difficult, indeed

---

[53] *The Open Secret*, p. 184.
[54] Ibid., p. 185.

impossible to reconcile them. Therefore, every program founded upon the unity of the religions is bound to fail. Like everyone else, Hick has his own standpoint from which he views all religions, but his personal view (liberal Protestant monotheism) cannot become normative for everyone in the world. His conception of God can be challenged by any one of the actual religions, because his position that God is revealed validly and sufficiently in every tradition is an affirmation of faith. As David Lochhead says, "It is no less a particular faith statement than the affirmation that God is uniquely and definitively revealed in Jesus Christ or in the Qur'an."[55] Hick's views are provocative, but they seem to demand a major modification of many accepted and deeply-held Christian doctrines, while at the same time undermining the specificity of every other actually existing religious tradition.

Newbigin objects to the dichotomy between a "confessional dialogue" and a "truth-seeking dialogue," as Hick suggests in his Younghusband Lecture.[56] These are said to be two different positions or attitudes within "discursive theological dialogue" which is concerned with the truth-claims of the different religions. According to Hick's scheme,

> At one extreme there is purely *confessional dialogue* in which each partner witnesses to his own faith, convinced that his has absolute truth whilst his partner's has only relative truth. At the other extreme is *truth-seeking dialogue* in which each is conscious that *Transcendent Being* is infinitely

---

[55] *The Dialogical Imperative* (Maryknoll: Orbis, 1988), p. 26.

[56] John Hick, "Christian Theology and Inter-Religious Dialogue," in *World Faiths*, No. 103 (Autumn 1977), p. 2. Hick speaks of a 'discursive theological dialogue' and a 'practical dialogue.' The latter notion is consistent with Newbigin's second type of dialogue described above.

greater than his own limited vision of it, and in which they accordingly seek to share their visions in the hope that each may be helped towards a fuller awareness of the Divine Reality before which they both stand. Dialogue sometimes takes place nearer to one pole and sometimes nearer to the other, but often varies in character as it proceeds, moving back and forth along the scale.[57]

According to Hick's scheme, each dialogue partner "has the impression of standing at the centre of the world of meanings, with all other faiths dispersed around its periphery."[58] But there are many "different circles of faith," with the inhabitants of each living under the impression of the unique centrality of their own. Hick urges that "Christianity must move emphatically from the confessional to the truth-seeking stance" in dialogue.[59]

However, the Christian can be confessional and truth-seeking at the same time. The Christian can say "Jesus Christ is Lord of all" and also that "Jesus Christ is infinitely greater than my limited view of him." These two affirmations are analogous. Both statements can be made by the same person seeking the truth. Therefore Hick's dichotomy has to be ruled out. The Christian's basic commitment is to a "historic person and to historic deeds."[60]

Newbigin also responds critically to Hick's concept of "Transcendent Being." This, he points out, is not a recorded event in history. Rather, it is an abstract idea, and a difficult one for those not trained in philosophy. He argues:

---

[57]Ibid., pp. 2-3. Emphases added.
[58]Ibid., p. 4.
[59]Ibid., p. 11.
[60]*The Open Secret*, p. 187.

> "Transcendent" is an adjective which literally refers to the position of something above or beyond something else. "Being" is a verbal noun from the verb "to be" which normally only has meaning in association with a subject. The idea of "being" which is devoid of any subject, that is, devoid of any reference to something which *is*, seems for most people to be very difficult to grasp.[61]

Newbigin sees that Hick can use this phrase because he is addressing people who are familiar with the long history of "philosophical idealism." Newbigin asks why it is preferable to use this very abstract mental construct, while there is a more reliable and concrete starting point for the adventure of truth seeking, namely, Jesus Christ. Reflecting again the epistemology of Michael Polanyi, he points out that

> Every attempt to form a coherent understanding of the whole human situation starts out from an initial act of faith. There is no possibility of knowing anything except on the basis of something which is, at least provisionally, taken for granted. In this respect the Christian believer and the idealist philosopher share the same human predicament. My point is that I know of no basis, no axiom, no necessity of thought which requires me to believe that a historic person and a series of historic events provide a less reliable starting point for the adventure of knowing than does the highly

---
[61] Ibid.

sophisticated mental construct of a philosopher.[62]

Hick's argument implies that those who take the confessional stance are not seekers of truth, and one cannot enter into real dialogue if one begins by denying the intellectual integrity of one's partner. However, Newbigin argues that under the guise of openness and teachability, Hick is asserting that his own presuppositions are the only way to arrive at truth, whereas those of Christ-centred Christians are not.

The Christian position in inter-religious dialogue has to be that of one ultimately committed to Jesus Christ. The Christian derives his/her authority from the gospel, and this authority cannot be replaced by a philosophical system or a mystical experience, or by the requirements of national and global unity.[63]

b. Manner of Dialogue

It is the doctrine of the Trinity, as we find in *The Open Secret* that offers the "true grammar of dialogue."[64] In accordance with this teaching, Christians and non-Christians share a "common nature" a "common patrimony." In dialogue, both parties meet as children of the one Father, regardless of whether or not the non-Christian partners have accepted their sonship.[65] This implies,

---

[62]Ibid., p. 188.

[63]Ibid., pp. 190-191.

[64]p. 207. As early as 1963, Newbigin stressed the importance of the "strong Name of the Trinity" for the missionary movement. See his *Trinitarian Faith and Today's Mission* (Richmond, Va.: John Knox Press, 1963), p. 31. He has expressed concerns that the trinitarian and christological foundations of the mission of the church are breaking down in the newer pluralistic theologies of religion.

[65]Ibid.

> We are eager to receive from our partners what God has given them, to hear what God has shown them. In Karl Barth's words, we must have ears to hear the voice of the Good Shepherd in the world at large.[66]

This eagerness to receive even what is new and strange is the mark of one who recognizes the words of Jesus: "All that the Father has is mine" (Jn 16:15a). This, Newbigin says, is a way of learning to share in the common patrimony as human beings made by the one God.[67]

Moreover, there is a shared context of things, of nonpersonal entities. Christians do not abstract themselves from the world of things. Dialogue cannot be conceived as the "encounter of pure naked spirits."[68] Christians share with non-Christians one common world which is the gift to both of the one Creator God. It also implies that the dialogue partners meet at a particular place in time in the ongoing history of the world, which Christians believe to be under God's rule and providence. Newbigin says that

> We meet, not as academics studying dead traditions from the past, but as men and women of faith struggling to meet the demands and opportunities of *this* moment in the life of our city, our nation, our world. ... We shall meet in the open country where all of us, of whatever faith, are being called upon to bring our faith to the test of decision and action in

---

[66]*The Open Secret*, p. 207.
[67]Ibid.
[68]Ibid.

new and often unprecedented situations.[69]

Newbigin believes that it is in this open encounter in the field of contemporary decision that true dialogue takes place. Christians participate in the dialogue as members of the body of Christ. This body of believers has been appointed by the Father to continue the mission of Jesus. In Newbigin's opinion, this has three consequences for the manner of dialogue.

First, Christians are vulnerable and exposed to temptation. They do not possess the truth in an unassailable form.[70] While they are so open to understanding the partner's view of the world, they may not move away from or ignore the example of Jesus, who remained faithful to God. He was exposed to all the power of human religion and ideologies and yet committed his spirit into his Father's hands. The true disciple, in the same way, should remain bound to Jesus in dialogue.

It is at this juncture that Newbigin uses the model of Walter Freytag of Hamburg.[71] This model, which can be illustrated by means of a picture, has its origin in an Indonesian theological seminary. It consists of two flights of steps, each with seven stairs, the one going up to the right and the other to the left, and between them a cross, its base level with, and very near, the lowest step of each stairway. Its cross-beam was at the same height as the two topmost steps. The model originally illustrated in the Javan culture

---

[69] Ibid., p. 208.
[70] Ibid.
[71] Walter Freytag, *The Gospel and the Religions* (London: SCM Press, 1957), p. 21. This was originally published as *Das Rätsel der Religionen und die Biblische Antwort* (Wuppertal-Barmen, Germany: Jugenddienst-Verlag, 1956) to address a widespread interest in the relation between Christianity and non-Christian faiths.

the relationship between Javanese mysticism and the message of the Bible. The summary is that the higher the mysticism ascends, the more it departs from the cross, although it reaches the same height, and the deeper is the cleft separating the Bible message and mysticism.[72]

For Newbigin, the staircases in the picture represent the many ways by which the human person learns to rise up towards the fulfillment of God's purpose.[73] These ways include all the "ethical and religious achievements" which so richly adorn the human cultures. The cross in the middle represents a "historic deed in which God exposed himself in a total vulnerability to all our purposes and in that meeting exposed us as the beloved of God who are, even in our highest religion, the enemies of God."[74] Furthermore,

> The picture expresses the central paradox of the human situation, that God comes to meet us at the bottom of our stairways, not at the top; that our real ascent towards God's will for us takes us further away from the place where he actually meets us.[75]

Newbigin affirms the biblical truth that Jesus came to call not the righteous, but sinners. Christians meet non-Christians at the bottom of the stairway, not at the top, because `Christianity' as it develops in history takes on the form of one of the stairways. In inter-religious dialogue, Christians do not meet their partners as the exclusive possessors of the truth and the holiness of God but as those who bear witness to a truth and holiness which are God's

---

[72]Ibid.
[73]*The Open Secret*, p. 205.
[74]Ibid.
[75]Ibid.

judgment on them. This meeting at the bottom of the stairway, as Newbigin calls it, is a *kenosis*, a self-emptying.[76] In this self-emptying, much of what is called Christianity may have to be left behind. Further, much of its intellectual construction, its piety and the practice, may also have to be called into question. This meeting place for religions is central in Newbigin's scheme of inter-religious dialogue, because it is the place of the cross of Christ. It is also true that a person's 'Christianity' may be put at risk in this meeting of partners. It may even give rise to an occasion where Christians are challenged to a "radical reconsideration" of their long-accepted Christian formulations. But this reconsideration can be done only within their "ultimate commitment to Jesus Christ as finally determinative of his way of understanding and responding to all experience."[77]

Newbigin uses a term "dialogue *of* the religions," which I believe is indicative of this task as a normally occurring phenomenon in the daily life of the Christians and non-Christians.[78] The Christian participation is rooted in the life of the church, namely, its worship, teaching, sacraments, and shared discipleship. The Christian has to be "deeply rooted in Christ" and only in this way can the Christian enter into the world of religion with complete self-emptying.[79] The Christian is not only rooted in Christ and the life of his church, but also believes and expects that the Holy Spirit will use the dialogue to glorify Jesus by converting to him both the partners in the dialogue. Here conversion with respect to the Christian is the self-consciousness and possible reassessment of self in the light of other religions. There is a

---

[76]Ibid.
[77]Ibid., p. 210.
[78]Ibid.
[79]Ibid. Newbigin sees here the world of the religions as the world of the demonic.

profound change in the life of the Christian as a result of the dialogue. The example may be cited from the story of Peter and Cornelius. Newbigin describes the story of this meeting as "radical conversion" for both the apostle and Cornelius. The Holy Spirit, who convicts the world of sin, of righteousness, and of judgment, may use the non-Christian partner in dialogue to convict the church. For Newbigin, dialogue also means "exposure to the shattering and upbuilding power of God the Spirit."[80]

Is it proper for the Christian not to expect the conversion of the partner to Jesus Christ? Although Newbigin says that inter-religious dialogue is not for converting the non-Christian partner, he maintains that the Christian should expect that the Holy Spirit might use this occasion for the conversion of the non-Christian partner to faith in Jesus.[81] To exclude this belief and expectation is to "reduce dialogue to something much less than its proper importance."[82] The "conversion of St. Peter" in the example quoted above should not be used to overshadow the conversion of the Gentile, without which there would have been no conversion of Peter. A dialogue which is safe from all possible risks is no true dialogue. Here Newbigin is affirming the conviction of an Indian philosopher,[83] who criticizes certain false notions of inter-religious dialogue. One of them is the understanding that the purpose of dialogue is mutual confirmation of each other's position. Sundara Rajan says that stating the aim of dialogue in this way does not even consider the possibility of "mutual destruction of faith."[84] If it

---

[80]Ibid., p. 211.
[81]Ibid.
[82]Ibid.
[83]R. Sundara Rajan, "Negation: An Article on Dialogue among Religions," in *Religion and Society*, Vol. 21, No. 4 (December 1974), p. 74.
[84]Ibid.

is impossible to lose one's faith as a result of encounter with another faith, then that dialogue has been made safe from all possible risks. This guaranteed safety, says Sundara Rajan, reinforces the tendency towards mutual confirmation.[85] Newbigin shares this view and affirms that the Christian will go to dialogue expecting a radical conversion of himself or herself and the non-Christian partner. Dialogue cannot be made safe from all possible risks. But he says that "to put *my* Christianity at risk is precisely the way by which I can confess Jesus Christ as Lord."[86]

In accordance with the trinitarian framework which Newbigin employs in inter-religious dialogue, the Holy Spirit is the one who glorifies Christ, by taking all the gifts of God and showing them to the Church as the treasury of Christ (Jn 16:14-15). The work of the Spirit is the confession of Christ (1 Jn 4:2-3; 1 Cor 12:3). He is the one who guides the church into the fullness of the truth in Jesus. The Christian comes to believe because of the work of the Spirit and not of the Antichrist (Acts 11:1-18). As this biblical witness shows,

> It is only as the church accepts the risk that the promise is fulfilled that the Holy Spirit will take all the treasures of Christ, scattered by the Father's bounty over all the peoples and cultures of mankind, and declare them to the church as the possession of Jesus.[87]

Newbigin goes on to state the nature of the church's stewardship in relation to the gospel. The church and all those who are called to its leadership are servants entrusted with the gospel.

---

[85]Ibid.
[86]Ibid.
[87]Ibid.

The mystery of the gospel is not entrusted to the church to be buried in the ground, but to be "risked in the change and interchange of the spiritual commerce of humanity."[88] The purpose of inter-religious dialogue for the Christian is to be faithful to this task of the church.

c. Purpose of Dialogue

The purpose of inter-religious dialogue for Christians is "obedient witness" to Jesus Christ. Newbigin says,

> Any other purpose, any goal which subordinates the honor of Jesus Christ to some purpose derived from another source, is impossible for the Christian. To accept such another purpose would involve a denial of the total lordship of Jesus Christ. A Christian cannot try to evade the accusation that, for him, dialogue is part of obedient witness to Jesus Christ.[89]

However, this witness is not to secure the conversion of others. It is not to "acquire one more recruit," although the Christian would long to see that others might come to faith in Christ. On the contrary, it means that whenever we come into the presence of the cross with another person, whether Christian or not, we receive judgment and correction. But one should also remember that the Spirit of God can use the occasion for the conversion of the partner to faith in Christ. Therefore, the Christian's task is to tell the story

---

[88] Ibid., p. 214.

[89] Ibid., p. 205. Cf. "The Basis, Purpose and Manner of Inter-Faith Dialogue," *Scottish Journal of Theology*, Op. cit., p. 265.

of Jesus, the story of the Bible.[90] This biblical story is itself the power of God for salvation. The Christian must tell the story, not because of any lack of respect for the partner, but because God has chosen the Christian to be part of the company which is entrusted with the story. But conversion cannot occur unless the Holy Spirit, through his mysterious work, touch the hearts of people and cause them to put their trust in Jesus.[91] So faithfulness is telling the story of Jesus and, as part of a congregation, the Christian has to so conduct himself or herself as to embody the truth of the story.

It is also true, as we have seen, that participating in dialogue will change and hopefully deepen the "Christianity" of the participant, and this is part of its purpose. This is because genuine dialogue is challenging to both partners in a very profound way. Newbigin agrees with the observation of Klaus Klostermeier,[92] who says that in the dialogue with his Hindu friends, he feels the need for a *metanoia* from an unknown depth. Dialogue occasions the need for one to become more "essential, more human, more Christian."[93] Newbigin approvingly quotes Klostermeier when he says that, he through dialogue feels more "inadequate, shattered and helpless before God."[94] It is Klostermeier's opinion that God challenges the church in inter-religious dialogue. Dialogue is a transforming experience for the participants because it exposes the

---

[90] *The Gospel in a Pluralist Society*, p. 182. The Church, as the chosen people of God, exists in mission for the world. This missionary motif must find expression in its mission to the world. See "The Bible and Inter-faith Relations," p. 185.

[91] *The Gospel in the Pluralist Society*, p. 182.

[92] "Dialogue - the Work of God," in *Inter-Religious Dialogue* (Bangalore: The Christian Institute for the Study of Religion and Society, 1967), p. 120.

[93] Ibid., p. 121.

[94] Ibid., p. 120.

shallowness of routine religious life, the compromises with the ways of the world, and the essentially unchristian character of so much that bears the name Christian.[95] Newbigin relates this encounter to that of Peter and Cornelius in which the church is changed, the world is changed, and Christ is glorified.[96]

On the basis of the manner and purpose of dialogue which Newbigin has outlined, what approach should one take to devout adherents of non-Christian religions? As we shall see in the following section, it should not be an attitude of arrogance or ignorance. He offers some practical suggestions which are in conformity with his understanding of the exclusive nature of the gospel.

d. Attitude to Non-Christians

Detailed guidance about the relations which Christians ought to have with Muslims, Hindus, and Buddhists, and others is not provided by the Bible. But the New Testament shows something about the relations between Jews and Christians.

Inter-religious dialogue is not about who is saved and who is lost. The last Day of Judgment, as the New Testament teaches, will be a day of surprise both among the saved and among the lost (Mt 25:31-46).[97] Christians are warned against judging anything before the time (1 Cor 4: 1-5). Refusing to answer the question about the number that is saved, as the Lord himself refused, is simply honest. This, for Newbigin, determines the way in which Christians should approach the person of another faith.[98] He says,

---

[95] Ibid.
[96] *The Open Secret*, p. 206.
[97] *The Open Secret*, p. 196.
[98] Ibid.

> It is almost impossible for me to enter into simple, honest, open, and friendly communication with another person as long as I have at the back of my mind the feeling that I am one of the saved and he is one of the lost. Such a gulf is too vast to be bridged by any ordinary human communication.[99]

Newbigin does not want to enter into a dialogue assuming that he has access to the secret of his partner's ultimate destiny. Such an assumption would go beyond his authority as a Christian and would destroy the possibility of a real meeting. Instead, he would take a much humbler stance, namely, the position of a witness. This is the position of one who has been laid hold of "by Another and placed in a position where I can only point to Jesus as the one who can make sense of the whole human situation which my partner and I share as fellow human beings."[100] This is the basis Newbigin outlines for dialogue.

The Christian attitude to people of other faiths should be one of recognizing and rejoicing in the "abundant spiritual fruits" to be seen in the lives of non-Christians.[101] It should be an attitude of friendship and peaceful co-existence. Since Jesus is the light that lightens every person, it is impossible to believe that non-Christians are devoid of the truth. One should be eager to discover and welcome all the evidence of the work of God's grace in them. He argues,

> If our starting point is God's revealing and atoning work in Jesus Christ, we know that Jesus is the

---

[99]Ibid., pp. 196-197.
[100]Ibid., p. 197.
[101]Ibid., p. 191.

eternal word of God active in all creation and in all human life. We know that as the ascended Lord, at the right hand of the Father he reigns over all and there is no limit to the reach of his gracious work. We know that he is the light that illuminates all being. We will rejoice in every reflection of that light wherever it is found.[102]

Therefore, it will not be the Christian attitude "to probe the soul of the other person in order to discover the sins, the weaknesses, the anxieties which might provide the "point of contact" for the Gospel.'[103] Nevertheless, the recognition of sins and weaknesses will come, but it comes by the work of the Holy Spirit mediated by the telling of the gospel story. As Harold Wells argues," If the Christian gospel is to give offense, let it be the offense of the cross and not the offense of proud Christian superiority."[104] Therefore, the Church must not only tell the unsubstitutable story of the Gospel, but also "acknowledge with thankfulness and without reservation all that is of God wherever that is found, whether outside of the walls of the Church and beyond the sound of the Gospel."[105] According to Scripture, both

---

[102]Lesslie Newbigin, "Religious Pluralism: A Missiological Approach," in *Studia Missionalia*, Vol. 42 (1993), p. 237.

[103]Ibid.

[104]"The Holy Spirit and Theology of the Cross: Significance for Dialogue," in *Theological Studies*, Vol. 53 (1992), p. 486. This essay, which warns against a reductionistic theological stance in inter-religious dialogue, emphasizes the importance of paying attention to the universality of the Spirit's presence and work in the world, without removing the particularity or reducing the scandal of the cross.

[105]Lesslie Newbigin, "Religious Pluralism: A Missiological Approach," p. 238.

the apostolic recognition of the work of God outside the Church and the necessity of telling the gospel story are evident.[106] Newbigin holds together the paradox of fallen human nature, both made in the image of God and alienated through sin.[107] In a pluralistic milieu, dialogue has often been used as a substitute for telling the story. Newbigin does not favour the notion of "Christian presence" as a substitute for "evangelization" in today's world.[108] This is a "confusing half-truth." The Church has to both embody and proclaim the gospel. Christ's own commission to his disciples (Jn 20: 19-23) is the basis for this proclamation.

Newbigin suggests that Christians should reach out in friendship to other people. They should share in hospitality with others. Also, Christians can accept invitation to non-Christian worship places. They should reciprocate this invitation. This is certainly not to be part of the worship that they offer, but "to sit there quietly with respect and reverence their reverence."[109]

e. Newbigin On the Quest for the Unity of Religions

Is it possible to achieve the unity of humankind through religion? And is it possible to reconcile the conflicting claims of all religions? In an earlier article Newbigin examined questions such as these with special reference to the claims of Hinduism for

---

[106] Particular examples are St. Paul affirming the religious devotion of the citizens of Athens and at the same time telling them the act of God in Christ (Acts 14:8-18; 17:22-31), and the story of St. Peter and Cornelius (Acts 10).
[107] "Religious Pluralism: A Missiological Approach," p. 238.
[108] Ibid., p. 239.
[109] "Confessing Christ in a Multi-Religion Society," p. 131.

unity.[110] He recognized the need for the unity of humankind, but did not think that Hinduism could provide the means of unity as has been believed by many.[111] It is appropriate here to consider how Newbigin evaluated the claims of Hinduism to be a religion that can unite humankind.

Newbigin's analysis of Hinduism brings out several conflicting truth claims which are irreconcilable with historic Christianity. First of all, `experience of mystical union with the ultimate' is the basis of the Hindu position, and it is this experience which provides the certitude upon which the Hindu attitude to other religions rests.[112] According to this experience, every expression of the religious sense is seen as a refraction of the one ultimate truth. Therefore, any ultimate claim to truth such as is evident in the preaching of the gospel, becomes unacceptable and intolerable according to Hinduism. Newbigin argues, however, that no tolerance can be infinite, and Hinduism eventually becomes "intolerant of intolerance."[113]

The clue to all experience, according to the Hindu Vedantin, is a "particular kind of individual experience" which is equally available to all at all times and places. Therefore, no universal truth can be established on the basis of a particular event in history. Newbigin is not denying the reality of the mystical experience of the individual;[114] rather he is pointing out the difficulties of its a-historical character. This experience or enlightenment does not

---

[110] Lesslie Newbigin."The Quest for Unity through Religion," in The Journal of Religion, Vol. 35 (Chicago: Chicago University Press, 1955), pp. 17-33.
[111] Ibid., pp. 21, 33.
[112] Ibid., pp. 20, 21.
[113] Ibid., p. 21.
[114] Ibid., p. 22.

form community. The Hindu sage or *sannyasi* is an isolated person. His experience frees him from the bonds of all human community, including those of the family. Newbigin says that Hinduism has no doctrine of the church.[115] Therefore, this mystical experience is an unsuitable basis for the unity of humankind.

As far as Christianity is concerned, its faith rests upon a "particular historic event, unique, unrepeated, and unrepeatable." It is a "once-and-for-all event" that took place "under Pontius Pilate" which for the Vedantin is folly, because its truth is established on the basis of a "particular event in the flux of history."[116] Again, for the Christian, there is a strong notion of community. The Christian is related to this once-and-for-all event through a "continuous, living, historic process."

Secondly, according to the Vedantin, the disunity of humanity is the product of the human person's involvement in *maya*; it is the result of *aviddya* (lack of knowledge) which fails to know and to realize the individual's identity with the one spirit.[117] This claim is in conflict with the Christian's understanding of the cause of disunity, namely, sin. According to the Christian claims, every individual is alienated from God because of sin. The alienation from God has also resulted in the breakdown of the interpersonal relationships in the human community. This is where Newbigin brings in the doctrine of atonement, which for him underlines the idea of unity. He says,

> It is an event by which atonement is wrought between God and men and therefore between man and his fellow-man. The unity thus created between

---

[115]Ibid.
[116]Ibid., p. 25.
[117]Ibid

men is not simply an intellectual one; it does not consist in the sharing of a common set of beliefs, though that is involved in it. It is the reconciliation of persons in their totality to one another. It is the mutual forgiveness of sins, based upon the fact that in Christ the sins of all have been forgiven by God. It is the replacement of mutual hostility by mutual love.[118]

The atonement and reconciliation have dealt with the cause of disunity and they have brought about a "complete inward revolution, a death and rebirth, a redirecting of all vital powers" of the human person both to love and forgive which are essential to unity.

A third point in Newbigin's analysis of Hinduism has to do with how both Hindus and Christians understand the term `salvation.' In Hinduism, salvation is by absorption of the individual soul into the Supreme Being, whereas in Christianity, it is by receiving God's forgiveness and being reconciled to him.[119]

What, then, is the basis upon which the unity of humankind can be affirmed? Because of the differing truth claims, Newbigin is convinced that Hinduism cannot offer the basis for unity. Its claim to be the truth transcending all religions is necessarily at the same time a "negation of the truth of those religions as their adherents understand them", and can even be understood as a "declaration of war upon all religion which claims to be based upon a historic revelation."[120]

---

[118] Ibid.
[119] Ibid., p. 22.
[120] Ibid., p. 23.

Furthermore, every claim to reconcile conflicting religious claims is itself in some sense a claim to religious truth and must be examined on its merits as such. Unity can be achieved only around some centre, and what that centre is, is a vital question. There cannot be a unity "except as a unity in the truth" and "truth cannot make concordats with falsehood." The quest for unity around a false centre must be rejected. He adds,

> There is no way to unity by mere amalgamation, wholesale syncretism, or universal toleration. Men are not made one except by something which draws them together. When the Hindu says, "All rivers flow into the ocean; all ways lead to God," he is, in fact, bearing witness to a very definite faith as to the ultimate nature of man, of the world, and of God, and we cannot avoid asking the question "Is it true?" Once that question is raised, we are again in the realm of conflict between religions.[121]

Each religion has its own truth claims which normally contradict the claims of other religions. "Religion deals with the sacred," says Newbigin. It makes upon human persons a claim to which every other claim has to be subordinated. For a believer, every life experience is related to the sacred. Thus every mature and universal religion will have its own interpretation of other religions. Such an interpretation would be part of its own claim to be the ultimate and universal truth.[122] Newbigin stresses the need for carefully examining every claim of religion that is said to be drawing people together, because such claims rest upon some 'truth'. One has to scrutinize the particular standpoint from which such claims are produced.

---

[121] Ibid.
[122] Ibid.

f. Christ and the Unity of Humanity

Newbigin is concerned about the need for human unity, but this unity cannot be achieved through religion. He acknowledges the desire for harmony and for coherence.[123] Unity among peoples of all faiths, ideologies and cultures is highly desirable, and therefore this is urgent and imperative.[124] The problem, however, is that here 'Unity' is a "formal concept" until one reveals the centre and basis of unity.[125] Unless the centre and basis are established, one is seeking unity only on one's own terms. This is difficult to achieve as long as there are differing and conflicting commitments among peoples of various religions. Speeches about 'world peace' are not rare in a world of power politics, but Newbigin argues that the true meaning of the word 'peace' depends on who speaks it and where it is spoken. In other words, 'unity' is an empty word until one is clear about its content and the commitment which will hold it together.[126]

In the discussion about human unity, Newbigin often refers to an illumination on this topic by André Dumas[127], who urges that the Church can be a "centred diversity."[128] He goes on to say that if

---

[123]"Religious Pluralism: A Missiological Approach," Op. cit., p. 234.
[124]Lesslie Newbigin, *Christian Witness in a Plural Society* (London: British Council of Churches, 1977), p. 3.
[125]Ibid.
[126]Ibid.
[127]"The Unity of the Church and the Unity of Mankind," in the *Study Encounter*, Vol. 10, No. 2 (1974) pp. 1-16. Dumas contends that philosophies of the unity of humankind remain the ideologies of the select few, and that the real unity has to have a common centre.
[128]Ibid., p. 15.

there is no centre, one cannot speak of unity. The absence of the centre creates a communication gap which neither language, action nor the heart can bridge. In his words, the affirmation of a centre other than the individual self is a summons to remove oneself from the centre.[129] Dumas states his case clearly:

> The existence of the centre brings to an end what I would call the dogmatic solitude of the individual point. The centre means the birth of a diversity which is no longer a lonely diversity, the emergence of a universe where the One does not discredit the Many. .... The centre we are speaking of is not a point of convergence nor a government, but a name and a life.[130]

The views of Dumas and Newbigin converge at this point. For both of them, the questions of 'particularity' and 'universality' are not mutually exclusive. Only a particularity which has a name is not replaced by universality. Moving from the Abrahamic covenant to the covenant in Jesus Christ, one sees both particularity and universality. There is one centre common to all and there is the diversity of the circumferences. Thus, Dumas points out that the basis of unity is "not a monolithic, centralized system but a 'centred diversity.'[131] What comes at the centre of unity is not synthesis, but the uniqueness of God's love in Christ.[132]

In similar vein, Newbigin asserts the centrality of Christ at the heart of unity. Any programme for unity has to be examined to see if the centre around this unity has been revealed. As long as

---

[129]Ibid.
[130]Ibid.
[131]Ibid., pp. 2, 3.
[132]Ibid., p. 15.

this centre is not revealed, the proposer is proposing himself as the centre.[133] In offering a Christian proposal, Newbigin expresses his position in the following way:

> Obviously we must all agree that the centre of all things is God - God as he truly is. Certainly the centre is not Christianity, which is a highly ambiguous and vastly diversified and constantly changing historical phenomenon. The Christian faith is that it is Jesus Christ who, being part of history and being part of the world accessible to our knowledge, is `God as he truly is'. Therefore Jesus Christ is the centre, and all the phenomena of religion (including Christianity) and the phenomena of irreligion and all anti-religion are to be judged and valued by their relation to him.[134]

This means, even if one puts together the essential truth from different religions, the fundamental predicament cannot be escaped, namely, that the result is still only one proposal which has to be defended against others. Newbigin says that "a variety of relative truths do not become absolute by being combined."[135]

What is unique in the Christian story is the centrality of the cross and resurrection of Jesus. To state this as the central point of the story is not imperialism. But there are rival imperialisms (including Christian imperialism) which are the result of deep corruption in human nature which leads one to see oneself as the centre of the world and to judge everything from that centre. That

---

[133]Lesslie Newbigin, *Christian Witness in a Plural Society*, Op. cit., pp. 4, 7.
[134]Ibid.
[135]Ibid., p. 5.

corruption, says Newbigin, has been met, exposed and dealt with in the atoning work of Jesus Christ.[136] It is not the human self that should occupy the centre, but the Christ who has displaced one's self.[137] Here Jesus, who has become the centre of the believer, is the same Jesus through whom and for whom all things exist and in whom they all hold together (Col. 1: 16, 17). Therefore, human unity is possible only through the Christ who says, "But I, when I am lifted up from the earth, will draw all men unto myself."[138] The secret of human unity, therefore, is

> The one place where our self-centred human wills can be drawn together is the place where this radical corruption has been met and dealt with, where sin has been forgiven and atonement made, the mercy-seat where we can meet together as common debtors to the immeasurable grace of God.[139]

For Newbigin, the real centre of human unity is Jesus Christ. He speaks particularly about the 'mercy-seat' which was provided by God in the dying of Jesus.[140] For both Christian unity and for the

---

[136]"Religious Pluralism: A Missiological Approach," p. 235.

[137]"I have been crucified with Christ and I no longer live, but Christ lives in me. The life I live in the body, I live by faith in the Son of God, who loved me and gave himself for me" (Gal 2:20). See Ibid.

[138]John 12:32.

[139]Ibid.

[140]Lesslie Newbigin, *Is Christ Divided?: A Plea for Christian Unity in a Revolutionary Age* (Grand Rapids: Wm. B. Eerdmans Publishing Company, 1961), p. 6. Here the author notes that the Greek word *hilasterion*, translated as "expiation" in Romans 3: 25 (RSV), is the word used for the 'mercy-seat' in the Septuagint rendering of Exodus and Leviticus and in Hebrews 9:5.

unity of humankind, this `mercy-seat' is the focal point. It is to this one `mercy-seat' that nations will be drawn. And it is only there the chasm between Jew and Gentile can be healed. It is, as Paul says (Eph 2:13), "in the blood of Christ," that those who were far off can be brought near. Christ draws the nations to himself through the expiation by his blood, through the one atoning act by which all are reconciled to God and thereby to one another.[141]

Newbigin recognizes the many and varied ways in which people of different religions and ideologies have tried to unify the world, which become themselves the most fearsome causes of strife. He firmly believes that

> There is no place at which mankind can receive the gift of unity except the mercy-seat which God has provided. We can only be made one at the point where our sins are forgiven and we are therefore enabled to forgive one another. There is no other place where "righteousness and peace have kissed each other." Every other righteousness becomes self-righteousness, and every other peace becomes appeasement. Only he who is lifted up from the earth can fulfill the promise to draw all men to Himself.[142]

Here the importance of the Church as the agent of unity has been stressed, because it is the "household of God" to manifest to the world "the manifold wisdom of God" (Eph 3:7-10). The atoning work of God is so "deep and all-embracing" that "the deepest divisions between men are transcended," and "men of

---

[141]Ibid.
[142]Ibid., p. 9.

every sort and kind are drawn together."[143] The Church, which is the body of Christ, is not distinguished from the rest of humankind by any peculiarities of race, or tradition, or education, or temperament; it is just the recreated humankind, recreated in the image of Christ.

In this respect, the unity of Christians is a unity in Christ for the sake of the world, the world which God made and loved. It should be a supernatural unity, which transcends all human groupings and parties. What occupies its centre is not the name of one of the great human religious leaders, but the name of Jesus Christ.[144]

Thus, for Newbigin, Jesus is the "determinative centre of all history, as He is its beginning and its end."[145] There can be no human unity without having at its centre the name and work of Christ. Newbigin affirms that the one real crisis of human history is the cross of Christ and it is at this point that the ultimate issues between human beings and their Maker are exposed and settled.[146]

Concluding Critical Comment

In conclusion, it can be said that Newbigin has paved the way for a theology of inter-religious dialogue which both respects and challenges the people of non-Christian faiths. It does not compromise the biblical teaching about the uniqueness of Jesus

---

[143] Ibid., p. 7.
[144] Ibid., pp. 22-23.
[145] Ibid., p. 28.
[146] Ibid., p. 30. See also Newbigin's *Unfinished Agenda*, p. 254 for his affirmation of the uniqueness of the Cross of Christ as the only point at which the mysteries of sin and forgiveness are finally dealt with.

Christ as the only way of salvation. At the same time, he wants to appreciate the work of God's grace in people of other religions. By making the Trinity the true "grammar of dialogue," Newbigin rejects the impersonal conceptions of God which some theocentric theologians have proposed. The trinitarian framework affirms the given unity of humanity, since all are objects of God's creation and reconciliation. It also requires that dialogue must take place from the Christian side on the basis of the uniqueness of Jesus Christ. Newbigin shows that the trinitarian grammar confirms the work of the Holy Spirit, who can use the dialogue for his own purpose. Thus dialogue, in an attitude of learning from non-Christians what God has given them in His grace and goodness, is an aspect of the mission of the triune God to the whole of humankind. It is clear that Newbigin cannot be slotted into any of the three categories,- `exclusivism', `inclusivism', and `pluralism'. The rigorous stance that he takes is distinctive, both in its Christ-centredness, and its generous openness to the work of God's Spirit in others.

Newbigin is very critical, as we have seen, of the Reformed tradition's idea of *gratia communis*, which he calls an unbiblical idea. However, we may question whether Newbigin's rejection of this concept stems from an adequate understanding of its use in Reformed theology. An example of a Reformed theologian who uses this concept is Abraham Kuyper. For him, *gratia particularis* and *gratia communis* are not two kinds of grace, but only one. The preservation of some sense of truth, morality, and religion among human beings are seen as the fruits of common grace. It accrues from the general operation of the Holy Spirit, which is well attested biblically (Acts 17:22; Rom 1:18-25, 2:15). There are several passages of Scripture in which it is abundantly evident that God bestows many of his good gifts on all indiscriminately, that is, upon the "just and the unjust" (such as Gen 39:5; Ps 145:9, 15, 16; Mt 5:44, 45; Lk 6:35, 36; Acts 14:16, 17; 1 Tim. 4:10). On the one hand, this concept takes the conception of sin in the most "absolute sense," and on the other, it explains that which is good in fallen human beings.[147] The extent of special grace is determined by the decree of election, while common grace is not so limited. It is a useful concept to explain the sense of truth, morality and religion of sinful human beings, who are entirely devoid of the new life that is in Jesus.

---

[147] Abraham Kuyper, *Calvinism* (New York: Fleming H. Revell Co., 1898), p. 162. See also John Calvin, *Institutes of the Christian Religion*, Vol. 1, ed. by John T. McNeill (Philadelphia: The Westminster Press, 1960), Bk. 2. 2. 17, n63, 64; Herman Bavinck, "Common Grace," Trans. Raymond C. Van Leeuwen, in *Calvin Theological Journal* 24, 1 (April 1989), pp. 38-65.

BIBLIOGRAPHY

PRIMARY SOURCES

1. Books by Lesslie Newbigin
   (Chronologically Listed)

Newbigin, Lesslie. *Christian Freedom in the Modern World.* London: SCM Press, 1937.

--------. *What is the Gospel?* SCM Study Series No. 6. Madras: CLSI, 1942.

--------. *The Reunion of the Church: A Defense of the South India Scheme.* London: SCM Press. Republished in a revised second edition in 1960.

--------. *A South India Diary.* Revised edn. London: SCM Press, 1951. Republished in 1952 in an American edition entitled *That All May Be One.* New York: Association Press. A revised edition was published in 1960 by SCM Press, London.

--------. *The Household of God: Lectures on the Nature of the Church.* London: SCM Press. The Kerr Lectures given at Trinity College, Glasgow, in November 1952. An American edition was published in 1954 by Friendship Press, New York, with more complete sectioning. Republished in a slightly revised edition in 1964 by SCM Press.

--------. *Sin and Salvation.* London: SCM Press, 1956.

--------. *One Body, One Gospel, One World: The Christian Mission Today.* London and New York: International Missionary Council,

1958. Partially published in the *Ecumenical Review* 11 (1958): 143-156.

--------. *Is Christ Divided? A Plea for Christian Unity in a Revolutionary Age*. Grand Rapids: Wm. B. Eerdmans Publishing Company, 1961.

--------. *A Faith for this One World?*. London: SCM Press, 1961.

--------. *Joint Action for Mission*. World Council of Churches, Commission on World Mission and Evangelism, Geneva: WCC, 1962.

--------. *The Ordained Ministry and the Missionary Task*. Geneva: WCC, 1962.

--------. *The Relevance of Trinitarian Doctrine for Today's Mission*. London: Edinburgh House Press, 1963. Republished in an American edition entitled *Trinitarian Faith and Today's Mission*. Richmond, Virginia: John Knox Press, 1964.

--------. *Honest Religion for Secular Man*. Philadelphia: Westminster Press and London: SCM Press, 1966. The Firth Lectures, University of Nottingham, November 1964.

--------. *Christ our Eternal Contemporary*. Madras: CLS, 1968. Meditations given at the Christian Medical College, Vellore, July 1966.

--------. *Behold I Make All Things New*. Madras: CLS, 1968.

--------. *Set Free to be a Servant: Studies in Paul's Letter to the Galatians*. Madras: CLS, 1969.

--------. *The Finality of Christ*. London: SCM Press and Richmond, Virginia: John Knox Press, 1969.

--------. *The Holy Spirit and the Church*. Madras: The Christian Literature Society, 1972.

--------. *Journey into Joy*, Madras: CLS and Delhi: ISPCK, 1972. Republished in an American edition, Grand Rapids: Wm. B. Eerdmans Publishing Company, 1973.

--------. *The Good Shepherd: Meditations on Christian Ministry in Today's World*. Madras: CLS, 1974. Revised and Republished by Leighton Buzzard, Beds: The Faith Press, 1977.

--------. *The Open Secret*. Grand Rapids: Wm. B. Eerdmans Publishing Co., 1978. Second rev. edn., 1995.

--------. *Context and Conversion*. London: Church Missionary Society, 1978. The 1978 annual sermon delivered at St. Andrew's Church, London, December 4, 1978. Republished in the *International Review of Mission* 68: 301-312.

--------. *Priorities for a New Decade*. Birmingham, U.K.: National Student Christian Congress and Resource Centre, 1980.

--------. *Sign of the Kingdom*. Grand Rapids: Wm. B. Eerdmans Publishing Co., 1980. First Published in Britain under the title, *Your Kingdom Come*. Leeds: John Paul the Preacher's Press.

--------. *The Light Has Come: An Exposition of the Fourth Gospel*. Grand Rapids: Wm. B. Eerdmans Publishing Co., 1982.

--------. *The Other Side of 1984: Questions for the Churches*. With a Postscript by S. Wesley Ariarajah. Geneva: WCC, 1983.

--------. *Unfinished Agenda: An Autobiography*. Grand Rapids: Wm. B. Eerdmans Publishing Co., 1985. First Published in London: SPCK, 1985.

--------. *Foolishness to the Greeks: The Gospel and Western Culture*. Geneva: World Council of Churches and Grand Rapids: Wm. B. Eerdmans, 1986.

--------. *Mission in Christ's Way*. Geneva: WCC Publications, 1987.

--------. *The Gospel in a Pluralist Society*. Geneva: WCC Publications and Grand Rapids: Wm. B. Eerdmans Publishing Co., 1989.

--------. *Mission and the Crisis of Western Culture*. Edinburgh: The Handsel Press, 1989.

--------. *Come Holy Spirit, Renew the Whole Creation*. Occasional Paper No. 6. Birmingham, U.K: Selly Oak Colleges, 1990. An address on the theme chosen for the 1991 Assembly of the World Council of Churches in Canberra, Australia.

--------. *Truth to Tell: The Gospel As Public Truth*. Geneva: WCC Publications and Grand Rapids: Wm. B. Eerdmans Publishing Co., 1991.

--------. *Unfinished Agenda: An Updated Autobiography*. Edinburgh: St. Andrew Press, 1993.

--------. *A Word in Season*. Grand Rapids: Wm. B. Eerdmans Publishing Co., 1994.

--------. *Proper Confidence*. Grand Rapids: Wm. B. Eerdmans Publishing Co., 1995.

--------. *Truth and Authority in Modernity*. Valley Forge, PA.: Trinity Press International, 1996.

2. Articles and Addresses by Lesslie Newbigin (Chronologically Listed)

Newbigin, Lesslie. "The Student Volunteer Missionary Union." *The Christian Faith Today*. pp. 95-104. London: SCM Press, 1933.

--------. "Revelation." Unpublished theology paper presented at Westminster College, Cambridge, 1936.

--------. "Can I be Christian? --VIII." *The Spectator* (May 6, 1938): 800.

--------. "Things not Shaken: Glimpses of the Foreign Missions of the Church of Scotland in 1937." Unsigned. Edinburgh: Church of Scotland Foreign Mission Committee, 1938.

--------. "Living Epistles: Impressions of the Foreign Mission Work of the Church of Scotland in 1938." Unsigned. Edinburgh: Church of Scotland Foreign Mission Committee, 1939.

--------. "The Kingdom of God and the Idea of Progress." Unpublished notes of four lectures given at United Theological College, Bangalore, 1941.

--------. "The Church and the Gospel." *The Church and Union*, by the Committee on Church Union, SIUC. pp. 46-59. Madras: CLSI,

1944.

--------. "Foreword" to *The Church and Union*, by the Committee on Church Union. SIUC. Madras: CLSI, 1944.

--------. "Ordained Foreign Missionary in the Indian Church." *International Review of Missions* 34 (1945): 86-94.

--------. "I Believe." In *I Believe*, ed. by M. A. Thomas, pp. 73-88. Madras: SCM Press, 1946. Address given at the Regional Leaders' Conference, Madras, December 1945.

--------. "I Believe in Christ." In *I Believe*, ed. by M. A. Thomas, pp. 101-114. Madras: SCM Press, 1946. Address given at the Regional Leaders' Conference, Madras, December 1945.

--------. "I Believe in God." In *I Believe*, ed. by M. A. Thomas, pp. 89-100. Madras: SCM Press. Address given at the Regional Leaders' Conference, Madras, December 1945.

--------. "The Ceylon Scheme of Union: A South India View." *South India Churchman* (June 1948): 162-163. Acknowledgement to the *Morning Star*, Jaffna.

--------. "The Duty and Authority of the Church to Preach the Gospel."
in *The Church's Witness to God's Design*, Amsterdam Assembly Series, Vol. II, pp. 19-35. New York: Harper and Brothers, 1948.

--------. "The Heritage of the Church of South India: Our Presbyterian Heritage." *South India Churchman* (January 1948): 52-54.

--------. "The Evangelization of Eastern Asia." *The Christian*

Prospect in Eastern Asia: Papers and Minutes of the Eastern Asia Christian Conference, Bangkok, December 3-11, 1949. pp. 77- 87. New York: Friendship Press, 1950. Republished in the *International Review of Missions* 39 (1950): 137-145.

--------. "Comments on 'The Church, the Churches and the World Council of Churches'." *Ecumenical Review* 3 (1951): 252-254.

--------. "Our Task Today: A Charge to be given to the Fourth Meeting of the Diocesan Council, Tirumangalam, 18-20 December, 1951." Unpublished paper.

--------. "The Christian Layman in the World and in the Church." *National Christian Council Review* 72 (1952): 185-189.

--------. "The Nature of the Christian Hope." *Ecumenical Review* 4 (1952): 282-284.

--------. "Odd Theologians." *South India Churchman* (August 1953): 3-4.

--------. Review of *The Communication of the Gospel*, by David H. C. Read. *International Review of Missions* 41 (1952): 526-528.

--------. "Ambassadors for Christ." *South India Churchman* (August 1953): 3-4.

--------. "Can the Churches give a Common Message to the World?" *Theology Today* 9 (1953): 512-518.

--------. "The Christian Hope." *Missions Under the Cross* ed. by Norman Goodall, pp. 107-116. London: Edinburgh House Press, 1953. Address given at the Enlarged Meeting of the IMC at

Willingen.

--------. "The Ministry of the Church." *National Christian Council Review* 73 (1953): 351-355. Published form of a draft entitled, "Statement for the consideration of the Dioceses on the Ministry of the Church -- Ordained and unordained, Paid and Unpaid; Madura, 1953."

--------. Review of *God's Order: The Ephesian Letter and This Present Time*, by John A. Mackay. In *Theology Today* 10 (January 1954): 543-547.

--------. "Conversion." *The Guardian (Madras)* (23 December 1954): 409.

--------. "The Life and Witness of the Local Church." *The Church in a Changing World: Addresses and Reports of the National Christian Council of India, Gumtur, November 5-10, 1953*. Mysore: Wesley Press, 1954.

--------. "The Present Christ and the Coming Christ." *Ecumenical Review* 6 (1954): 118-123.

--------. "Why Study the Old Testament?" *National Christian Council Review* 74 (1954): 71-76.

--------. "The Quest for Unity through Religion." *Journal of Religion* 35 (1955): 17-33. The Thomas Memorial Lecture at the University of Chicago in 1954. Republished in the *Indian Journal of Theology* 4, 2 (1955): 1-17.

--------. "National Missionary Society." *South India Churchman* (January 1956): 6-7. Address at a Meeting of the Golden Jubilee Celebration of the National Missionary Society, Madras,

November 1955.

--------. "The Wretchedness and Greatness of the Church." *National Christian Council Review* 76 (1956): 472-477. Sermon preached at the United service during the Triennial meeting of the NCCI, Allahabad.

--------. "When I am Lifted Up...." Unpublished sermon given at the Uniting Synod of the Congregational and Evangelical and Reformed Churches, Cleveland, 1957.

--------. "A Time for Decision." *Revolution in Missions*, ed. by Blaise Levai, Vellore: The Popular Press, 1957.

--------. "The Gathering up of History into Christ." *The Missionary Church in East and West*, ed. by Charles C. West and David M. Paton, pp. 81-90, London: SCM Press, 1959. Address given in 1957 at the Ecumenical Institute in Bossey.

--------. "The Nature of the Unity We Seek." Unpublished paper, c. 1959

--------. "The Pattern of Partnership." *A Decisive Hour for the Christian World Mission*, by Norman Goodall, J. E. Lesslie Newbigin, W. A. Wisser 't Hooft, and D. T. Niles, pp. 34-45. London: SCM Press. One of the John R. Mott Memorial Lectures at the Founding Assembly of the East Asia Christian Conference, Kuala Lumpur, May 1959.

--------. "The Work of the Holy Spirit in the Life of the Asian Churches." *A Decisive Hour for the Christian World Mission*, by Norman Goodall, J. E. Lesslie Newbigin, W. A. Wisser 't Hooft, and D. T. Niles, pp. 18-33, London: SCM Press, 1960. One of the John R. Mott Memorial Lectures at the Founding Assembly of the

East Asia Christian Conference, Kuala Lumpur, May 1959.

--------. "The Summons to Christian Mission Today." *International Review of Missions* 48 (1959): 177-189. Address given at the Annual Dinner of the North American Advisory Committee of the International Missionary Council, New York, November 1958.

--------. "Will God Dwell Upon Earth?" *National Christian Council Review* 79 (1959): 89-102. Text of a sermon preached at the dedication of a chapel in a Christian College.

--------. "Basic Issues in Church Union." *We are Brought Together*, ed. by David M. Taylor, pp. 155-169. Sydney: Australian Council for the WCC. Address given at the National Conference of Australian Churches, Melbourne, February 1960.

--------. "Bishop Newbigin's Final Word." *We are Brought Together*, ed. by David M. Taylor, pp. 128-130. Sydney: Australian Council for the WCC. Address given at the National Conference of Australian Churches, Melbourne, February 1960.

--------. "Bible Studies: Four Talks on 1 Peter by Bishop Newbigin." *We are Brought Together*, ed. by David M. Taylor, pp. 93-123. Sydney: Australian Council for the WCC. Addresses given at the National Conference of Australian Churches, Melbourne, February 1960.

--------. "The Cup of Blessing which We Bless." Unpublished sermon preached at Grace Cathedral, San Francisco, December 9, 1960.

--------. Letter to the Editor: "Church of South India." *Faith and Unity* 5, 8 (1960): 24.

--------. "Forgetting What Lies Behind...." Unpublished sermon preached at the Riverside Church, New York City, at the 50th Anniversary Observance of the Edinburgh 1910 World Missionary Conference, May 25, 1960.

--------. "The Life and Mission of the Church." *We are Brought Together*, ed. by David M. Taylor, pp. 59-69. Sydney: Australian Council for the WCC. Keynote Address at the National Conference of Australian Churches, Melbourne, February, 1960.

--------. "The Ministry of the Church of South India: A Letter from Bishop Lesslie Newbigin to Fr. Dalby, S. S. J. E." *Faith and Unity* 5, 7 (1960): 12- 14.

--------. "Mission and Missions." *Christianity Today* 4, 22 (August 1, 1960): 911.

--------. Review of *God's People in India*, by John Webster Grant. In *International Review of Mission* 49 (1960): 353-355.

--------. "The Mission and Unity of the Church." Grahamstown: Rhodes University. The Eleventh Peter Ainslee Memorial Lectures, October 17, 1960. Republished under the title, "Is there Still a Missionary Job Today?" *563 St. Columba: Fourteenth Centenary 1963*. Glasgow: The Iona Community Publications Department, for the Church of Scotland.

--------. "The Truth as it is in Jesus." Pamphlet. U. S. A: North American Ecumenical Youth Assembly. Address given at a Faith and Order Luncheon in San Francisco, December 1960.

-------- ."The Unification of the Ministry." *Faith and Unity* 6 (1960): 4-10.

--------. "Address by Bishop Lesslie Newbigin to Africa Committee, January 27th, 1961." Unpublished address, refined and published as "Sugar in the Coffee" in *Frontier* 4 (1961): 93-97.

--------. "Ecumenical Comments" in *Lutheran World* 8 (1961): 74-77. An invited Response to an article by Peter Brunner entitled "The LWF as an ecclesiological problem." *Lutheran World* 7: 237 ff.

--------. "Foreword" to *The Theology of the Christian Mission*, ed. by Gerald Anderson, pp. xi- xiii. Nashville and New York: Abingdon Press, 1961.

--------. "Bringing Our Missionary Methods Under the Word of God." *Occasional Bulletin from the Missionary Research Library* 13 (1962): 1-9. Address at a Mission Consultation of the Presbyterian church, U S.

--------. "The Church-- Local and Universal." *The Church--Local and Universal:Things We Face Together* No. 2, by Lesslie T. Lyall and Lesslie Newbigin, pp. 20-28, London: World Dominion Press, 1962.

--------. "Foreword" to *Missionary Methods: St. Paul's or Ours?*, by Roland Allen, American edition, pp. i-iii. Grand Rapids: Wm. B. Eerdmans Publishing Co., 1962.

--------. "Foreword" to *Upon the Earth*, by D. T. Niles, London: Lutterworth Press, 1962. pp. 7-8.

--------. "The Missionary Dimension of the Ecumenical Movement." *Ecumenical Review* 14 (1962): 207-215. Republished in the *International Review of Mission* 70 (1981): 240-246.

--------. "Preface." in *Survey of the Training of the Ministry in the Middle East*, by Douglas Webster and K.L. Nasir. Geneva, London, New York: Commission on World Mission and Evangelism, WCC, 1962.

--------. "Report of the Division of World Mission and Evangelism to the Central Committee." *Ecumenical Review* 15 (1962): 88-94.

--------. "Rapid Social Change and Evangelism." Unpublished paper, c. 1962

--------. "Developments During 1962: An Editorial Survey." *International Review of Missions* 52 (1963): 3-14. Unsigned.

--------. "Editor's Notes." *International Review of Missions* 52 (1963): 242-246, 369-373, 508-512. Unsigned.

--------. "Gesta Dei per Tamulos." *Frontier* 5 (1963): 553-555. Review of *The Dispersen of the Tamil Church* by N.C. Sargant, 1963.

--------. "Jesus the Servant and Man's Community." Unpublished address given at a Congress of the SCM, 1963.

--------. "The Message and the Messengers. Notes of Bible Studies given at the Singapore Situation Conference. (1 Cor. 1-4)." *South East Asia Journal of Theology* 5 (1963): 85-98. Republished in *One People--One Mission*, ed. by J.R. Fleming. East Asia Christian Conference, 1963.

--------. "World Christianity: Result of the Missionary Expansion." Unpublished address given at Biblical Seminary, New York City, c. 1963.

--------. "The Church: Catholic, Reformed, and Evangelical." *Episcopalian* 129 (1964): 12-15, 48.

--------. "Editor's Notes." *International Review of Missions* 53: (1964): 248-252, 376-379, 512-517. Unsigned.

--------. "Foreword" to *God for All Men*, by Robert C. Latham, London: Edinburgh House, p. 4. New York: Friendship Press and Geneva: WCC, 1964.

--------. "Survey of the Year 1962-3: By the Editor" *International Review of Missions* 53 (1964): 3-82. Unsigned.

--------. "From the Editor" *International Review of Missions* 54 (1965): 145- 150 (Unsigned), 273-280 (Unsigned), 417-427 (Initialed).

--------. "The Healing Ministry in the Mission of the Church." in *The Healing Church*, pp. 8-15. Geneva: Division of World Mission and Evangelism, WCC, 1965.

--------. "Introduction" in *The Programme Fund of the Division of World Mission and Evangelism*, WCC, 1965.

--------. "Introduction by Lesslie Newbigin." *All Africa Conference of Churches*, Geneva: WCC, 1965.

--------. "Integration et Mission" *Rythmes du Monde* (Brugge-Paris) 13: (1965):139-147.

--------. "Ministry and Laity." *National Christian Council Review* 85 (1965): 479-483. Summary of a Talk given to the United Mission of Nepal at Kathmandu, March 1965.

--------. "Preface" in *The Healing Church* pp. 5-6. Geneva:

Division of World Mission and Evangelism, WCC, 1965.

--------. "Survey of the year 1963-4: By the Editor." *International Review of Missions* 54 (1965): 3-75. Unsigned.

--------. "Conversion." *National Christian Council Review* 86 (1966): 309-323. Notes of an Address given at the Nasrapur Consultation, March 1966. Republished in *Religion and Society* 13, 4 (1966): 30-42 and in *Renewal for Mission*, ed. by David Lyon and Albert Manuel, pp. 33-46. Madras: CLS, 1967.

--------. "A Survey of the Year 1964-65." *International Review of Missions* 55 (1966): 3-80. Unsigned.

--------. "Church in its World Mission." *Outlook for Christianity: Essays for E. A. Payne*, ed. by L. G. Champion. pp. 109-118. London: Lutterworth, 1967.

--------. "Glory, Glory, Glory." *The Lutheran Standard (USA)* (30 May 1967): 13, 16. Bible Study on John 17 given at the 1966 meeting of the National Council of Churches of Christ of the USA, Miami Beach.

--------. "Just Who is the Enemy?" *The Lutheran Standard (USA)* (2 May 1967): 12-13. Bible Study on John 17 given at the 1966 Meeting of the National Council of Churches of Christ of the USA, Miami Beach.

--------. "A Point from Which to Move the World." *The Lutheran Standard (USA)* (16 May 1967): 9, 30. Bible Study on John 17 given at the 1966 meeting of the National Council of Churches of Christ of the USA, Miami Beach.

--------. "The Spiritual Foundation of Our Work." *The Christian*

College and National Development, pp. 1-8. Madras: CLS, 1967.

--------. "Strong Roots of Driftwood." *The Lutheran Standard (USA)* (18 April 1967): 9-10. Bible Study on John 17 given at the 1966 meeting of the National Council of Churches of Christ of the USA, Miami Beach.

--------. "Anglicans, Methodists and Intercommunion: A Moment for Decision." *The Churchman* 82: (1968): 281-285.

--------. "Behold I Make All Things New." Madras: CLS. Talks given at Youth Conferences in Kerala, May 1968.

--------. "Bible Studies Given at the National Christian Council Triennial Assembly, Shillong" in the *National Christian Council Review* 88 (1968): 9-14, 73-78, 125-131, 177-185. Four Studies given in October 1967. Republished in 1968 in *Renewal for Mission*, ed. by David Lyon and Albert Manuel, pp. 192-213. Second Revised and Enlarged Edition. Madras: CLS, 1968.

--------. Review of *Theology in Reconstruction*, by T.F. Torrance. *Indian Journal of Theology* 17 (1968): 43-45.

--------. "The World Mission of the Church." *South India Churchman* (September 1968): 2-4.

--------. "The Call to Mission--A Call to Unity." *The Church Crossing Frontiers*, ed. by Peter Bayerhaus and Carl F. Hallencruetz, pp. 254-265. Lund: Gleerup, 1969. Contribution to a collection of essays on the Nature of Mission in honour of Bengt Sundkler.

--------. "Church Union: Which Way Forward?" *National Christian Council Review* 89 (1969): 356-363.

----------. "Which Way for 'Faith and Order'?" *What Unity Implies: Six Essays After Uppsala*, World Council Studies No. 7, ed. by Reinhard Groscurth, pp. 115- 132, Geneva: WCC, 1969.

----------. "The Bible Study Lectures." *Digest of the Proceedings of the Ninth Meeting (COCU)*, pp. 193-231. Princeton, N. J: Consultation on Church Union, 1970. Lectures given in March 1970.

----------. "Cooperation and Unity." *International Review of Mission* 59 (1970): 67-74.

----------. "Mission to Six Continents." *The Ecumenical Advance: A History of the Ecumenical Movement, Vol. 2, 1948-1968*, ed. by Harold E. Fey, pp. 171-197, London: SPCK, 1970.

----------. "Stewardship, Mission and Development." Unpublished address given at the Annual Stewardship Conference of the British Council of Churches, Stanwick, June 1970.

----------. "Conversion." *Concise Dictionary of the Christian World Mission*, ed. by Stephen Neill, Gerald H. Anderson, and John Goodwin, pp. 147-148. Nashville and New York: Abingdon Press, 1971.

----------. "The Church as a Servant Community." *National Christian Council Review* 91 (1971): 256-264. Lecture given at the consultation on Love and Justice in the World of Tomorrow, October 1970.

----------. "Jesus Christ." *Concise Dictionary of the Christian World Mission*, ed. by Stephen Neill, Gerald H. Anderson, and John Goodwin, pp. 307-309, Nashville and New York: Abingdon Press,

1971.

--------. Review of *Salvation and Humanization*, by M.M. Thomas. *Religion and Society* 18 (1971): 71-80.

--------. "Salvation." *Concise Dictionary of the Christian World Mission*, ed. by Stephen Neill, Gerald Anderson, and John Goodwin, pp. 537-538. Nashville and New York: Abingdon Press, 1971.

--------. "Trinitarianism." *Concise Dictionary of the Christian World Mission*, ed. by Stephen Neill, Gerald H. Anderson, and John Goodwin, pp. 607. Nashville and New York: Abingdon Press, 1971.

--------. "Address on the Main Theme, 'Jesus, Saviour of the World', at the Synod Assembly of January 1972." *South India Churchman* (February 1972): 5-8.

--------. "Baptism, the Church and Koinonia: Three Letters and a Comment," *Religion and Society* 19 (1972): 69-90. An exchange of letters between Lesslie Newbigin and M.M. Thomas with a comment by Alfred C. Krass. Letter of 17th November 1971 ("18-11-71") by Lesslie Newbigin, pp. 75-84. Republished in *Some Theological Dialogues*, by M.M. Thomas, pp. 110-144, Madras: CLS, 1977.

--------. "The Church of South India--Twenty-five Years After." *Christian Advocate* (21 December 1972): 13-14.

--------. "Faith and Order in India Now." *National Christian Council Review* 92 (1972): 433-436. Guest Editorial.

--------. "The Secular-Apostolic Dilemma." *Not Without a Compass: JEA Seminar on Christian Education in the India of*

Today, ed. T. Mathias, et al., pp. 61-71. New Delhi: Jesuit Educational Association of India, 1972. With reaction by Pierre Fallon, G. Casimir and G. Soares, pp. 72-78.

--------. "Servants of the Servant Lord." *Vivekananda Kendra Patrika* (February, 1972): 153-155.

--------. "Twenty-five Years of C.S.I." *National Christian Council Review* 92 (1972): 141-145.

--------. "Twenty-five Years Old: How Fares the Church of South India." *Presbyterian Life (Philadelphia)* 25, 9 (1972): 38-40.

--------. "The Churches and CASA." *National Christian Council Review* 93 (1973): 543-549. A Paper written for the Consultation between CASA and Heads of Churches at Delhi, September 1973.

--------. "The Form and Structure of the Visible Unity of the Church." *So sende Ich Euch: Festschrift fur D. Dr. Martin porksen zum 70. Geburtstag*, Otto Wack et. al., Eds., pp. 124-141. Korntal bei Stuttgart: Evang. Missionsverlag, 1973.

--------. Review of *Christ and the Younger Churches*, by Georg F. Vicedom. *Indian Journal of Theology* 22 (1973): 183-185.

--------. "Salvation, the New Humanity and Cultural-Communal Solidarity." in *Bangalore Theological Forum* 5, 2 (1973): 1-11.

--------. "The Taste of Salvation at Bangkok." *Indian Journal of Theology* 22 (1973): 49-53.

--------. "Christian Faith and Marxism." *Madras Christian College Magazine* (1974): 21-26.

--------. "Living with Change." *Religion and Society* 21, 4 (1974): 14-28.

--------. "... But What Kind of Unity?" *National Christian Council Review* 95 (1975): 487-491.

--------. Review of *Crisis of Dependency in Third World Ministries*, by James A. Berquist and P. Kambar Manickam. *Religion and Society* 22 (1975): 81-81.

--------. Review of *Canterbury Pilgrim*, by A. Michael Ramsey. *Ecumenical Review* 27 (1975): 171.

--------. Review of *Great Christian Centuries to Come*, ed. Christopher Martin. *Ecumenical Review* 27 (1975): 171-172.

--------. Review of *India and the Latin Captivity of the Church*, by Robin Boyd. *Scottish Journal of Theology* 28, 1 (1975): 90-92.

--------. "Reflections on an Indian Ministry." *Frontier* 18 (1975): 25-27.

--------. "All in One Place or All of One Sort: On Unity and Diversity in the Church." *Creation, Christ and Culture: A Festschrift in Honour of Professor Thomas F. Torrance*, ed. by Richard W.A. Mckinney, pp. 288-306. Edinburgh: T & T Clark, 1976.

--------. "The Centrality of Christ." *Fraternal* 177 (1976): 20-28.

--------. "Christian Unity at Nairobi: Some Personal Reflections." *Mid-Stream* 15 (1976): 152-162. Excerpts republished under the title, "Nairobi 1975: A Personal Report." *National Christian Council Review* 96: 345-356.

--------. Review of *New Ways for Christ*, by Michael Wright. *International Review of Mission* 65 (1976): 228-229.

--------. "The Bishop and the Ministry of Mission." *Today's Church and Today's World*, ed. by J. Howe, pp. 242-247. London: CIO Publishing, 1977. A Contribution to the preparatory volume for the Lambeth Conference, 1978.

--------. "The Basis, Purpose and Manner of Inter-faith Dialogue." *Scottish Journal of Theology* 30 (1977): 253-270. Originally prepared for the Lutheran Church in America, Division for World Mission and Ecumenism. It was written in November 1975 and distributed by the LCA in pamphlet form under the title *Interfaith Dialogue* (1976). Republished in 1977 in two German translations: "Christem im Dialog mit Nichtchristem." *Theologie der gegen wart* 3: 159-166; and "Dialog zwischen verscheidenen Glauben." *Zeitschrift fur Mission* 3, 2: 83-98. Republished in Rousseau 1981: 13-31. Modified as chapter ten of *The Open Secret* (1978), "The Gospel Among the Religions," republished in *Mission Trends No. 5: Faith Meets Faiths*, ed. by Gerald H. Anderson and Thomas F. Stransky, C.S.P., PP. 3-19, New York: Paulist Press.

--------. "Conciliar Unity: A Letter to the Editor." In *South India Churchman* (March 1977): 10.

--------. "Christian Witness in a Plural Society." A Paper presented to the Assembly of the British Council of Churches, April 1977.

--------. "The Future of Missions and Missionaries." In *Review and Expositor* 74, 2 (1977): 209-218.

--------. "Recent Thinking on Christian Beliefs: VIII. Mission and

Missions." *The Expository Times* 88, 9 (1977): 260-264. A Review of Mission Theology from 1950 to 1976.

--------. "Teaching Religion in a Secular Plural Society." *Learning for Living* 17, 2 (1977): 82-88. Address given at the annual General Meeting of the Christian Education Movement. Republished in 1978 in Christianity in the Classroom, pp. 1-11. London: Christian Education Movement. Republished in 1982 in *New Directions in Religious Education*, ed. by John Hull, pp. 97-108. London: Falmer Press.

--------. "What is a `Local Church Truly United'?" *In Each Place*, by J. E. L. Newbigin et. al., pp. 14-29. Geneva: WCC, 1977. Republished in the *Ecumenical Review* 29: 115-128.

--------. "The Church as Witness: A Meditation." *Reformed World* 35 (March 1978): 5-9.

--------. Review of *Denominationalism*, ed. by Russell E. Richey. In *Ecumenical Review* 30 (April 1978): 189.

--------. "Christ and the Cultures." *Scottish Journal of Theology* 31 (1978): 1-22. A paper read to the 1977 Conference of the Society for the Study of Theology. Adapted as part of chapter nine of *The Open Secret* (1978).

--------. "Episcopacy and the Quest for Unity." Unpublished notes of a contribution to a discussion at the Annual Conference of CCLEPE and Ecumenical Officers at Stanwick, September 1978.

--------. Review of *Faith Meets Faith: Some Christian Attitudes to Hinduism in the Nineteenth and Twentieth Centuries*, by Eric J. Sharpe. *Theology* 81 (March 1978): 142-143.

--------. "The Right to Fullness of Life." *A Vision for Man: Essays on Faith, Theology and Society*, ed. by Samuel A. Amirtham, pp. 339-347. Madras: CLS, 1978. A contribution to a collection of essays in honour of Joshua Russell Chandran on the occasion of his sixtieth birthday.

--------. *This is Our Life*. Leeds: John Paul the Preacher's Press. Moderator's address to the General Assembly of the United Reformed Church, Southport, 1978.

--------. "The Centrality of Jesus for History." *Incarnation and Myth: The Debate Continued*, ed. by Michael Goulder, pp. 197-210. Grand Rapids: Wm. B. Eerdmans Publishing Co., 1979. Followed by a "Comment on Lesslie Newbigin's Essay," by Maurice Wiles, pp. 211-213.

--------. "Not Whole without the Handicapped." *Partners in Life: The Handicapped and the Church*, Faith and Order paper No. 89, ed. by Geiko Muller-Fahrenholz, pp. 17-25. Geneva: WCC., 1979.

--------. "Presiding at the Lord's Supper." An unpublished paper written as a contribution to the discussion in the United Reformed Church regarding "the Presidency at the Lord's Supper of Members other than those Ordained," 1979.

--------. "Preaching Christ Today." Birmingham: Overdale College. The Eighteenth Joseph Smith Memorial Lecture, published as a pamphlet, 1979.

--------. "Theological Education in a World Perspective." *Ministers for the 1980s*, ed. by Jock Stein, pp. 63-75. Edinburgh: The Handsel Press, 1979.

--------. "Toespraak tot de gezamenlijke vergadering van de

Synoden van de Nederlandse Hervormde Kerk en de Gereformeedde kerken in Nederland op 22 November 1978 in De Blije Werelt te Lunteren." *Wereld en Zending* 8, 1: (1979): 96-109.

--------. "Common Witness and Unity." *International Review of Mission* 69 (1980): 158-160. Written for the Joint Working Group Study on Common Witness of the Roman Catholic Church and the World Council of Churches, Venice, May 29-June 2, 1979.

--------. Review of *The Meaning and End of Religion*, by Wilfred Cantwell Smith. Theology 82, 688 (1979): 294-296.

--------. "He that Sitteth in the Heavens Shall Laugh." *Imagination and the Future*, ed. by J. Henley. pp. 3-7. Melbourne: Hawthorn Press, 1980.

--------. "Mission in the 1980s." *Occasional Bulletin of Missionary Research* 4, 4 (1980): 154-155.

--------. "Priorities for a New Decade." Reprinted from *Reform* (URC). Birmingham, U.K.: National Student Christian Congress and Resource Centre, 1980.

--------. "South Africa: A Fabric of Fear and Hope." *One World* No. 62 (December 1980): 10-11.

--------. "Integration--Some Personal Reflections 1981." *International Review of Mission* 70 (1981): 247-255.

--------. "Politics and the Covenant." *Theology* 84 (1981): 356-363.

--------. Review of *Red Tape and the Gospel*, by Churchman 95, 3 (1981): 273-274.

--------. Review of *Beyond Ideology*, by Ninian Smart. *Theology* 85 (September 1982): 381-383.

--------. Review of *Christ's Lordship and Religious Pluralism*, ed. by Gerald Anderson, Thomas F. Stransky. *International Bulletin of Missionary Research* 6 (January 1982): 32.

--------. "Bishops in a United Church." *Bishops, But What Kind?*, ed. by Peter Moore, pp. 149-161. London: SPCK, 1982.

--------. "Cross-currents in Ecumenical and Evangelical Understanding of Mission." *International Bulletin of Missionary Research* 6, 4 (1982): 146-151. Responses by Paul G. Schrotenboer and C. Peter Wagner, pp. 152-154 and a reply by Lesslie Newbigin, pp. 154-155.

--------. "L' Eglise de L' Inde du Sud." *Unitié Chretienne* 65 (1982): 9-15.

--------. "Living Together." *Now* (The Methodist Church Overseas Division, London) (June 1982): 18-19.

--------. "Ministry." Unpublished Address given at a Conference in Croydon, c. 1982

--------. "Text and Context: The Bible in the Church." *Theological Review (Near East)* 5, 1 (1982): 5-13. Originally written for the *Festschrift* in honour of Bishop Kulandran published in India in 1981 under the title *God's Word in God's World*, ed. by D. J. Ambalavanar.

--------. "Christ, Kingdom and Church: A Reflection on the Papers of George Yule and Andrew Kirk." Unpublished paper, c. 1983.

--------. "Christ and the World of Religions." *The Churchman* 97 (1983): 16-30. Written for a collection of reflections on the theme of the Vancouver 1983 WCC Assembly, "Jesus Christ, the Life of the World." Republished in the *Reformed Review* 37, 3: 202-213.

--------. "How should we Understand Sacraments and Ministry?" Unpublished paper. Written for a consultation jointly mandated by the Anglican Consultative Council and the World Alliance of Reformed Churches, London, January 1983.

--------. "Renewal in Mind." *GEAR* (Group for Evangelism and Renewal in the URC) No. 29 (1983): 4-7. Text of an address given at the Birmingham (U.K) GEAR Day, February 26, 1983.

--------. Rejoinder to "Mission and Unity in the Missionary Ecclesiology of Max A. C. Warren." by Ossi Haaramaki. *International Review of Mission* 72 (1983): 271-272.

--------. "The Basis and the Forms of Unity." *Mid-Stream* 23 (1984): 1-12.

--------. "The Bible and our Contemporary Mission." *The Clergy Review* 69, 1 (1984): 9-17. The Fourth Thomas Worden Memorial Lecture, given at the Upholland Northern Institute, May 4, 1983.

--------. "Faith and Faithfulness in the Ecumenical Movement." *Faith and Faithfulness: Essays on Contemporary Ecumenical Themes*, ed. by Pauline Webb. pp. 1-7. Geneva: WCC, 1984. Essays in tribute to Philip A. Potter.

--------. "The Sending of the Church-- Three Bible Studies." *New Perspectives on World Mission and Unity*. Occasional Paper No. 1: 1-14. Church of Scotland Board of World Mission and Unity. Addresses given at a Conference on World Mission and Unity,

Edinburgh, November 1984.

--------. "Can the West Be Converted?" in *Princeton Seminary Bulletin* 6 (1985): 25-37. Originally published by the Friends of St. Colm's, the Education Center and College of the Church of Scotland. Republished in 1987 in the *International Bulletin of Missionary Research* 11, 1 (1985): 2-7.

--------. "Does Society Still need the Parish Church?" Transcript of a taped address given at the Centre for Explorations in Social Concern on November 5, 1985 and distributed "for private circulation only."

--------. "A Fellowship of Churches." *Ecumenical Review* 37, 2 (1985: 175-181.

--------. "'Going Public' Operates with...." Unpublished notes following correspondence with Rev. Peter Wright about *Going Public: A Report on Ministry of Full-Time Chaplains in Polytechnics*. London: National Standing Committee of Polytechnic Chaplains, 1985.

--------. "How I arrived at the Other Side of 1984." *Selly Oak Journal* No. 2 (1985): 6-8. An introduction to a series of six responses to *The Other Side of 1984*.

--------. "The Role of the Bible in Our Church." Unpublished remarks given at a meeting of the URC Forward Policy Group, April 17-18, 1985.

--------. "Re. `Going Public'." Unpublished Letter to Rev. Peter Wright regarding *Going Public: A Report on Ministry of Full-Time Chaplains in Polytechnics*. London: National Standing Committee of Polytechnic Chaplains, 1985.

--------. Review of *A New World Coming*, by Andrew Kirk. prepublication draft, 1985.

--------. "A Response to the Responses." *Selly Oak Journal*, No. 2 (1985): 33-36. Newbigin's comments on the series of six responses to the *Other Side of 1984*.

--------. "The Welfare State: A Christian Perspective." Oxford Institute for Church and Society. Republished in *Theology* 88 (1985): 173-182.

--------. Review of *A History of Christianity in India: The Beginnings to AD 1707*, by Stephen Neill C. In *Journal of Theological Studies* 36 (October 1985): 530-531.

--------. "A British and European Perspective." In *Entering the Kingdom: A Fresh Look at Conversion*, ed. by Monica Hill, pp. 57-68. Middlesex, U.K.: British Church Growth Association and MARC Europe, 1986.

--------. "By Faith Abraham Obeyed...." Unpublished address given at a celebration of the seventy-fifth anniversary of the Edinburgh 1910 World Missionary Conference. Abridged version published under the title, "Ecumenical Pilgrims," in the *Catholic Gazette* (The Catholic Missionary Society) 77, 2 (1986): 6-8.

--------. "The Biblical Vision: Deed and Word Inseparable." *Concern* 28, 8 (1986): 1-3, 36.

--------. "England as a Foreign Mission Field." Reproduced text of an address given at the Assembly of the Birmingham Council of Christian Churches, March 10, 1986.

--------. "Foreword" to *Redeeming Time: Atonement Through Education*, by Timothy Gorringe, pp. ix -x. London: Darton, Longman and Todd, 1986.

--------. "One of the Loveliest of the Psalms...." Unpublished address given on the BBC, 1986.

--------. "Witness in a Biblical Perspective." *Mission Studies* 3, 2 (1986): 80-84.

--------. Review of *The Catholicity of the Church*, by Avery Dulles. In *The Journal of Theological Studies* 38 (April 1987): 273-274.

--------. Review of *The Christ and the Faiths*, by Kenneth Cragg. London: SPCK, 1986, in *The Journal of Theological Studies*. New Series, 38 (1987): 585-588.

--------. "The Pastor's Opportunities 6: Evangelism in the City." In Expository Times 98 (September 1987): 355-358.

--------. "The Christian Faith and the World Religions." In *Keeping the Faith: Essays to Mark the Centenary of Lux Mundi*. Geoffrey Wainwright, Ed., pp. 310-340. Philadelphia: Fortress Press and Pennsylvania: Pickwick Publications, 1988.

--------. "The Enduring Validity of Cross-Cultural Mission." *International Bulletin of Missionary Research* (April 1988): 50-53.

--------. "On Being the Church for the World." *The Parish Church?*, ed. by Giles Ecclestone. pp. 25-42. London: Mowbray, 1988.

--------. "Religion, Science and Truth in the School Curriculum." *Theology* 91 (May 1988): 186-193.

--------. "A Sermon Preached at the Thanksgiving Service for the Fiftieth Anniversary of Tambaram Conference of the International Missionary Council." *International Review of Mission* 77 (1988): 325-331.

--------. "The Significance of Tambaram - Fifty Years Later." *Missionalia* 16 (August 1988): 79-85.

--------. "Gospel and Culture - - But Which Culture?" *Missionalia* 17 (November 1989): 213-215.

--------. "Religious Pluralism and the Uniqueness of Jesus Christ." *International Bulletin of Missionary Research* 13, 2 (April 1989): 50-54.

--------. Review of *The Myth of Christian Uniqueness*, by John Hick and Paul Knitter, eds., Maryknoll, New York: Orbis Books, 1988 in *The Ecumenical Review* 41, 3 (July 1989): 468-471.

--------. "Vision for the City." *The Renewal of Social Vision*, ed. by A. Elliot and I. Swanson. pp. 39-41. Edinburgh: University of Edinburgh Press, 1989.

--------. "Episcopacy and Authority [and evangelism]." *The Churchman* 104, 4 (1990): 335-339.

--------. "Religion for the Marketplace." *Christian Uniqueness Reconsidered: The Myth of a Pluralistic Theology of Religions*. ed. by Gavin D'Costa, Maryknoll, New York: Orbis Books, 1990, pp. 135-148.

--------. "A Missionary's Dream." *Ecumenical Review* 43, 1 (July

1991): 4-10.

--------. "A Christian Vedanta?" *The Gospel and Our Culture* (News Letter No. 12), Birmingham, U.K. (Spring 1992): 1-2.

--------. "Whose Justice?" *Ecumenical Review* 44, 3 (1992): 308-311.

--------. "The Legacy of W. A. Wisser 't Hooft." *International Bulletin of Missionary Research* 16, 2 (April 1992): 78-81.

--------. "The Gospel as Public Truth." Editorial. *Touchstone: A Journal of Ecumenical Orthodoxy (US)* 5 (Summer 1992): 1-2.

--------. "Way Out West: The Gospel in a Post-Enlightenment World." *Touchstone: A Journal of Ecumenical Orthodoxy (US)* 5 (Summer 1992): 22-24.

--------. "Culture and Theology." *The Blackwell Encyclopedia of Modern Christian Thought*, ed. by Alister E. McGrath. pp. 98-100. Cambridge, MA, U.S.A: Blackwell Publishers, 1993.

--------. "The Kingdom of God and Our Hopes for the Future." *The Kingdom of God and Human Society*, ed. by R. S. Barbour. pp. 1-12. Edinburgh: T & T Clark, 1993.

--------. "Religious Pluralism: A Missiological Approach." *Studia Missionalia* 42 (1993): 227-244.

--------. "Ecumenical Amnesia." Newbigin's Assessment of *Ecumenism in Transition: A Paradigm Shift in the Ecumenical Movement?* by Konrad Raiser, Geneva: WCC Publications, 1991, in the *International Bulletin of Missionary Research* 18, No. 1 (January 1994): 2-5. Raiser, Konrad. "Is Ecumenical Apologetics Sufficient? A Response to Lesslie Newbigin's 'Ecumenical Amnesia'." *International Bulletin of Missionary Research* 18, No. 2 (April 1994): 50-51. Newbigin's Reply to Konrad Raiser, pp. 51-52.

--------. Review of *Sharing a Vision*, by Archbishop George Carey. London: Darton Longman & Todd, 1993 in *Theology* 97, No. 776 (March - April 1994): 132-133.

--------. "Certain Faith: What Kind of Certainty?" *Tyndale Bulletin* 44 (1993): 339-350.

--------. "Confessing Christ in a Multi-Religion Society." *Scottish Bulletin of Evangelical Theology* 12 (Autumn 1994): 125-136.

--------. Interview with Lesslie Newbigin. Duke University, North Carolina, 24 October, 1994.

--------. "Blessed be the God and Father...." An Unpublished Paper given at the World Alliance of Reformed Churches Conference, Edinburgh, August 1995. pp. 1-17.

--------. "Foreword" to *Roland Allen*, by Hubert J. B. Allen. Cincinnati: Forward Movement Publications, 1995. pp. xiii-xv.

SECONDARY SOURCES

1. Books (Alphabetically Listed)

Ahlers, Rolf. *The Barmen Theological Declaration of 1934: The Archeology of a Confessional Text*. Toronto Studies in Theology,

Vol. 24, Lewiston/Queenston: The Edwin Mellen Press, 1986.

Arendt, Hannah. *The Human Condition*. Chicago: University of Chicago, 1958.

--------. *On Revolution*. New York: The Viking Press, 1963.

Ariarajah, Wesley. *The Bible and People of Other Faiths*. Geneva: WCC, 1985.

Augustine, Aurelius. *On the Trinity*. Nicene and Post-Nicene Fathers, Schaff, Philip. ed., Buffalo, New York: Christian Literature Co., 1887.

--------. *On Free Choice of the Will*. Trans. by Benjamin, Anna S. and Hackstaff, L. H. New York: The Bobbs-Merrill Co., 1964.

Barth, Karl. *Church Dogmatics*. 1/2. Edited by Bromiley, G. W. and Torrance, Thomas F. Edinburgh: T & T Clark, 1956.

--------. *Church Dogmatics*. 3/2. Edited by Bromiley, G. W. and Torrance, Thomas F. Edinburgh: T & T Clark, 1956.

--------. *Church Dogmatics*. 4/3. Edited by Bromiley, G. W. Edinburgh: T & T Clark, 1962

Bavinck, J. H. *The Church Between Temple and Mosque*. Grand Rapids, Michigan: Wm. B. Eerdmans Publishing Co., 1967, Reprinted, 1981.

Berger, Peter L. *The Heretical Imperative: Contemporary Possibilities of Religious Affirmation*. Garden City, New York: Anchor Press, 1979.

Berkhof, Hendrikus. *Christ the Meaning of History*. Trans. by Buurman, Lambertus from the 4th edition. London: SCM Press, 1966.

--------. *Christ and the Powers*. Trans. by John Howard Yoder. Scottdale, Pa: Herald Press, 1962.

Berkhof, Louis. *Systematic Theology*. Grand Rapids: Wm. B. Eerdmans, 1939.

Bevans, Stephen. *John Oman and His Doctrine of God*. Cambridge, U.K.: Cambridge University Press, 1992.

Bloom, Allan D. *The Closing of the American Mind*. New York: Simon and Schuster, 1987.

Bosch, David J. *Believing in the Future: Toward a Missiology of Western Culture*. Valley Forge, Pennsylvania: Trinity Press International, 1995.

Braaten, Carl E. *The Apostolic Imperative*. Minneapolis: Augsburg Publishing House, 1985.

Buber, Martin. *I and Thou*. New York: Charles Scribner's Sons, 1958.

Butterfield, Herbert. *Christianity and History*. London: G. Bell and Sons Ltd., 1949.

Calvin, John. *Institutes of the Christian Religion*. Vol. I. Philadelphia: Westminster Press, 1960.

Carr, E. H. *What is History?* London: Macmillan & Co., 1961.

Cochrane, Charles N. *Christianity and Classical Culture: A Study of Thought and Action From Augustus to Augustine*. New York: Oxford University Press, 1957.

Crossan, John D. *The Dark Interval: Towards A Theology of Story*. Niles, Illinois: Argus Communications, 1975.

D'Costa, Gavin. *Christian Uniqueness Reconsidered: The Myth of a Pluralistic Theology of Religions*. Maryknoll, New York: Orbis Books, 1990.

--------. *Theology and Religious Pluralism*. Oxford: Basil Blackwell, 1986.

Denney, James. *The Atonement and the Modern Mind*. London: Hodder & Stoughton, 1903.

Dooyeweerd, Herman. *Roots of Western Culture: Pagan, Secular, and Christian Options*. Trans. by Kraay, John. Toronto: Wedge Publishing Company, 1979.

Dulles, Avery R. *Models of Revelation*. First edition. Garden City, New York: Doubleday, 1983.

Eck, Diana. *Encountering God*. Boston: Beacon Press, 1993.

Einstein, Albert. *Ideas and Opinions*. New York: Crown Publishers, 1954.

--------. *The World As I See It*. New York: Covici, Friede, Inc., 1934.

Freytag, Walter. *The Gospel and the Religions*. IMC Research

Pamphlet No. 5. London: SCM Press, 1957.

Gairdner, W. H. T. *Echoes From Edinburgh, 1910: An Account and Interpretation of the World Missionary Conference.* London and Toronto: Fleming H. Revell Co., 1910.

Geertz, Clifford. "Religion As a Cultural System," in *The Interpretation of Cultures*, New York: Basic Books, Inc., 1973.

Guardini, Romano. *The End of the Modern World: A Search for Orientation.* New York: Sheed & Ward, 1956.

Gutierrez, Gustavo. *A Theology of Liberation: History, Politics and Salvation.* New York: Orbis Books, 1973.

Hallencreutz, Carl F. *Kraemer Towards Tambaram: A Study in Hendrik Kraemer's Missionary Approach.* Uppsala, Sweden: Almqvist & Wiksells, 1966.

Hick, John. *God and the Universe of Faiths: Essays in the Philosophy of Religion.* London: The Macmillan Press Ltd., 1973.

--------. *God Has Many Names.* London: The Macmillan Press, 1980.

--------. *An Interpretation of Religion: Human Responses to the Transcendent.* New Haven and London: Yale University Press, 1989.

--------. *The Metaphor of God Incarnate.* Louisville, Kentucky: Westminster/ John Knox Press, 1993.

--------. *The Myth of God Incarnate.* Philadelphia: Westminster Press, 1977.

Hick, John and Hebblethwaite, Brian. ed., *Christianity and Other Religions*. Philadelphia: Fortress Press, 1981.

Hick, John & Knitter, Paul. Ed., *The Myth of Christian Uniqueness*. Maryknoll, New York: Orbis Books, 1987.

Hick, John & Meltzer, Edmund. Eds., *Three Faiths - One God: A Jewish, Christian, Muslim Encounter*. Albany, New York: State University of New York Press, 1989.

Hocking, William E. *The Coming World Civilization*. London: Allen & Unwin, 1956.

Horton, W. M. *Contemporary English Theology*. New York: Harper & Brothers, 1936.

Hunsberger, George. *The Missionary Significance of the Biblical Doctrine of Election as A Foundation for a Theology of Cultural Plurality in the Missiology of J. E. Lesslie Newbigin*. Ph.D. Thesis. Princeton, New Jersey: Princeton Theological Seminary, 1987.

International Missionary Council. *The World Mission of the Church, Tambaram 1938*. London and New York: IMC, 1938.

--------. *Jerusalem Meeting of the International Missionary Council, March 24 - April 8*. London: Oxford University Press, 1928

Jai Sing, Herbert. *Inter-Religious Dialogue*. Bangalore: Christian Institute for the Study of Religion and Society, 1967.

James, William. *The Will to Believe*. London: Longmans, Green, 1912.

Jüngel, Eberhard. *Christ, Justice and Peace: Toward a Theology of the State in Dialogue with the Barmen Declaration.* Trans. by Bruce Hamill, D. and Torrance, Allan J. Edinburgh: T & T Clark, 1992.

Kittel, Gerhard. ed., *Theological Dictionary of the New Testament,* Vol. 1. Trans. and ed. by Bromiley, G. pp. 574-593. Grand Rapids: Eerdmans, 1964.

Knitter, Paul. *No Other Name?: A Critical Survey of Christian Attitudes Toward the World Religions.* Maryknoll, New York: Orbis Books, 1985.

Kraemer, Hendrik. *The Christian Message in a Non-Christian World.* London: Edinburgh House Press, Reprinted June, 1947.

--------. *Religion and the Christian Faith.* London: Lutterworth Press, 1956.

--------. *Why Christianity of All Religions?* London: Lutterworth Press, 1962.

--------. *World Religions and World Cultures.* London: Lutterworth Press, 1960.

Kristensen, Brede W. *The Meaning of Religion.* The Hague: Marinus Nijhoff, 1960.

Kuhn, Thomas. *The Structure of Scientific Revolutions.* Chicago: The University of Chicago Press, 1962.

Küng, Hans. *On Being a Christian.* Trans. by Quinn, Edward.

London: Collins, 1977.

Kuyper, Abraham. *Lectures on Calvinism*. Grand Rapids: Wm. B. Eerdmans Publishing Co., 1931.

Lindbeck, George A. *The Nature of Doctrine*. Westminster Press, 1984.

Lochhead, David. *The Dialogical Imperative: A Reflection on Interfaith Encounter*. Maryknoll, New York: Orbis Books, 1988.

Locke, Hubert G. Ed., *The Barmen Confession: Papers from the Seattle Assembly*. Toronto Studies in Theology, Vol. 26. Lewiston/Queenston: The Edwin Mellen Press, 1986.

Locke, John. *A Third Letter for Toleration*. London: Awnsham & John Churchill, 1692.

Lonergan, Bernard. *Method in Theology*. Toronto: University of Toronto Press, 1971.

Luzbetak, Louis J. *The Church and Cultures*. Techny, IL: Divine Word Publications, 1970.

MacIntyre, Alasdair C. *After Virtue*. University of Notre Dam Press, 1981.

Macnicol, Nicol. *Is Christianity Unique?*. London: SCM Press, 1936.

Martin, Hugh. *Beginning at Edinburgh: A Jubilee Assessment of the World Missionary Conference, 1910*. London: Edinburgh House Press, 1960.

Marvin, Francis Sydney. *The Living Past: A Sketch in Western Progress*. Oxford: Clarendon Press, 1917.

Moltmann, Jürgen. *The Crucified God: The Cross of Christ as the Foundation and Criticism of Christian Theology*. London: SCM Press, 1974.

--------. *The Church in the Power of the Spirit*. London: SCM Press, 1977.

Montefiore, Hugh. *The Gospel and Contemporary Culture*. London: Mowbray, 1992.

Munby, Denys L. *The Idea of a Secular Society, and Its Significance for Christians*. London: Oxford University Press, 1963.

Netland, Harold A. *Dissonant Voices: Religious Pluralism and the Question of Truth*. Grand Rapids: Wm. B. Eerdmans Publishing Co., 1991.

Niebuhr, H. Richard. *Christ and Culture*. New York: Harper & Row, 1951.

Nida, Eugene A. *Customs and Cultures: Anthropology for Christian Missions*. New York: Harper & Row, 1954

Oman, John. *The Church and the Divine Order*. London: Hodder & Stoughton, 1911.

--------. *Grace and Personality*. London: Hodder and Stoughton, 1917.

--------.*The Natural and the Supernatural*. Cambridge: Cambridge

University Press, 1931.

--------. *Vision and Authority: The Throne of St. Peter.* London: Hodder, 1902.

Osborn, Robert T. *Barmen Declaration as a Paradigm for a Theology of the American Church.* Lewiston, New York: E. Mellen Press, 1991.

Otto, Rudolf. *The Idea of the Holy: An Inquiry into the Non-rational Factor in the Idea of the Divine and its Relation to the Rational.* London: Oxford University Press, 1923.

--------. *India's Religion of Grace and Christianity Compared and Contrasted,* Translated by Foster, Frank Hugh. London: SCM Press, 1930.

Panikkar, K.M. *Asia and Western Dominance.* London: George Allen & Unwin, 1959.

Panikkar, Raimundo. *The Unknown Christ of Hinduism.* London: Darton, Longman and Todd, 1964.

Pannenberg, Wolfhart. *Jesus - God and Man.* Trans. Wilkins, Lewis and Priebe, D. London: SCM Press, 1968.

Pinnock, Clark. *A Wideness in God's Mercy: The Finality of Jesus Christ in a World of Religions.* Grand Rapids: Zondervan Publishing House, 1992.

Polanyi, Michael. *Personal Knowledge.* Chicago: The University of Chicago Press, 1958.

--------. *Science, Faith and Society.* Chicago and London: The

University of Chicago Press, 1946.

--------. *The Tacit Dimension*. Garden City, New York: Doubleday & Co., 1966.

The Logic of Personal Knowledge: Essays Presented to Michael Polanyi on His Seventieth Birthday. London: Routledge & Kegan Paul, 1961.

Polkinghorne, John. *One World: The Interaction of Science and Theology*. London: SPCK, 1986.

Portalie, Eugene. *A Guide to the Thought of Saint Augustine*. Edited by Bastian, Ralph A. London: Burns & Oates, 1960.

Rahner, Karl. *Theological Investigations*. Vol. 5. Trans. by Kruger, Karl-H. Baltimore: Helicon Press and London: Darton, Longman and Todd, 1966. pp. 115-134.

--------. *Theological Investigations*. Vol. 6. Trans. by Karl-H and Boniface Kruger. London: Darton, Longman and Todd and New York: Seabury Press, 1969. pp. 390-398.

Ramsey, Michael. *The Gospel and the Catholic Church*. London: Longmans, Green & Co., 1936.

Reilly, John. *Evangelism and Ecumenism in the Writings of Lesslie Newbigin and Their Basis in His Christology. Excerpta ex dissertatione ad Doctoratum in Facultate Theologiae Pontificiae Universitatis Gregorianae*. Rome: Pontifical Gregorian University, 1979.

Russell, Bertrand. *The Scientific Outlook*. London: George Allen & Unwin, 1931.

Samartha, Stanley. *Courage for Dialogue: Ecumenical Issues in Inter-Religious Relationships*. Geneva: WCC, 1981.

--------. Ed. *Faith in the Midst of Faiths: Reflections on Dialogue in Community*. Geneva: World Council of Churches, 1977.

Sanders, John. *No Other Name: An Investigation into the Destiny of the Unevangelized*. Grand Rapids: Wm. B. Eerdmans, 1992.

Schleiermacher, Friedrich. *The Christian Faith*. Philadelphia: Fortress Press, 1928.

-------- *On Religion: Speeches to its Cultured Despisers*. Trans. by Oman, John. New York: Harper & Row Publishers, 1958.

Scott, Drusilla. *Everyman Revived: The Commonsense of Michael Polanyi*. Lewes, Sussex: Book Guild, 1985.

Sharpe, Eric. *Comparative Religion*. London: Lutterworth Press, 1975.

Shenk, Wilbert R. *Write the Vision: The Church Renewed*. Valley Forge, Pennsylvania: Trinity Press International, 1995.

Shorter, Aylward. *Toward a Theology of Inculturation*. Maryknoll: Orbis Books, 1988.

Simpson, Carnegie P. *The Fact of Christ*. 3rd edn., London: Hodder & Stoughton, 1901.

Smith, Wilfred Cantwell. *Towards a World Theology*. Philadelphia: Westminster Press, 1981.

--------. *The Meaning and End of Religion: A New Approach to the Religious Traditions of Mankind.* Toronto: The New American Library of Canada Ltd., 1962.

--------. *The Faith of Other Men.* New York: New American Library, 1962.

Song, C.S. *Tell Us Our Names: Story Theology from an Asian Perspective.* Maryknoll, New York: Orbis Books, 1984.

[Speer, Robert E]. Ed., *The Christian Message in Relation to Non-Christian Systems.* Vol. 1. London: Oxford University Press, 1928.

Stuhlmacher, Peter. *Historical Criticism and Theological Interpretation of Scripture.* Trans. by Roy A. Harrisville. Philadelphia: Fortress Press, 1977.

Swidler, Leonard. Ed. *Toward a Universal Theology of Religion.* Maryknoll, New York: Orbis Books, 1987.

Tacitus, Cornelius. *The Annals of Imperial Rome.* Translated by Grant, Michael. Harmondsworth, U.K.: Penguin Books, 1956.

Tambaram Madras Series. *The Authority of the Faith.* Vol. 1. London: Oxford University Press, 1939.

Thomas, M. M. *Salvation and Humanization: Some Crucial Issues of the Theology of Mission in Contemporary India.* Madras: CLS, 1971.

Thomson, Alexander. *Tradition and Authority in Science and Theology With Reference to the Thought of Michael Polanyi.* Edinburgh: Scottish Academic Press, 1987.

Torrance, Thomas. F. ed., *Belief in Science and in Christian Life: The Relevance of Michael Polanyi's Thought for Christian Faith and Life*. Edinburgh: The Handsel Press, 1980.

--------. *Theological Science*. London: Oxford University Press, 1969.

--------. *Transformation and Convergence in the Frame of Knowledge: Explorations in the Interrelations of Scientific and Theological Enterprise*. Grand Rapids, Michigan: Wm. B. Eerdmans Publishing Co., 1984.

--------. *The Trinitarian Faith: The Evangelical Theology of the Ancient Catholic Church*. Edinburgh: T & T Clark, 1988.

Turner, Harold W. *New Religious Movements in Primal Societies [Microform]: A Collection of Primary Source Documents*. edited by Stan Nussbaum. Birmingham, England: Selly Oak Colleges, 1993.

Van Buren, Paul. *The Secular Meaning of the Gospel*. New York: Macmillan and London: SCM Press, 1963.

Van Leeuwen, Arend Th. *Christianity in World History: The Meeting of the Faiths of East and West*. New York: Charles Scribner's Sons, 1964.

Whitehead, A.N. *Essays in Science and Philosophy*. New York: Philosophical Library, 1948.

Wiles, Maurice. *Christian Theology and Inter-Religious Dialogue*. London: SCM Press and Pennsylvania: Trinity Press International, 1992.

Wink, Walter. *Naming the Powers: The Language of Power in the New Testament*. Philadelphia: Fortress Press, 1984.

[World Missionary Conference, 1910]. *The Missionary Message in Relation to Non-Christian Religions*. Vol. IV. New York, Chicago, and Toronto: Fleming H. Revell Co., 1910.

Yu, Carver T. *Being and Relations: A Theological Critique of Western Dualism and Individualism*. Edinburgh: Scottish Academic, 1987.

2. Other Articles
(Alphabetically Listed)

Barns, Ian. "Christianity in a Pluralist Society: A Dialogue with Lesslie Newbigin." *St. Mark's Review*, No. 158 (Winter 1994): 27-37.

Bavinck, Herman. "Common Grace." Trans. by Raymond C. Van Leeuwen, *Calvin Theological Journal* 24, No. 1 (April 1989): 38-65.

Beeby, Daniel H. and Newbigin, Lesslie. "The Bible and Inter-faith Relations." In *Using the Bible Today*. Ed., Cohn-Sherbok, Dan. pp. 180-187. London: Bellew Publishing, 1991.

Bevans, Stephen. "Doing Theology in North America: A Counter-Cultural Model?" Unpublished Paper, 1995.

Conway, Martin. "Lesslie Newbigin's Faith Pilgrimage." *Mission Studies* 11, 2 (1994): 191-202.

Dumas, André. "Unity of Mankind - Unity of the Church," *Study Encounter* 10, No. 2 (1974): 1-16.

Eck, Diana L. "The Religions and Tambaram: 1938 and 1988." *International Review of Missions* 77 (July, 1988): 375-389.

Fackre, Gabriel. "The Scandals of Particularity and Universality." *Mid-Stream* 22 (January 1983): 32-52.

Hick, John. "Christian Theology and Inter-religious Dialogue." *World Faiths: Journal of the World Congress of Faiths* No. 103 (August 1977): 2-19.

Hunsberger, George. "Acquiring the Posture of Missionary Church." *Insights* 108 (Fall 1993): 19-26.

--------. "The Newbigin Gauntlet: Developing a Domestic Missiology for North America." *Missiology* 19 (October 1991): 391-408.

Lindbeck, George A. Review of *The Gospel in a Pluralist Society*, by Lesslie Newbigin. *International Bulletin of Missionary Research* 14, 1 (January 1990): 182.

McGrath, Alister E. "The Challenge of Pluralism for the Contemporary Christian Church." *Journal of the Evangelical Theological Society* 35 (September 1992): 361-373.

McSorley, Harry. "God's Saving Activity and The Mission of the Church." Unpublished Paper. Toronto: St. Michael's College, 1992.

Mulder, D. C. "The Dialogue Between Cultures and Religions:

Kraemer's Contribution in the Light of Later Developments." *The Ecumenical Review* 41 (January 1989): 13-19.

--------. "Professor Hick on Religious Pluralism." *Religious Studies* 22 (1986): 249-261.

Samartha, Stanley J. "Looking Beyond Tambaram 1938." *International Review of Mission* 78, No. 307 (July 1988): 311-324.

Smith, Wilfred Cantwell. "Mission, Dialogue, and God's Will for Us." *International Review of Mission* 78, No. 307 (July 1988): 360-374.

Starkloff, Carl. "Aboriginal Cultures and the Christ." *Theological Studies* 53 (June 1992): 288-312.

--------. "Inculturation and Cultural Systems." Pt. 1. *Theological Studies* 55 (March 1994): 66-81.

Thomas, J. M. "Continuity, Discontinuity, and the Finality of Christ: A Theological Essay on the Relationship between Non-Christian Religions and Christianity." *Dharma Deepika*, Vol 13, #1 pp. 25-34 (January-June, 2009).

--------.*The Church as Cultural Critic in the Missiology of Lesslie Newbigin* (*Missio Apostolica*, Vol. 15., (Nov. 2007)

--------. "Exclusivism, Inclusivism, and Pluralism: Distinctive Contribution of Lesslie Newbigin to a Theology of Religion." in *Trinity Theological Journal*, Vol. 14, (Singapore, Sept., 2006).

--------. "Dissonant Themes in Inter-Religious Dialog: A Study of John Hick and Lesslie Newbigin." in *Mission Studies*, (January,

2007).

--------. "The Concept of Religion and Salvation of Non-Christians in the Writings of Lesslie Newbigin." *Mission Today* (April-June, 2006)

-------. "The Nature and Task of Inter-Religious Dialogue in the Theology of Lesslie Newbigin" *Mission Studies (Internet Edition, October, 2005.)*

Thomas, M. M. "Baptism, the Church, and Koinonia: Three Letters and a Comment." By M. M. Thomas, Lesslie Newbigin and Alfred C. Krass. Letters dated 21 October, 1971 (pp. 69-74) and 20th December 1971 (pp. 87-90) in *Religion and Society* 19 (1972): 69-90.

Thorogood, Bernard G. "Apostolic Faith: An Appreciation of Lesslie Newbigin, Born 8 December 1909" *International Review of Mission* 79 (January 1990): 66-84.

"In Tribute to Bishop Lesslie Newbigin" by various authors in the *International Review of Mission* 79 (January 1990): 86-100.

Wells, Harold G. "Holy Spirit and the Theology of the Cross." *Theological Studies* 53 (Spring 1992): 476-492.

Wiles, Maurice. "Comment on Lesslie Newbigin's Essay." *Incarnation and Myth: The Debate Continued*, ed. by Michael Goulder, pp. 211-213. Grand Rapids: Wm. B. Eerdmans Publishing Co., 1979.

Williams, John. "The Gospel As Public Truth: A Critical Appreciation of the Theological Programme of Lesslie Newbigin." *Anvil* 10, 1 (1993): 11-24.

www.ingramcontent.com/pod-product-compliance
Lightning Source LLC
Chambersburg PA
CBHW071236300426
44116CB00008B/1062